D1236335

THE HORSEMAN'S MANUAL

The Horseman's Manual

Lt-Col. C. E. G. Hope

CHARLES SCRIBNER'S SONS

NEW YORK

1 3 5 7 9 11 13 15 17 19   I/C   20 18 16 14 12 10 8 6 4 2

Printed in Great Britain
Library of Congress Catalog Card Number 73-9303
SBN 684-13622-8 (cloth)

To
The Gentleman of the Party – the Horse

Contents

Illustrations

Preface by William Luscombe

(Managing Director, Pelham Books)

We all called him 'Charles'.

As the co-founder and Editor of the magazines *Light Horse* and *Pony*, he was known and loved by followers of the equestrian scene everywhere. Always cheerful, whatever the pressures, and ready to give advice, patiently and with enthusiasm, Charles Hope observed and reported on equestrian events for over thirty years and was still the active Editor of his two magazines at the time of his death.

He finished *The Horseman's Manual* a few weeks before he went into hospital. His last letter to me said, modestly, that this, his seventeenth book, was, he felt, the best he had ever written.

In my view, his claim was entirely true.

The Horseman's Manual is the culmination of many instructional books by Charles Hope. It aims at being a comprehensive textbook on riding theory and practice today, based on personal experience and on the wisdom of the many masters of the subject all of whom were personal friends of the author.

The book starts with an introductory section containing a survey of the development of horsemanship through the ages to the present day. There are chapters on the 'Points of the Horse', conformation, psychology and equipment. Then the training of the rider and the training of the horse are treated in separate sections, with step-by-step instruction in each case for the complete novice up to high school. Other sections include the practical application of teaching to equestrian sports on driving. Here, then, is the complete book for all horselovers.

Charles Hope will be sadly missed.

He will never be forgotten.

THE HORSEMAN'S MANUAL

ONE

Setting the Scene

1 The Development of Horsemanship

It has been suggested that early man rode other, easier animals before he got round to mounting a horse – the ox, perhaps, or, as a child, goats and sheep. As a universal carrier the ass certainly precedes the horse, and, most likely, the camel. The ancient inhabitants of Arabia are known to have ridden the latter long before the horse.

There is a clay figurine, found at Susa in southern Iraq and dated about 3000 B.C., which shows a just recognisable human astride an unrecognisable quadruped. It could be an ass. That gives a visible starting point in time for equitation of a sort, but the idea could well have been borrowed from the wilder lands to the north, the steppes of Central Asia, the plains of Mongolia, which were the cradle of the horse in the Eurasian continent after the Behring contact with America was broken. A combination of unlimited numbers of wild horses and the nomad herdsman with his flocks of domesticated cattle makes horsemanship inevitable.

The moment anybody, at any time, first sits on the back of a horse he has problems. Today there is an instructor at hand to help him solve them, to show him how to sit, how to hold his hands, how to use his legs; and there are all sorts of equipment available. It is hard to imagine a situation in which these problems had to be solved for the first time, but it is not fanciful to suggest that prehistoric man, who was no fool, began to think about them and, within the limitations of his means and requirements, to solve them. A reasonable parallel from more recent times is the case of the American Indian, who had never seen a horse until the Spaniards brought it to America in the sixteenth century. By various means the Indians quickly acquired horses of their own and learned to ride them with no equipment to begin with but a rope.

The earliest document on the breaking in and backing of a horse is a frieze on a Kumis jug, dated the fourth century B.C. at Chertomlyk found in the Ukraine in the last century. It shows a group of men with ropes stalking wild horses on the steppe, shepherding them into a *cul de sac* in the hills, lassoing a horse,

17

playing it on the long rein, mounting it and belting it on at a gallop over the boundless plain, free forward movement. Later the exhausted horse is brought back, the rider dismounts, and with his assistants makes much of the horse, handling its whole body and legs, picking up its feet; then the horse is quietly thrown. Finally a pad is put on its back. A not unfamiliar process today, and one which must have been repeated many times before it was so realistically depicted.

Kikkuli's famous book, *The Training of Horses*, written in the fourteenth century B.C., presumably for the Hittite monarch, Suppliluliumas, to whom it is dedicated, precedes the Chertomlyk jug by 1,000 years, but the horses to be trained to the chariot were probably broken in, in the same way. The programme is a progressive, and tough course of 148 days, which includes selection, conditioning, and work at the walk, amble and gallop over increasing distances. Stable management and feeding is included. The object of the work was the training of chariot horses, but there is no reason to suppose that the horses were not ridden also, although we do not see documentary evidence of a mounted man until the Assyrian records of the ninth century B.C.

It is interesting to note the riding positions and accoutrements of these first cavalry men as portrayed on the reliefs from the bronze gates of Shalmaneser III of Assyria (859–824 B.C.). They ride bareback, of course, sometimes with a square cloth, sitting well back on the horses' croups, knees up and legs wrapped round the flanks, heels tucked in just in front of the stifle joints, which is in fact the most comfortable and secure way to ride when you have neither saddle nor stirrups.

The soldiers are either archers or spearmen. The archer is fully occupied handling his composite type bow, so he has a half-section who carries a small shield and handles the reins of both horses. The spearman has a small round shield on his left arm, holding the reins with the left hand, spear wielded in the right hand rather like a hoghunter's stabbing spear. While the archers ride on saddle cloths, the lancers are completely bareback. Their bits are snaffles, with all kinds of murderous devices in the mouthpiece, studs, discs, and spikes on the outside. They have long, sometimes rectangular cheekpieces, attached to divided straps from the bridle cheekpieces, with or without a noseband. The bits were jointed, and the effect of the rein action was to close the cheekpieces, with all their spikes and protuberances on to the sides of the mouth. Equitation was not of a high order: go and stop, and turns and circles were probably the limit of it, with perhaps some rearing and prancing to show off. Two hundred years later, in the reign of Ashurbanipal, the bitting is much the same, but the riders are sitting forward, just behind the withers, with straighter legs. This style of riding continues to the time of Xenophon, and after.

Hippike, Xenophon's book on horsemanship is a high water mark in the study of the art, after which the tide ebbs away to very low levels until the work was rediscovered in the Renaissance. Like the work of his predecessor, Kikkuli, his book is so finished and detailed, that it must be the culmination of a considerable body of thought and discussion and writing. We know of one such author, Simon of Athens, who seems to have flourished round the turn of the fifth and fourth centuries B.C. He was obviously known to Xenophon, who refers to and quotes him with respect in *Hippike*, which was probably written about 360 B.C.

'It is true,' he says, 'that a book on horsemanship has already been written by Simon . . . who dedicated the bronze horse at the Eleusinion in Athens with his own exploits in relief on the pedestal. Still, I shall not strike out of my work all the points in which I chance to agree with him, but shall take much greater pleasure in passing them on to my friends, believing that I speak with the more authority because a famous horseman, such as he, has thought as I do.' In Chapter XI, he cites Simon in support of his remark that 'what the horse does under compulsion is done without understanding'. It is a pity that, apart from a few isolated references such as these, nothing remains of Simon's book but a brief description of the points of the horse.

Xenophon was a man of parts, soldier of fortune, horseman and writer. His most famous work is, of course, the *Anabasis*, the story of how he conducted the Greek mercenaries of Cyrus back to the Black Sea after the latter's defeat and death in the battle of Cunaxa in 401 B.C. As he was only a supernumerary staff officer when he took over command, his feat is all the more remarkable. Exiled by Athens for serving against Artaxerxes, he took service with the Spartans and settled at Scillus in Elis, about 387 B.C., where he wrote several books. Before that he was almost certainly a member of the equestrian *corps d'elite* of the Athenians, and, obviously had considerable experience of horses and cavalry work, as well as the ability to write freely and lucidly. His book on the Cavalry Commander (*Hipparchikos*) was written about 362 B.C. before the Battle of

Mantinea where one of his sons was killed, and *Hippike* shortly after.

This book of twelve short chapters, admirably clear and concise, sets the pattern for all the many books on equitation that have succeeded it. First there is a description of the horse so that one may 'escape being cheated in buying a horse'. Xenophon is not aware of the anatomy of the fore limbs, nor of the shock-absorbing function of the frog, but he insists on good bone and well-muscled upper limbs, broad chest, cresty neck, and small, clean-cut head with large eyes and wide nostrils. He likes high withers and a 'double back', i.e. one broad and well covered with flesh on either side of the spine, a great comfort to a bareback rider. The horse he describes would be well coupled with a short back and strong hindquarters.

The breaking-in of young horses he leaves to the professional trainers, who must have been fairly plentiful, for he considers the cavalryman, for whom he is primarily writing, should not waste his time over a routine job. 'For states lay the duty of cavalry service upon those who are best provided with money and who play the major part in politics, and a young man should see to his own health and horsemanship, or, if he is already a good rider, should practise riding. And a grown man, rather than breaking-in horses had far better pass his time in looking after his estate and friends and political and military affairs.' But he should make it quite clear to the horsebreaker in writing exactly what he is to teach the colt.

However, before being sent to the horsebreaker the colt should be well gentled and taught to associate everything good and pleasant with man and to seek his company. He must also be got used to crowds and strange sights and noises, again rough treatment is to be avoided. It is astounding how all Xenophon's words and thought about the horse ring with sympathy and understanding far ahead of his time, and are combined with shrewd common sense.

When buying a made horse he likes him to be about five years old, not having lost his milk teeth; he must be easily bridled and be a quiet ride; he must be willing to pass or to leave other horses, and must not be nappy or one-sided. The test for this is to try them on turns to right and left; he must be good across country; and above all he must have courage.

There then follow instructions in stable management with emphasis on routine, mounting – without stirrups of course – then riding. Xenophon's riding position is well-known, not sitting as if on a chair but 'like a man standing upright with his legs apart', an instruction not to be repeated until Piero Santini's interpretation of the ideas of Caprilli twenty-three centuries later. Actually such a position is extremely rare, if one is to judge by the art of the period. Nothing could be sounder, however, than his recommendation that the upper part of the body should be as supple as possible, or that, once mounted, the horse should be taught to stand still while the rider adjusts his dress. The Greeks rode usually in the normal skirted tunic (*chiton*) or in nothing at all. If dressed for battle he wore a helmet (Xenophon recommends the Boeotian pattern), cuirasses, a kilt of tassets (overlapping flaps attached to the waist of the cuirasse), greaves and boots. Xenophon also recommends that the cloth on which the warrior sits should be padded; a first step surely towards a saddle, and it is a wonder that the highly intelligent Greeks never pursued the matter.

Xenophon talks about signals for movement but unfortunately never describes them in detail. As he deprecated violent methods with the whip, it may be safe to assume that he means leg and voice aids. The aid for the gallop (canter) on the left lead is to be given when the right foot is in the air. Turns and figures of eight are used extensively in the training, equally on both reins. The horse should be checked on the turns, and the rider should keep upright; after the turn the horse is urged forward again at greater speed. Turning here means a half-turn of 180 degrees, 'for in active service one turns either in order to pursue or to retreat'. Practice is also given in direct halts from the gallop, and turns; in fact the well-trained Greek horse must have been almost as handy and supple as a polo pony. Of course we do not know how long it took to bring the horse to a stop in full gallop. All this was done in a snaffle bit; not unlike a modern jointed snaffle but a good deal more severe. The mouthpiece was covered with prickles or small spikes, rounded or pointed according to the degree of severity required. For a highly-couraged, excitable horse Xenophon recommends a smooth bit, and the opposite for a slug; but he also adds that a rough bit must be used with 'lightness of hand'. He deprecates showy, meretricious performances obtained by misuse of the bit, whip and spurs. The Greek spur was a small goad without rowels strapped to the heel.

Jumping lessons for the horse start by leading in hand over obstacles, with a man behind with a whip to be used only if he refuses. One such treatment is deemed to be enough. When the horse leads freely over jumps, mounted work begins, first over small ones and gradually progressing, using the spur at the take-off. The rider leans forward when the horse goes forward, back when he stops; in jumping or going uphill the rider should hold on to the mane. Going down a steep slope 'you must lean backwards yourself and hold the horse with the bit, so that neither horse nor rider may be carried headlong down the slope'. Throughout calmness is the watchword, avoiding unnecessary hurt to the horse, and all training is progressive. Reward and punishment, especially the former, is emphasised, and, it is interesting to note, in connection with the handling of the reins that 'you must pull on the horse's mouth, neither too roughly, so that he throws up his head to evade the bit, nor too gently, so that he does not feel it. And when the action of the bit makes him raise his neck, give rein at once.' And, 'when he curvets (or rears?) beautifully you should at once dismount and unbridle him. If you do this, you must know well that he will come to curvet of his own free will.'

There has been great debate as to whether Xenophon taught, or performed, anything approaching modern high school airs. Probably not, but he certainly liked a showy, prancing horse, with his hocks well under him. Not every horse, however, was suitable. 'If you want,' he says, 'to train a horse for parade, for high school, it is certainly not every horse that can develop the necessary qualities.' He suggests one 'naturally endowed with greatheartedness of spirit and strength of body . . . with loins supple and short and strong (meaning not the part under the tail, but that between the ribs and the haunches, along the flank) . . . able to bring his hindlegs further forward under him'. And he goes on to describe the movement: 'When he has gathered them well in, if you take him up with the bit, he falls back on his hocks and raises his forehand so that his belly and sheath can be seen from the front.' He adds, 'You must give him the bit when he does this, and it will look to the spectators as if he were doing all of his own accord.' What else can this movement be but a levade? There is a monument in Athens to an Athenian knight, Dexileus, who fell in battle near Corinth in 394 B.C., which shows his horse doing just this over a prostrate foeman. And the action of the horses of the famous Parthenon frieze shows a close approximation of it.

No other movements are mentioned, but it might be possible to discern the rudiments of piaffe and passage in the following excerpt: 'If you teach your horse to go with a light hand on the bit, and yet to hold his head well up and to arch his neck, you will be making him do just what the animal himself glories and delights in. A proof that he really delights in it is

22

that when a horse is turned loose and runs off to join the other horses, and especially towards mares, then he holds his head up as high as he can, arches his neck in the most spirited style, lifts his legs with a free action, and raises his tail.'

One must not exaggerate Xenophon's influence on horsemanship. He was a man of his time, working with the means and techniques that were available to him and limited by them. It is not suggested that the strutting and prancing and rearing that he describes to be compared with the ordered, disciplined and methodical airs produced by the training of the Spanish Riding School of Vienna. Lateral movement appears to have been unknown to him; he would surely have mentioned it otherwise. Both he and his contemporaries were primarily interested in producing efficient officers' chargers and troop horses. But he has laid down in lapidary sentences the foundations of horse management and schooling, teaching a psychological approach and humane methods, which are not always followed, even now. For this reason his name comes first in the long line of equestrian writers, and towers above many of them.

Xenophon died in about 355 B.C. at the age of about ninety. His works disappeared, and it was some eighteen centuries before anything constructive on equitation was written again.

2 The Development of Horsemanship — Renaissance to Modern Times

The study of horsemanship flashes into the equestrian scene like a comet, makes its brilliant appearance, in the form of Xenophon's book, then vanishes into the outer darkness suddenly to reappear nearly two thousand years later in Renaissance Italy. Then the analogy breaks down; instead of a mighty flash there starts a gentle stream which quickly expands to a torrent, quickly swollen to a spate which never seems to lessen.

There was no lack of interest in the horse in the intervening centuries, but it centred on the animal's appearance and stable management rather than upon the art of riding. When classical authors like Virgil wrote on rustic or agricultural matters they could not fail to mention the horse. The Romans do not seem to have been great horsemen; when the army wanted cavalry it had to fall back on auxiliaries furnished by the barbarian horsemen. Chariot racing was the great sport of the age. Trick riding was popular in Rome, as it must have been at all times, and we still have the term 'Roman riding' to describe that kind of display.

The Middle Ages produced some works on stable management, veterinary care, and equipment, with only a few scattered references to actual horsemanship. The best known of these medieval writers was Rusius (Lorenzo Rusio), who wrote on the care of the horse and equipment (*Hippiatrica Sive Marescalia*). He died in 1350, but the book, first in manuscript then in print (1486), was current until the seventeenth century.

Thought about equipment and saddlery was slow in application. One must avoid the temptation, enticing though it is, to turn this study into a history of horse equipment, but the accoutrements of the horse do have a bearing on the development of horsemanship so a summary of the important events is relevant. The only instrument which has had a full and detailed treatment from the beginning of recorded history is the bit. The two main concerns of the early horsemen were to make their mounts go, and then to stop them – they still are.

The bit has been coeval with the tamed horse; as soon as there was metal available the bit appeared, in the Bronze Age, say 2000 to 1400 B.C. according to the area. There is a Yorkshire Bronze Age double-jointed snaffle in the British Museum, most modern in appearance and mild, compared with eastern contraptions of about the same period which stopped the horse by pressing spikes and knobs into the sides of the horse's mouth. The true curb bit, with its lever action on a curb chain fitting into the chin groove, was a long time coming. In Europe it seems to appear during the age of chivalry, from about the ninth century A.D. From being long and murderous, with mouthpieces filled with painful ironmongery it gradually reduced in size and severity as ideas about horsemanship grew more sophisticated. In this case it was not the bit that made horsemanship but the reverse.

A true landmark in the development of riding is the saddle. Until a proper bearing surface to protect the back from direct contact with the weight of the rider, in other words a tree, was devised it was impossible for the horse to carry efficiently the increasing burden of warrior and his armour. This development took place in the East, and came to the West via Byzantium in late Roman times. The Column of Marius in Rome of the second century A.D. shows a saddle with a pommel and cantle. These became more exaggerated during the Middle Ages, when the principle military action was the charge with couched lance, to keep the jousting knight in his saddle, and subsequently were reduced with the demise of the armoured knight and the beginnings of equitation for its own sake in the seventeenth century. But it is doubtful whether the age of chivalry, which rested on the power of the mounted man in armour with lance and sword, mace or battle axe, would ever have happened but for the stirrup.

The introduction of the stirrup into the West was the real turning point of equitation, and, it is said, of the feudal system. By giving his followers lands filched from the Church, Charles Martel was able, in the eighth century, to put a strong cavalry force into the field, his followers then being rich enough to buy and maintain the costly horses. But it was the stirrup which made this cavalry efficient, because at last the mounted soldier was secure in the saddle.

Historical and archaeological opinion places the origin of the true stirrup in China in perhaps the sixth century A.D. It spread westwards through Central Asia, Persia and the Middle East and Russia, reaching the Francs sometime in the eighth century.

The idea of supporting the foot of the rider had of course occurred to people earlier than that. Sculptures in India of the second century B.C. show a rider supporting himself with his big toe in a loop from the girth, all right so far as it went, but no good for a cold climate. A Kushan engraved gem of 100 A.D. shows a rider apparently booted, resting his foot on a sort of hook hanging from the saddle. But the real metal stirrup with its platform for the sole of the foot did not appear for another 400 years. The way was then prepared for real equitation, once the English longbow and the cannon and the musket had driven the armoured knight from the battlefield.

The process was a slow one, and European thought, even in the enlightened Renaissance, was a long way from Xenophon when Rusius, already mentioned, could write:

'The nappy horse should be kept locked in a stable for forty days, thereupon to be mounted wearing large spurs and a strong whip; or else the rider will carry an iron bar, three or four feet long and ending in three well-sharpened hooks and if the horse refuses to go forward he will dig one of these hooks into the horse's quarters and draw him forward; alternatively an assistant may apply a heated iron bar under the horse's tail, while the rider drives the spur in with all available strength.'

The book in which this was written only stopped being current in the sixteenth century when Federico Grisone was founding a new school of riding, which was to start an equestrian revolution. His book, *Ordini di Cavalcare*, published in 1550 was the first serious approach to systematic training of the horse since Xenophon, but there the resemblance to the Greek work ends.

Grisone was a pioneer in teaching the use of combined aids, leg and hand, getting a horse on the bit, obtaining collection, reining back, lateral movement, and so on. The methods of obtaining these results had none of the humanity and gentleness of Xenophon. The aim was the complete subjugation of the horse by violent and painful means. For a horse that refused to be mounted Grisone recommended that 'you will hit with a stick between the ears (but be careful of the eyes) and on all parts of the body where it seem best to you, and also threatening him with a rude and terrible voice...' until he gives in through fear, when 'you must also pat and caress him'. The time-honoured principles of punishment and reward are there.

A most potent instrument of coercion and punishment was the bit, still of medieval proportions. A drawing of one of

Grisone's bits shows cheekpieces nearly as long as the medieval ones, with an absolute mouthful of iron. Spurs were still pretty murderous. Extreme collection was certainly achieved, and high school movements were performed, including rearing and the capriole. Whether these latter, as often suggested, were of any use for military purposes is debatable. Grisone and his successors may have thought so, but the execution of them in the hurly-burly of combat must have been extremely difficult. Even with the highly trained horses of the Spanish Riding School of Vienna quite a lengthy process of preparation and winding up is necessary to get a horse into the air for a courbette or capriole and a rearing horse would be extremely vulnerable to a bold pikeman on foot. Indeed, cavalry at any time have never been consistently successful against infantry.

However that may be, Grisone and other Italian riding masters like Cesar Fiaschi of Ferrara and Jean-Baptiste Pignatelli, who was the instructor of the Frenchman, de la Broue, started a vogue of sophisticated, elegant riding in the grand manner, which was immediately followed by the horsemen of the rest of Europe, particularly France. As Vladimir Littauer says, 'The sixteenth century's cultivated approach to horsemanship originated in Italy as a part of that refinement of material living that accompanied the Renaissance.' (*Horseman's Progress.*)

The Baroque age seemed just made for showy but deliberate form of riding, with its high stepping Andalusian stallions, the pirouettes, the levades and all the rest, all performed by wealthy men of rank, superbly dressed and their horses clad in most ornamental accoutrements. Such arts were not for the common man, who had to be content with his ambling palfrey or even mule. One doubts if they ever thought much of riding as an art, though probably their mounts were far happier than the horses of the manège.

At the end of the sixteenth century the focus on horsemanship switched to France. There were writers in England, such as Thomas Blundeville, Gervaise Markham, and John Astley, but the authority from now on is French. The first of these writers and the direct link with the Italian school was Salomon de la Broue whose book, *Le Cavalerie François* appeared in 1594. More than a hundred years later de la Guérinière, deploring the decadence of horsemanship in his day, wrote: '... we can only seek the truth in the principles of those who have left us in writing the fruits of their work and inspiration. Among a large number of authors we have only two, by the unanimous consent of all connoisseurs, whose works are worth considering, those of M. de la Broue and the Duke of Newcastle.' Praise indeed from such a weighty authority.

De la Broue was the first to advocate the use of the snaffle in the preliminary stages of training, and developed the use of direct flexions and of the legs (and/or spurs) to bring the horse to hand. His contemporary, Antoine de Pluvinel, also a pupil of Pignatelli, followed him with his book, *Instruction du Roi*, in 1623. He took an important step forward to the more humane and understanding approach to the training of the horse, insisting on an appeal to the intelligence and goodwill of the horse instead of the use of brute force, and seeking to find the reasons for resistances and evasions, which, he said, came not usually from malice but from misapprehension. And the prevailing severity of bits and spurs was greatly softened.

The second of de la Guérinière's recommendations, William Cavendish, Duke of Newcastle, published his book, *A General System of Horsemanship* in 1657 in French, while he was a refugee on the Continent from the Cromwell government. Not being concerned with mere money, he only had fifty copies printed which he distributed free to sundry noblemen, and then broke up the plates. The work was later printed again in English and translated into French.

The Duke understood the use of the snaffle for softening the mouth and the suppling of the shoulders, which he sought to obtain by work on the circle, a practice opposed by de la Guérinière, who substituted the shoulder-in and kindred movements. He divided the body of the rider into mobile and immobile parts: the former comprised the upper part of the body down to the waist, and the legs from the knees downwards; the latter being the part in between. He objected to the pillars, for the invention of which de la Guérinière credits de Pluvinel, because 'on them one unnecessarily overburdens and torments a horse in order to make him lift his forehand, hoping thereby to put him on his hocks'. De la Guérinière defends them, however, when used to obtain the piaffe.

The real turning point in the study and teaching of equitation comes with François Robichon de la Guérinière, who opened his riding academy in Paris in 1715 and published his great work, *Ecole de Cavalerie*, in, 1733. This book is probably the most complete manual of the horse ever written. It begins with a comprehensive section on the points of the horse, ageing, colours, different breeds, the bridle, bits, bitting, shoeing, saddlery; the second part deals with the training of the horse, and its use in outdoor sports as well as in the manège; a third part covers anatomy (skeleton), veterinary details and breeding.

He castigates the practical horseman – still with us – who dismisses theory as unnecessary. 'Without theory practice is always uncertain . . . theory teaches us to work on sound principles, which instead of opposing nature should be a means of perfecting nature with the help of art. Practice gives us the ability to put into execution what theory teaches us. And to acquire this ability one must *love the horse, be strong and bold, and have great patience*. These are the principal qualities which go to make a true horseman.' (The italics are mine.) And he defends work in the manège because its 'object is to make a horse supple, gentle and obedient and to come back on its haunches'.

He then spends considerable time on the psychology of the horse, describing its physical and mental characteristics and seeking causes for its so-called vices and resistances. He finds them in the varied characters of horses, lack of courage, sluggishness, impetuosity, bad temper, not all of which, he admits are necessarily inherent in the creature but the 'fault of those who have broken them in badly' or 'punished them excessively', or asking of them 'things of which they are not capable'. Another interesting reason, very pertinent in this age, he gives for the various faults he finds in horses is 'riding them too young. It makes them weak in the loins and hocks, and sickens them permanently of the whole process.' The right age, in his view, to start training a horse is six, seven or eight years, 'according to the climate of the place of his birth'.

Contrary to present dressage practice the reins were for the most part held in the left hand only, the right holding the whip. 'One uses separated reins with horses that are not yet accustomed to obey the bridle hand; or with horses that resist and refuse to turn on one hand.' A good hand must be 'light, soft and firm'. The light hand has no contact, the soft hand very light contact, and the firm hand full contact; and de la Guérinière describes very clearly the process of give and take in the handling of the reins, also the combined action of hands and legs. It must be remembered that the basis of all the work described is extreme collection, the horse still controlled by a severe curb bit, an instrument of torture in the wrong hands, of which there are always many in every age. The only slight relaxation is that allowed in hunting.

The short chapter on hunting insists that the manège training is the foundation of the preparation of the hunter, but he is allowed more galloping in a less elevated manner, with the angle of the head in front of the perpendicular. De la Guérinière, by the way, much admired the English hunter. The progressive training for the gallop, however, is well on modern lines. Jumping receives scant attention, but the short paragraph, based directly on de la Broue, is very well in line with modern principles and practice. 'Take a hurdle, about three to four feet wide and ten to twelve feet long; first of all lay it flat on the ground and take the horse over it at the walk and trot and then at the gallop; if it steps on it instead of clearing it, punish him with whip and spur. Then raise the hurdle about a foot, and, as the horse jumps freely, raise it its full height, embellishing it with branches and leaves. This method, which he (de la Broue) says he has often practised, certainly teaches a horse to extend and stretch itself for jumping hedges and ditches; but this lesson, necessary for a war horse and a hunter, should not be used until he turns obediently to either hand, nor until his head is set and his mouth accepts the bit.'

Ecole de Cavalerie sets the tone for all future manège riding and what we now call dressage until the present time, and is acknowledged to be the fountainhead of the riding at the two remaining great high school riding establishments of Europe – Vienna and Saumur (now removed to Fontainebleau). But in the eighteenth century another school of thought (if you can call it that, for its proponents were not much given to thought of that kind), takes the field with that peculiarly English sport of hunting.

The pursuit of game is common to all nations, but the equable climate and open countryside of England, together with a plentiful supply of deer and foxes, were ideally suited for hunting on horseback with packs of hounds; and the squires of England were admirably placed financially and temperamentally to exploit them to the full. They were not concerned with the niceties of the manège; all they wanted of their horses was that they should carry them safely and fast across country. They were in their way superb horsemen and had something to teach the Continentals, but it was a long time before the lessons went home, by which time their descendants had realised that the manège had a meaning for them too.

Side by side with hunting went racing, requiring still greater speed and lighter saddlery. The English took their horses and their riding habits to North America, mingled with the descendants of the Spanish horses, to produce the range rider of the pioneer West and the whole school of Western riding. It was a case, as always, of adapting methods to needs and circumstances.

The development of military tactics also had its effect on the Continental ideas of horsemanship. Until the age of mechanisation the ultimate object of all equitation was to produce a cavalryman. As the cavalries of Europe assumed the function of shock assault in orderly formed bodies, it was felt that the prolonged and sophisticated training of the manège, of establishments like the School of Versailles, and the Spanish Court Riding School of Vienna (founded in 1580) was no longer necessary. Frederick the Great in Germany and the Earl of Pembroke in England were chiefly responsible for this changed approach. Pembroke published his book, *A Method of Breaking Horses and Teaching Soldiers to Ride*, in 1762, which was followed in France in 1776 by *Traité sur la Cavalerie* by a French soldier of Scottish descent, Count Drummond de Melfort. Both were an attack on the conventional manège riding as out of date for practical people and in need of modification. All that a trooper needed to know in their opinion was 'to make his horse go forward, to make it stop when he wishes, to make it back, turn to the right and the left, walk, trot and gallop'. For jumping they still relied on de la Broue. The School of Versailles, on which the Spanish Riding School is based, continued, but a School of Instruction for Cavalry Officers was opened at Saumur in 1771. Closed during the revolutionary and Napoleonic period, they re-opened afterwards, Saumur to continue into the twentieth century, Versailles to close finally in 1830.

The nineteenth century saw the refinement of military riding and the expansion of cross-country riding, the *campagne* school. The English foxhunters carried on more or less regardless of these developments. The two great figures of the first half of the century were Viscount d'Aure, who came to Saumur from Versailles, and François Baucher. Both were outstanding horsemen, both in direct opposition. The former a soldier and riding master stood for sporting riding, in the freedom of the horse to co-operate with the rider rather than to be coerced into obedience; the latter, a circus rider, went back to the classical school in requiring complete submission of the horse to the will of the rider, principally by extreme collection at the halt followed by forward movement. The one represented the outdoor school of riding, the other the indoor – Fillis said that he never saw Baucher ride outside the school – and never the twain should meet. Their controversy made headlines in the 1840s, and was, of course, never resolved. But d'Aure won in the end, his ideas and methods helped to produce much of the riding of today, and foreshadowed perhaps the doctrine of Caprilli, the inventor of forward riding. Baucher's tricks and innovations mostly remained where they started, in the circus.

This is not to decry the circus. Much brilliant riding is seen there, even if the effects are not always obtained by classical means, and it is observable that the lighter horses used in circus equitation perform airs above the ground with a great deal more apparent freedom and lack of obvious effort than the classically trained ones. James Fillis (1834–1913), who studied high school under a pupil of Baucher and ended by disagreeing flatly with the latter's methods, spent his early career in the circus, until he became chief instructor at the Officers' Cavalry School in St Petersburg. Fillis was a very great high school rider and his influence on equitation at the end of the nineteenth and even in the present century has never been fairly acknowledged.

Equitation in the Continental armies had become very artificial and entirely unsuited for jumping when in 1892 at the Italian Cavalry School of Tor Di Quinto a young officer, Federico Caprilli, began to develop his ideas on the natural schooling and riding of the horse which gave birth to the last great revolution in horsemanship, the forward seat. He left very little in writing himself; he died too young in 1907; but was fortunate in having as his interpreter, the late Piero Santini, who died in 1960.

Before his time the English foxhunters and steeplechasers sat well back over fences; the latter mostly still do. The military riders taught that one should lean forward at the take-off and lean back on landing. Although even after World War I there were archaic cavalry officers like a major in my regiment who instructed his young officers thus: 'Take a firm hold of the reins, lean well back, and let him *pull* you over.' At that time Caprilli was not so well known in British cavalry circles, but Colonel M. F. McTaggart, of the 5th Royal Irish Lancers, invented an exaggerated form of forward seat of his own which aroused so much heated controversy that, in India, an Army Order was issued banning all discussion of the subject in Messes.

So, at the beginning of the twentieth century there were four main streams of horsemanship: the classical school, which still continued, revived by the introduction of Grand Prix dressage in the Olympic Games of 1912; the new forward riding school of Caprilli; the untutored 'practical' horsemanship of the English squires; and the 'Western' riding of the cowboys of the Americas. The soldiers developed a compromise between de la Guérinière and Caprilli, which the latter would never have have countenanced. 'Manège and cross-country equitation,' he said, 'are,

32

in my opinion, antagonistic: one excludes and destroys the other.' (This and other statements by Caprilli are taken from *The Caprilli Papers*.)

He maintained that 'we must strive to leave a horse as nature fashioned him, with his balance and attitude of head un-altered', which eliminated collection from the training of the military or outdoor horse. He described the riding position based on the knee grip, shortened leathers and pressure on the stirrup irons, buttocks off the saddle except at rest – the forward seat. 'The hands must be held naturally on either side of the withers, always low and ready to advance towards the horse's mouth. The lightest possible contact must, however, always be preserved between the horse's mouth and the rider's hands. A horse has never fallen because of galloping on the wrong lead. I therefore consider it useless to trouble a pupil regarding the lead his horse may happen to be galloping on.'

The Caprilli Papers take up less than forty pages, but the teaching of Caprilli, interpreted and expanded by Piero Santini in his three key books, *Riding Reflections, The Forward Impulse,* and *The Riding Instructor,* spread all over the world. The 'proof of the pudding' was in the Italian show jumping successes in the early 1900s, and all the countries of Europe took it up. Inevitably the purity of 'Il Sistema' has been adulterated by compromise, but the foundations remain. All the cavalry equita-tion schools had their version of it, but the most thoughtful and practical exposition of its modifications are those of Captain Vladimir Littauer, a Russian cavalry officer who became a successful riding master in New York between the wars, especially in his books, *Be a Better Horseman* and *Common-sense Horsemanship.*

School riding, now called 'dressage', long neglected in England, also had a revival between the wars, thanks to the efforts of Colonel and Mrs V. D. S. Williams, Henry Wynmalen and Mr E. Schmit-Jensen, and with the establishment of the three-day event at Badminton in 1949 there occurred, amazingly, a sort of marriage between the hunting man and the dressage rider. The former wanted to compete in a galloping cross-country event, but had to perform a dressage test in order to do so. Coming to scoff, he stayed to practise.

So, at long last, two opposing schools of thought have come together. The extremes in either direction, represented by racing and high school, still remain on their own, just to show that rigidity in horsemanship, whether of mind or body, is a negation of the art.

3 The Points of the Horse — Anatomy

The horse is a vertebrate mammal of the order of hoofed animals; that is to say it has an internal bony framework – the skeleton – built round a more or less rigid series of bones down the back (we shall qualify the term 'rigid' later on), covered with muscles and hair.

The beauty of any living vertebrate depends, so say the artists, on the bone structure, which is the chassis, as it were, setting the external proportions which we see when we look superficially at a horse, or any other animal. The effect of the bones, combined with the muscles, is also functional. 'When we speak of the conformation of a horse, we refer to the adaptability of his body for general or special work.' (Hayes, *The Points of the Horse*.) And the proportions of the bones and muscles of any animal are appropriate to that work. Generally speaking a very strong, slow-moving animal, adapted for carrying or pulling heavy weights, will have short legs in proportion to the length of the body; while a creature built for speed will have long legs in relation to the body. One has only to compare a racehorse with a heavy draught horse.

The purpose of all living things is to move, so, to quote Hayes again, 'The chief duties of bones in the act of progression are: 1. To bear weight; 2. To resist in combination with the ligaments the effects of concussion; 3. To act as levers. Capability for performing (1) and (2) is dependent on conditions of texture ("quality"), size ("substance") and arrangement.' Hence the preoccupation of all horsemen with 'bone' and its quality, especially below the knees and hocks.

Bone is composed partly of animal matter (fibrous tissue) and partly of earthy matter (phosphate and salts of lime). The latter give rigidity and hardness to the bone, the former bind it together. The denser the composition of these parts, the stronger the bone, and so the greater endurance and soundness of the horse. And one can see the importance of good, dry limestone soil for the breeding and keeping of horses. In the main dry climates and hard food make for tougher animals.

The picture (Fig. 1) shows the outline of the skeleton and lists

34

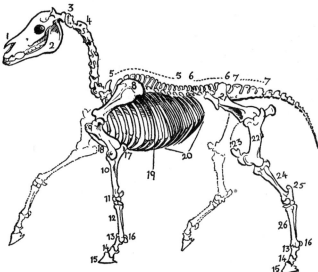

Fig. 1.   The Skeleton of the Horse

1. *Nasal Bone*   2. *Lower Jaw*   3. *Atlas*   4. *Axis*   5. *Back (Dorsal Vertebrae)*   6. *Loins (Lumbar Vertebrae)*   7. *Croup (Sacral Vertebrae)* 8. *Shoulder Blade (Scapula)*   9. *Upper Arm (Humerus)*   10. *Forearm (Radius)*   11. *'Knee' Bones*   12. *Cannon Bone (Metacarpal)*   13. *Long Pastern Bone*   14. *Short Pastern Bone*   15. *Pedal Bone*   16. *Sesamoid* 17. *Point of Elbow (Ulna)*   18. *Breast Bone (Sternum)*   19. *True Ribs* 20. *False Ribs*   21. *Pelvis*   22. *Thigh Bone (Femur)*   23. *Stifle (Patella, true knee)*   24. *Tibia (Shin)*   25. *Point of Hock*   26. *Cannon Bone (Metatarsal)*

the bones in order. It should be realised that the forelegs of a horse are the equivalent of the human arm and hand. So the term 'knee' given to the bony structure above the cannon bone is only a conventional, and convenient, way of describing that part. It is in fact the carpus or wrist. From the fetlock joint downwards the formation corresponds to the human finger, except that the long process of evolution has reduced it all to one, the same of course in the hindquarters, so the horse walks literally on finger and toe.

The skeleton sustains and protects the vital organs of the body, the heart and lungs, in the rib-cage, and to the rear of them, separated by a sheet of muscle known as the diaphragm, the stomach, bowels, liver, kidneys, bladder, spleen and glands. These work involuntarily and continuously all through life, without having to be actuated by nerves carrying instructions from the brain, e.g. the heart, which pumps blood over the whole body.

The main axis of the body is the backbone, the vertebra, which runs from the head to the tail. It is divided into sections: the neck or cervical vertebrae, the back or dorsal vertebrae, the loins or lumbar vertebrae, the croup or sacral vertebrae, and the tail or coccygeal vertebrae. From the base of the neck to the loins there are eighteen vertebrae, from which spring eighteen pairs of ribs. The first eight pairs are anchored to the breastbone (sternum) and are known as true ribs, constituting the rib-cage; the remaining ten pairs grow out of each other in a steadily diminishing scale and are the false ribs.

There is great variety of mobility in the various parts of the backbone. The neck bones have considerable power of move-

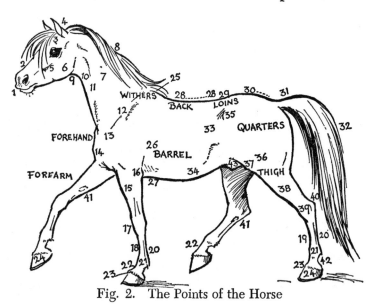

Fig. 2. The Points of the Horse

1. *Mouth (nostril, muzzle, lips)* 2. *Face* 3. *Forehead* 4. *Poll* 5. *Cheekbone* 6. *Cheek* 7. *Neck* 8. *Crest* 9. *Throat* 10. *Windpipe* 11. *Jugular Groove* 12. *Shoulder* 13. *Point of Shoulder* 14. *Breast* 15. *Forearm* 16. *Elbow* 17. *Knee* 18. *Cannon* 19. *Shannon (hindleg)* 20. *Back Tendons* 21. *Fetlock Joint* 22. *Pastern* 23. *Coronet* 24. *Hoof* 25. *Withers* 26. *Chest* 27. *Girth* 28. *Back* 29. *Loins* 30. *Croup* 31. *Dock* 32. *Tail* 33. *Flank* 34. *Belly* 35. *Hip* 36. *Thigh* 37. *Stifle (True Knee)* 38. *Gaskin (Second Thigh)* 39. *Hock* 40. *Points of Hock* 41. *Chestnuts* 42. *Ergot* 43. *Sheath*

ment, a horse's neck can be too mobile at times. The loins have fair flexibility but not much power of lateral movement; there is little movement in the croup, but the tail is extremely flexible. Lateral movement is possible where the neck joins the dorsal vertebrae (the withers), and behind the lumbar vertebrae, but although the articulation of the bones of the back is flexible, having a play of about one eighth of an inch only very slight lateral curvature is possible, and that only in a highly trained horse. Nor is there much upward (arching) movement; though the whole backbone will sag in old age. The belief that a buck-jumper arches its back when making its bid to remove its rider is not borne out by countless photographs which show the back absolutely straight, the effect being obtained by the devastating upward drive of all four legs together and the lowering of the head and hindquarters. The ribs, having moveable joints with the vertebrae, can expand, the more so towards the rear.

The other bones of the body are mostly joined together with either ball and socket or hinge joints. The shoulder and hip joints are ball and socket, which give them a wide range of movement. The elbow is a hinge joint, which can be bent and extended. The whole system of the fore limbs, however, is attached through the shoulder blades to the backbone at the base of the neck by a very strong fan-shaped muscle (serratus magnus). The horse, by the way, has no collar bone.

The main bones of the forehand, below the shoulder blade are the humerus (upper arm), which slopes back from the shoulder blade to meet the radius (forearm), which goes straight down from the elbow to the 'knee', below which are the cannon bone, the long and short pasterns, sesamoid bones, and, inside the hoof, the pedal or coffin bone and the navicular bone.

In the hindquarters the thigh bone joins the pelvis at the hip joint, sloping forwards to meet the tibia (shin) and the patella (knee cap or true knee), the latter being held in a groove firmly at the top of the tibia by three vertical ligaments and two laterals. The tibia, sloping backwards to the hock joint and point of the hock, is known as the gaskin or second thigh. The bones below the hock joint are the same as those below the 'knee' in the foreleg.

The bones of a joint are held together by ligaments, which can be either cords or flat bands, and between the bones is a pad of hard cartilage to reduce concussion. A joint is covered with a sheet-like membrane – the joint capsule – which is composed of two layers, the outer being thick to support the joint, the inner containing cells which secrete the joint oil, synovia, which lubricates the joint. Damage to these ligaments and membranes causes much of the lameness that occurs in working horses.

The whole skeleton is covered with muscles, which go to make up what we call flesh, the red edible meat. There are voluntary muscles for every part of the body, which means that they act on the commands of the brain, received via the nerves, which also cover the whole body. Muscles are attached to bones – and also to cartilages by tendons. These are tough inelastic ropes, composed of many threads, and like ligaments rounded or flat, which enable the elastic muscles to do their work without damage. The sprain of any joint is usually due to the tendon giving way, not the muscle.

The muscles move the body by acting on the bones. One set of muscles will bend or flex a joint (flexors), and another will straighten the joint out (extensors). There are an enormous number of muscles in the body with varied functions, too complicated to be detailed here, but some of the more important ones should be noted.

An important muscle is the panniculus, a broad sheet of muscle which lies immediately underneath the skin covering the neck, sides of the chest and abdomen, being attached by sheets of fibrous tissue. This is the muscle that makes the skin twitch when a fly lights on it, caused by its contraction and relaxation, and it is a great blessing to horses.

Running from behind the ear to the shoulder is the brachiocephalicus, which is one of the muscles for moving the head and neck. The principal muscle connecting the fore limbs with the trunk is the serratus magnus, a powerful fan-shaped muscle; another is the trapezuis, a triangular muscle covering roughly the area before and behind the withers. The most powerful muscle in the body is the longissimus dorsi, which runs roughly from the croup to the neck, attached to the pelvis, sacrum, all the loin and dorsal vertebrae, the last four bones of the neck, and to the ribs.

All locomotion, preferably forward, with which we are most concerned in a horse, is brought about by displacement of the centre of gravity, in other words loss of balance. A man standing at attention is in balance; if he leans forward so that his centre of gravity is in front of his base of support, he loses his balance, and will fall forward unless he takes a step forward to adjust his centre of gravity; and so on. It is the same with a horse, when he starts from the walk into a halt: '... by the straightening of one or both hindlegs he brings the centre of gravity of his body beyond the toe of the most advanced forefoot, with the result that the other foreleg has to be carried forward in order to restore the equilibrium. In doing this, the first foot to quit the ground will usually be a fore one.' (Hayes, *The Points of the Horse.*)

The same authority describes the movements of the limbs as follows. Fore limb: 'The shoulder blade (scapula) is rotated, chiefly by its upper end being pulled downwards by the posterior portion of the serratus magnus, and by its lower end being drawn upwards by the levator humeri, which also draws the entire limb to the front; the flexor muscles of the forearm bend the knee and the points of the fetlock and pastern, so as to enable the foot to clear the ground; the flexor brachii assists in straightening the shoulder joint and raises the knee; and the extensor muscles of the forearm finally straighten the knee and all the joints below it. When full extension of the fore limb takes place all the bones of the leg (from the shoulder blade to the pedal bone) are straightened as far as possible. It is evident that the less upright (more sloping) the shoulder blade is, the more can the foot and knee be advanced and raised.' The reason why, of course, horsemen look for a sloping shoulder in a riding horse.

Hind limb: Propulsion by the hind limb of the horse takes place through the hip joint and pelvis. When a horse moves at any speed, there is a tendency to displace the centre of gravity first to one side and then the other, which gives a rocking effect. The wider the limbs are apart the more pronounced the rocking will be. The muscular effort needed to counteract it reduces that available for forward movement, and consequently for speed. So in schooling a principal object is to train the horse to go straight. It is a fault in conformation if either the forelegs or the hindlegs are too far apart. Being too close together is also a fault and leads to brushing, which is the knocking of the inside of the fetlock joint with the opposite hoof; more common in the forelegs than the hind.

Over the muscles is the outer covering of the body, the skin, consisting of two layers: the top one being the epidermis, of cellular material having in its turn two layers; the lower layer is the dermis or true skin, composed of fibrous tissue and elastic fibres. Out of the skin grows the hair, which in the horse is regularly shed and replaced twice a year, spring and autumn. In the skin are two kinds of glands, sweat glands, and sebaceous glands, the latter producing an oily secretion to lubri-

39

cate the hair, and give the coat its much prized glossy sleekness. The hoof is an extension of the skin, which, instead of growing hairs, produces a collection of closely connected tubular horn fibres, cemented together and forming the horn. The chief functions of the skin are to protect the muscles underneath, and to regulate the body temperature.

COLOURING AND MARKINGS

The hairs of the horse grow in different colours, with variations on the body which constitute various markings. In 1954 the Royal College of Veterinary Surgeons issued a pamphlet on colours and markings of the horse for the benefit of veterinary surgeons giving descriptions of animals so that there should be consistent uniformity of nomenclature. The descriptions below follow that pamphlet.

The four main whole colours are black, brown, bay and chestnut.

Black is wholly black, including the muzzle and eyelids, apart from white markings as described below.

Black-brown is predominantly black but with brown muzzle and sometimes brown or tan flanks.

Brown is a mixture of black and brown pigment, with black limbs, mane and tail.

Bay-brown has brown as the predominant colour, black limbs (black points), mane and tail, bay muzzle.

Bay is usually a reddish brown colour like a ripe horse chestnut, but it can vary towards brown and chestnut, but always accompanied by black limbs, mane and tail.

Chestnut has variations of yellow colouring, distinguished as light, dark, liver. 'A 'true' chestnut has a chestnut mane and tail, which may be lighter or darker than the body colour. Light chestnuts, verging on palomino, may have flaxen manes and tails.

Other colours are dun, cream (Palomino), grey, roan, piebald, skewbald, odd-coloured, spotted (Appaloosa).

Blue dun is diluted black in colour, evenly distributed, with black mane and tail and black skin. There can be a dorsal stripe or withers stripe.

Yellow dun has a widely diffuse yellow pigment in the hair, with or without dorsal and withers stripes and bars on the legs. The striping usually goes with black on the head and limbs. The skin is black.

Cream: The body is of a light cream colour with unpigmented skin. The eyes often have a pinkish or bluish appearance.

Palomino is officially described as a pure gold colour, as in a 'newly-minted gold coin' if such is available for comparison. Varying shades from light to dark are permissible. Mane and tail are pure white, varying from silver to flaxen, eyes dark. The skin is dark with no sign of albinism.

Grey: The body coat is 'a varying mosaic of black and white hairs, with the skin black. With increasing age the coat grows lighter in colour'. There is no such thing officially as a white horse. Grey horses are born almost black.

Flea-bitten grey is when the white is mixed with one or more of the other colours.

Roans vary according to the basic whole colours.

Blue Roan: The body colour is black or black-brown with a sprinkling of white hair which gives the coat its bluish tinge. Black hairs usually predominate on the lower limbs, but there can be white markings.

Bay or Red roan: The same as above except that the body colour is bay or bay-brown, with the white hairs giving a reddish tinge to the coat.

Strawberry, or chestnut, roan: The body colour is chestnut with an admixture of white hairs.

Piebald: Large irregular patches of black and white over the body, with usually clearly defined lines of demarcation between them.

Skewbald: Large irregular patches of white and any other colour but black on the body.

Odd coloured: Large irregular patches of more than two colours, which may merge into each other on the dividing lines.

Whole coloured is used where there are no hairs of any other colour on the body, head or limbs.

Spotted, or Appaloosa: Spots of various sizes and patterns on white, or white on other colours. This does not include piebald, skewbald, or dappled grey. The following markings are recognised by the societies in England and the U.S.A. governing the breeding of these types. *Leopard:* Spots of any colour on a white or light coloured background. *Blanket:* Animals having a white rump or back on which are spots of any colour. *Snowflake:* White spots on a foundation of any colour. Special characteristics of this type are: white scelera round the eye (like the white round the human eye); hooves striped, yellowish-white and black or brown in vertical stripes; bare skin is mottled; manes and tails are often very sparse.

The many and various markings superimposed on these colours are described as follows.

Head

Star: White mark on the head, of varying size, described as large, small, faint, triangular, round, etc. If there are only a few white hairs, they should be so described. *Stripe:* A narrow white strip down the face, with or without a star, not wider than the surface of the nasal bones. If separated from a star, it is called an 'interrupted stripe starting from...' It can be distinguished as broad, narrow, inclined to right or left, etc. *Blaze:* White marking covering almost the whole of the forehead between the eyes and extending beyond the width of the nasal bones and usually to the muzzle. *White face:* The white covers the forehead and front of the face, and extending on either side to the mouth, or one side only. *Snip:* An isolated white mark independent of those already named, usually found between or near the nostrils. *Lip markings:* Spots or marks round about the lips, which should be described as observed. *White muzzle:* White on both lips and up to the nostrils. *Wall-eye:* Caused by lack of pigment, partial or total, in the iris, giving a pinkish-white or bluish-white tinge to the eye. *Showing the white of the eye:* Where some part of the white sclerotic of the eye shows between the eyelids. *Whorls:* Irregular setting of the coat hairs, like little eddies or whirlpools.

Body

Grey ticked: White hairs sparsely distributed through the coat also called white hairs on coat. *Flecked:* Small collections of white hairs appearing irregularly in any part of the body. May be heavily or lightly flecked. *Black marks:* Small areas of black hairs among white or any other colour. *Spots:* Small, more or less circular collections of hairs differing from the general body colour, distributed in various parts of the body. (See also *Spotted.*) *Patch:* A term to describe any larger irregular area of differing colour not covered by previous definitions. *Zebra marks:* Stripes on the limbs, neck, withers or quarters. *Mane and tail:* If different in colour from the rest of the body, it should be stated in any description of the animal. *Whorls:* See under *Head,* above.

Limbs

Hoofs: Any variation in colour should be noted. *White markings:* These used to be described as 'stocking' or 'sock', but it is recommended that this be discontinued in official descriptions, the actual markings and their extent being exactly stated, e.g. 'white to half pastern', 'white to below the fetlock', etc. *Black points:* The name commonly used to describe the black legs of a bay horse below the knee.

General

Mixed: To describe a white marking which contains varying amounts of hairs of the general body colour. *Bordered:* To describe a marking that is surrounded by a mixed border, e.g. 'bordered star', 'bordered stripe'. *Flesh marks:* Patches where the pigment of the skin is absent. *Acquired marks:* Such as saddle marks, girth marks, brands, tattoo marks, docking, which have been acquired through human agency.

THE FOOT

It is superfluous to dwell on the importance of the foot to the horse and its rider and the work that it has to do. At every stride the weight of the horse – and rider – falls on each hoof in turn; at about forty strides to the minute and a weight of 1,000 lb. there is quite an accumulation of weight on each foot.

Contained within the hoof are three bones: the lower part of the short pastern bone, the navicular bone and the pedal or coffin bone (Fig. 3). The last-named, situated inside the actual

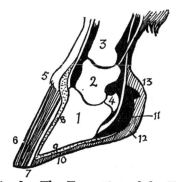

Fig. 3.   The Formation of the Foot

1. *Coffin or Pedal Bone*   2. *Short Pastern Bone*   3. *Long Pastern Bone*   4. *Navicular Bone*   5. *Coronary Band*   6. *Wall of Hoof*   7. *White Line*   8. *Fleshy leaves or Laminae*   9. *Fleshy Sole*   10. *Horny Sole*   11. *Fleshy Frog*   12. *Horny Frog*   13. *Plantar Cushion*

hoof, is a roughly semi-circular wedge, cut away at the back. Surrounding the top of this bone are the lateral cartilages, which can be felt at the bulges of the heel as 'springy' tissue. They act by helping to suspend the pedal bone. Above is the coronary band, which surrounds the hoof at the upper border and is made up of horn-producing cells from which the horn of the hoof is supplied; and at the rear of the foot the cushion of the heel or the plantar cushion. Behind the pedal bone, and protected by the plantar cushion is the navicular bone, a small boat-shaped bone, which acts as a pulley or roller for the deep flex or tendon (perforans) attached to the pedal bone. Resting in the socket at the top of the pedal bone is the lower end of the short pastern bone, to which is attached the superficial flexor tendon (perforatus). Anatomically the pedal bone is the third phalanx or finger tip. The short pastern bone and the long pastern above it correspond to the second and first phalanges of the human finger, or on the hindlegs to the toe. The horse, it will be realised, moves on its toes and finger tips.

The hoof proper consists exteriorly of the horny wall, a hard, black, insensitive horny substance which grows out of the coron-

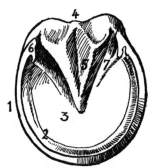

Fig. 4.   The Sole of the Foot

1. *Wall of the Hoof*   2. *White Line*   3. *Horny Sole*   4. *Cleft of the Frog*
5. *Frog*   6. *Angle of the Heels*   7. *Bars*

ary band. This horn grows downwards continually during life, its length having to be regulated either by natural means of wear and tear, or by rasping back with a file in the case of domesticated animals whether shod or unshod. The inside of this hard shelter dovetails into an enormous number of fleshy leaves or laminae, which are attached to the pedal bone and completely fill the interior of the foot. These laminae are copiously supplied with blood vessels, so that the foot inside literally floats in blood. If these parts are pricked in shoeing by a wrongly-directed nail, they bleed freely. They are extremely sensitive and subject to compression and expansion every time the foot strikes and leaves the ground. If these laminae become excessively filled with blood, through over-rich food or too much concussion, they expand against the hard casing of the wall and get inflamed, producing the troublesome and painful disease of laminitis or fever in the feet, which is very common amongst English ponies.

The horn of the wall grows out of the front of the coronary band at an angle of about 50 degrees in the case of the fore foot and at a steeper angle, about 30 degrees, in the hind foot. The hoof is rounded at the front, but straightens up somewhat on the inside and is also more upright; the outside curves and slopes more markedly, so that the foot presents a broad round surface to the ground. The hind foot is altogether steeper, narrower and more elongated.

At the back of the foot, on both sides, the wall curves sharply forwards, this part being known as the bars, to form a wedge-shaped area to accommodate the frog. This is a thick, wedge-shaped piece of rubbery horn, with a cleft in the middle, set point forward in the space between the bars. This exterior part, which shows, is extremely tough and resilient, and, with an unshod horse, was the first part of the shock-absorbing system which reaches up the leg via the pasterns, to the shoulders in the forehand and the pelvis in the hindquarters, touching the ground at every stride.

It grows out of an inner, fleshy frog which is closely connected with the interior bones and cartilages. Like the wall of the hoof it constantly replaces itself by growth. The under surface of the foot is occupied by the sole, a hard, insensitive substance on the outside, roughly crescent-shaped, with a soft laminated fleshy sensitive sole behind it. This sole, which is slightly concave, is part of the bearing surface of the foot, and it joins the horny wall, a white line marking the division between the hard and fleshy laminae. The appearance of this white line is a sign to the farrier that the wall of the hoof has been rasped back far enough. It is a guide also for the direction of the nails when putting on a shoe, which should never go inside it. The inner fleshy sole at the angle of the wall of the hoof and the bars is susceptible to bruising, through pressure and concussion brought about by excessive work on hard surfaces, picking up stones, lack of regular shoeing, showing as a red mark. This is a corn, and the area is known as the seat of corn.

4 The Points of the Horse — Conformation

When one judges a horse from the outside one of the first considerations will be the work it is expected to do. If speed is required, sloping shoulders and good length above the knees and hocks are desirable; for a harness horse a straight shoulder and longish back are acceptable; a heavy draft horse will have short, strong legs; a cutting horse will be found to have a powerful forehand and well-developed forearm muscles. But there are basic factors of conformation which are common to all equines.

Looked at from the side a well-shaped horse should give the general impression of proportion and symmetry. If the back looks too long, or the head appears overlarge for the rest of the body, or the body seems too far away from the ground, 'showing too much daylight', or the feet are too ponderous, then the proportions are wrong. For the purpose of judging and description, the horse is usually divided into three parts, forehand, middlepiece, hindquarters. The forehand takes in the head, neck, forelegs, shoulders and withers; the middlepiece all parts between the withers and the croup; the hindquarters, or quarters, comprise all the rear part of the body from the pelvis, exteriorly the hip, down to the feet. A horse must be judged, of course, from the front and rear as well from the side, but first impressions are always received from the side view. After first impressions one must assess each part individually from front to rear.

Head

A head can be too small for the body as well as too large, and a good guide estimating the right proportion is the fact that the length of the head from the poll to the nostrils should be about equal to the distance from behind the withers to the hip; and also to the depth of the girth taken from a point behind the withers. Other equal distances to the head are from the croup to the stifle, and from the point of the hock to the ground.

The length of the body of a well-proportioned horse from the point of the shoulder to the point of the buttock is roughly three times the length of the head.

The head itself should have a bony, rather ascetic, appearance, with a good straight or slightly concave profile, more pronounced in some breeds, e.g. the Arab, than in others. Heavy, cold-blooded horses, such as the Shire and some German breeds, will tend to have Roman noses. A horse with a pronounced lump between the eyes is widely considered to be unreliable in temperament. There should be a good deep jaw bone, and no thickness where the head joins the neck, so that the horse can bend its head easily downwards and backwards when called upon to do so by the action of the bit. This facilitates the very necessary process of flexion, without which there is no real control of the horse.

The eyes should be large, nearly horizontal, and generous in expression. A horse with small or shifty eyes, tending to show too much white, will usually have a mean disposition. The horse breathes through its nostrils, so they must be wide and fine and sensitive. The ears should be in proportion to the head, firm but mobile, continually switching backwards and forwards, displaying interest in all that is going on. A rider should always watch the movements of his horse's ears; they will tell him whether the horse is really *listening* to him or not. 'One must never,' said Willi Schultheis, the great German dressage rider and trainer, 'underrate the importance of the ears.' A horse that continually lays its ears flat back is one to be avoided. In any case it is a danger signal.

Neck

The neck should be long, graceful and muscular. A fair proportion is that, measured from withers to poll, it should be a little less than one and a half times the length of the head. Seen from the side it should appear light and slender, but when felt by the fingers along the crest it should be tough and full of muscle. A slack or stringy neck means weakness and unfitness. The muscles of the neck play a great part in movement, especially in jumping. When seen from above by a rider the crest should appear quite thick and broad.

The crest should start straight from the withers for the first half of its length, and then describe a slightly convex curve towards the head. The lower side of the neck takes the gullet and windpipe and goes straight into the space between the jaw bones, which is another reason for there having to be plenty of room at the join. When the neck starts from the withers with a concave curve the result is known as a ewe neck and it is a serious fault in conformation. It often appears in young horses that are unfit and under-fed, when it can sometimes be eradicated, or improved, by proper training and conditioning. A swan neck is when this concavity is more accentuated and the horse carries its head high, with a tendency to star gaze. A short, thick neck is ugly and usually goes with thickening and stiffness at the jowl, which makes the horse virtually unmanageable. The withers, which are formed by a group of bony processes growing out of the vertebrae, should be fairly high and narrow and well covered with muscle. Flat withers below the level of croup tend to give a downhill ride, and also allow a saddle to move forward, with the danger of rubbing and galling. Flat withers are often found with straight and loaded shoulders.

Fore limbs

The shoulders should be long, narrow and muscular, with a good slope forwards to the point of the shoulder, from which the upper arm or humerus slopes back and downwards to the point of elbow (ulna). The shoulder slope is made by the shoulder blade or scapula, which should be flat and merge into the withers and quite close to the opposite bone. When the shoulder blades are wide apart they cause a lumpy, 'loaded' shoulder. They are attached to the ribs by powerful muscles, which give the body a kind of elastic suspension, and are the top link in the shock-absorbing chain of the forelegs. A good shoulder should slope forwards at approximately an angle of 45 degrees, and the upper arm roughly at right angles to it.

The forelegs should be vertical from the point of the elbow to the fetlock joint. From the elbow to the 'knee' is forearm or radius, and it should be long in proportion to the rest of the leg, straight and broad and well covered with muscle. The knee (corresponding to the human wrist) should appear deep from front to rear, large and flat from the front view. Below this is the cannon bone, which it is desirable to have short in comparison with the forearm, and thick when seen from the side. Tendons and ligaments run down the rear edge of this bone, and the outer circumference of this part is measured to assess the amount of bone which a horse is said to have. This measurement is taken immediately below the knee, and in an average horse can be eight to nine inches. A horse with narrow 'bone' is not likely to be a weight carrier, but of equal importance to the dimensions is the quality of the bone itself which is gauged by the density of its composition. This, of course, is something you cannot discover until the horse is dead; but as a general rule the better the breeding the better the quality of the bone. Pure-bred Arab horses do not show a great deal of bone but they are renowned for their endurance and weight carrying over long distances. The circumference of an Arab horse's head may not appear as large as that of an Irish hunter, but because the Arab is capable of assimilating more from a given diet, its bone is denser and stronger.

The fetlock joint should be large, and below it the pasterns slope forward at an angle of about 45 degrees to the hoof, which they join at the coronet. Behind and between the two pastern bones are the small sesamoid bones, over which run the tendons and ligaments. Inflammation of this bone through excessive concussion or strain causes the condition known as sesamoiditis. The slope of the pasterns gives springiness, and they are another vital link in the shock-absorbing system. Too straight a pastern will subject the legs to considerable wear and tear; this and the opposite over-flat pastern are sources of weakness to be avoided. The foot has already been described, so we will now consider the rest of the body.

Middlepiece

The principal parts are the chest, back, barrel, flank and loins. The previous study of the skeleton shows that the ribs enclose most of the vital organs of the body. In front – the chest – are the heart and lungs; to the rear, separated by the diaphragm, are the digestive and other organs, which are partially protected by the false ribs and by strong abdominal muscles. There is an unprotected gap in the lumbar region, the loins, where lie part of the liver and kidneys. This gap should be as small as possible, thus making for a short back, regarded as a very great virtue in a horse. However, the requirements of this part vary with the type of horse and the work it has to do. A weight-carrying animal, such as a heavyweight hunter or polo pony, needs to have a short back, but in a hack, where a comfortable and smooth ride is essential, judges usually look for a rather longer back. Longer backs, and straight shoulders, are also favoured for harness horses of all kinds. Too short a back gives an uncomfortable ride, shortening the stride, and so sometimes, but not invariably, reducing speed. Very fast sprinters are likely to be very short in the back with accompanying well-developed largissimus dolsi, which enables them to muster an enormous effort. To the contrary, a long back means that the animal is standing over a larger area so that at each stride more ground is covered, which will tell over a staying distance.

The saddle-bearing surface of the back, behind the withers, should be well covered with flesh to protect the spine and the bony processes which project upwards from it. The barrel and chest should be well rounded, and there should be no slackness of the flanks, which occupy the sides of the horse between the ribs and the hindquarters. Excessive hollowness here, herring-gutted, shows weakness and difficulty in keeping in condition. The girth, which is the area round the chest from just behind the withers, where the saddle girth goes in fact, should be deep, providing more room for the vital heart and lungs.

Hindquarters

The true thigh of the horse slopes forward from the pelvis to the patella (stifle), and outwardly this area, which extends from the point of the hip to the buttocks, should be well rounded and muscular. From the stifle to the point of the hock runs the gaskin or second thigh (tibia or shin bone), which, like the forearm in front, should be long and thick and well muscled up, this being part of the propelling mechanism of the horse. The hock, which is composed of several bones, should be large, and the cannon (sometimes called shannon) bone, below, short in proportion to the gaskin. The lower parts, fetlock, pasterns, etc., are the same as in front and similar criteria apply, except that the hind pasterns, which do not have to endure the same sustained shocks as the front ones, have a straighter angle to the ground.

The sum and arrangement of all these various parts adds up to the qualities that one wants to see in a good riding horse. Looked at first from the side, the first impression, as has been said above, should be of symmetry and proportion: head not too large and heavy, or too small, or too coarse, well set on the neck and showing plenty of room at the union with it; the neck elegant but strong, about the same length as the head, rising out of moderately high and fairly narrow withers; shoulder should slope forward at an angle of about 45° and show clean but muscular lines; forelegs straight, with muscular forearm, short cannon, showing good bone, sloping pasterns, hoof well rounded with a moderate slope to the ground and good quality horn without cracks or flaking or horizontal lines indicating a laminitis condition; knees should not be bent forward (over at the knees), or sag back behind the vertical (back at the knees).

A good foot should always be proportionate to the size of the horse, neither too broad and heavy nor narrow and boxy with a steep angle to the ground. Heels should be wide to give room for a healthy frog. The two fore feet and hind feet should each make an exact pair, and the toes should point straight to front, neither turned in (pigeon toed) nor turned out (splay footed). The front pair are placed level and squarely on the ground, neither foot in advance of the other (pointing, and a sign of lameness). The hind pair, when the horse is standing alertly and to attention, are together, but when relaxed either hind foot can be raised on its toes (resting). When, however, a horse is being photographed all four legs must appear separately in the picture, otherwise there is the unsightly effect of the horse appearing to have only two legs; so the foreleg on the side furthest from the photographer is drawn back and the hindleg placed forward.

The chest should be broad, but not excessively wide, which will give the horse a rather waddling action. The back should be short, with no slackness between the barrel, which should be well rounded, and the quarters; the girth deep. The back should be straight, or rising slightly from behind the withers towards the croup. When the top line of the back is convex the horse is said to be roach-backed; the opposite condition of hollow back is usually a sign of old age, the ligaments which bind the vertebrae together becoming relaxed. The croup should be convex and high at the tail; a drooping croup, giving a lowly-placed tail (goose rump), is unsightly and a sign of weakness. The hips should be rounded; often prominent, pointed hips are a sign of poor condition.

The hindlegs should be placed directly under the quarters, and a line drawn down from the point of the buttocks should touch the point of the hock and the rear edge of the cannon bone and the back of the fetlock. The tail should be set high and carried gaily.

Two small parts not yet mentioned are chestnut and ergot. They are horny callosities found on the limbs, the chestnuts on the insides of the forearms and of the hind legs just below the hock joints, the ergots at the backs of the fetlock joints. They are skin growths, and are thought to be vestigial remains of extra foot pads or toes long since vanished.

Viewed from the front, the legs should appear straight and

clean, vertical from the point of the shoulder; chest neither too broad nor too narrow (legs coming out of the same hole), a sign of weakness and cause of brushing. The legs should not be bowed outwards nor knock-kneed. Similarly, from the rear, the quarters should show straight lines, with no turning in or out of the hocks, and again neither too broad (going wide behind) nor too narrow. When the hocks are turned in and the toes turned out the horse is said to be cow-hocked. Sickle hocks are those which show an ill-defined angle at the point permanently bent, hence the greater strain and predisposition to curbs – giving the impression of couching. Hocks set behind the buttocks is also a bad fault.

In all the foregoing the horse has been stationary; but a horse fulfils its being in movement. Again, the action of the horse in motion must be observed from the side and from each end. The walk stride should be long and energetic, the rear foot making an imprint well up to or in advance of that of the forefoot. It is generally reckoned that a good walker will make a good galloper. The trot should be active and well marked, feet picked up, with no dragging of the toes. Seen from the ends, the action should be straight, without throwing the feet outwards (dishing) or crossing one foot over the other (plaiting).

Obviously absolute perfection of form is rarely found in any horse, and one usually has to be content with the next best thing. It is true, also, that conformation and performance do not necessarily go together. Many great show jumpers and three-day eventers would find themselves in the back row of a show class; but they would be found, nevertheless to possess the basic attributes of good limbs, sound feet, plenty of bone, and good fronts. The art of assessing the conformation of the horse, expressed in the phrase 'having an eye for a horse', lies in the balancing of the good points against the bad.

However beautiful a horse may be, it is useless if it is not sound. We have already seen that a horse lame in his fore feet will tend to 'point' the affected foot, especially in the case of navicular disease but lameness shows more clearly when the horse is seen trotting, preferably on level and fairly hard ground. Pronounced lameness in front will reveal itself by an uneven action, the horse coming down more heavily on the sound foot and more lightly (favouring) on the lame foot, accompanied by a nodding of the head on the lame side. Detecting lameness in the hind limbs is more difficult, but a general guide is to watch the hips of the horse trotting away; if they tend to rise and fall alternately, the rising one will indicate the lame side.

So far we have considered the physical make-up of the horse, but equally important for both rider and trainer is an understanding of his mind.

5 The Mind of the Horse

Human appreciation of equine intelligence usually depends on the extent and quality of the horse's responses to the instructions given him, by various signals, which in its turn depends on the efficiency and clarity of those signals. This tells us as much about the limitations of the rider or instructor as it does about the understanding of the horse. Nevertheless the consensus of experienced opinion confirms that, whatever the capabilities of the trainer, the horse is *willing* to try to understand and to do what he is told. In spite of his great strength – and few riders really appreciate the truly enormous power of the horse – the horse seldom resists or rebels, not for long anyway. His is essentially docile and gentle, even a stallion, if he is intelligently treated.

Docility is the keynote of the horse's character, on which, combined with his excellent memory, all training is based. In a sense he is like a computer, which requires to be correctly programmed to produce the right answer. Only of course he is not just a computer; he is a creature of sense and sensibility, subject to aberrations and off days; which makes everything to do with riding and training horses at once frustrating and fascinating, and in the end supremely rewarding.

This willingness to co-operate helps to overcome the limitations of his intelligence, though we must be careful of our terms. If we measure his intelligence by his relations with the human race, it is of course negligible, in order of precedence below that of the primates and the dog, but above in some people's opinion that of the elephant. If we measure it in terms of survival, this particular quadruped had developed, improved and maintained itself for some sixty million years before man appeared on the scene, and since then has adapted itself to man's exacting requirements in a remarkable way. It should be a sobering thought.

One should pause, too, to consider how the horse learns to do all that it is asked to do by man, to solve all the conundrums that are put to it by exacting trainers. It has no common language; it cannot understand a word *qua* word. It has to translate in that small brain of his a series of external signs – movements of the body on its back, pressures of leg and spur and whip, tugs and vibrations on its mouth, movements of the hand or whip of a dismounted man – into actions, some simple, some very complicated and difficult, in the circus ring, in the Grand Prix dressage arena, playing polo, or just quietly hacking. And by and large, it does it so well that the achievement is taken for granted. Clever Hans was so responsive to the almost invisible signals of his master that many people credited him with human calculating powers. Perhaps, when a horse fails to translate the human sign language correctly, it may be conceded that he is not just a bloody fool but has not been given the signals correctly. Like the computer when it is given the wrong programme, it becomes confused, which makes it frightened and obstinate, and finally violent. Of course, there are horses which will not co-operate, deliberately resist, and appear to hate the human race, or will only tolerate it in certain ways. The Arabian mare, Nichab, bred by Lady Hester Stanhope in 1818 and later sold to France for breeding lived for twenty-eight years without once allowing a rider to stay on her back. Apart from this she had the sweetest of temperaments. Erika Schiele in *The Arab Horse in Europe* tells the story of how on her birth Turkish astrologers cast the filly's horoscope and prophesied that Nichab should never carry any common rider, unless she had first been ridden by the mightiest warrior on earth. The only candidate was Napoleon, who was by then not available.

Docility is a quality produced by domestication, but there is in the horse a conflicting characteristic inherited from millions of years of wildness, fear. For the most part docility and the regular routine imposed upon it overcomes fear, but it is still there in the horse, and cannot be ignored. It manifests itself in shying or spooking at unfamiliar objects or, sometimes, at nothing in particular, starting at sudden movements or noises, taking fright in traffic, bolting. For all his size and strength and apparent confidence the horse is a timid creature. His age-old instinct when confronted with anything potentially dangerous is to shy away and run.

Another characteristic of the horse is his gregariousness. He has always been used to going about in small, fairly close-knit communities, with a well-established leader. Several horses in a field will usually get on well together, and they quickly establish an hierarchy under a boss. Sometimes the members of a group will take a dislike to one of them, and make his life a hell; but this does not often happen. Normally mares and geldings get on well together. Domesticity has interfered with this natural order of things; horses in stables live a life of solitary confinement for twenty or more hours a day, only coming out for exercise. In the old-fashioned stables of the horse era they were usually in semi-darkness as well. No wonder the vices of crib-biting, wind-sucking, weaving and kicking of stable doors are so prevalent among the horses of civilised countries. I do not ever remember a troop horse kept in open horse lines becoming addicted to any of them. Modern stables are better, letting horses look out on some kind of living activity, and they are all the better for it. The bad temper of many thoroughbred stallions must have been mainly due to their lonely and boring lives. A much more enlightened treatment of that noble creature has had the most remarkable results.

Everybody knows that the horse has a good memory, and all his training depends on it; but it is an odd sort of memory. He certainly is able to connect effect with cause, provided the sequence is quick enough. If he is not corrected or rewarded at the very instant of his doing wrong or right, it will be too late; he will have forgotten why he is being punished or praised. That is why it is so futile to whip a horse after he has refused. It is not much use patting him either when he has got over the fence, unless it is done in the air. This is not to say that reward and punishment are not effective; they are essential, but their use has to be carefully thought out and very quickly applied.

On the other hand a horse will remember lessons he has learnt through constant repetition, and places where things have happened. A dressage horse will often learn the test as well as his rider, and anticipate the movements; while a milk horse will regularly stop his cart at the same places in the street every day. Horses obviously recognise places, such as their stables, for they will find their way to them unaided. I had a buggy horse in India who very well knew his way from the club to his stables, but he developed a habit of cutting his corners. Whether he would have done this from greater distances or after a lapse of time, I do not know. Many vast claims have been made for the horse in this way, but the evidence is not conclusive. Bernhard Grzimek, director of the Frankfurt Zoo, made some experiments with Arabs to test their homing instinct, with negative results. Perhaps the answer is that some horses have better memories than others.

Many people claim that their horses recognise them by sight, but here again the evidence is inconclusive. It is more likely that they identify people and things by their sense of smell, which is much more acute than their eyesight. I was told once of a pony which was very much attached to its young owner but could not stand her mother. I suggested that the mother should approach the pony wearing a coat belonging to her daughter. She did this and the pony accepted her quite readily, and then gradually got used to her. Ewart Evans in *The Horse and the Furrow* has suggested that the secret of the Horseman's Word which gave some Suffolk horsemen such power over their horses was the cunning application of the horse's sense of smell. This may have been the power behind the old Horse Whisperers but, as practitioners of this kind of horse control are few and far between, there must be something more to it than that. The practice described by Barbara Woodhouse of breathing into a horse's nostrils done by South American gauchos must be of the same *genre*. And horses, in common with most other animals, say how-do-you-do to each other by sniffing.

The horse's hearing is generally very acute, more so in finely bred, hot-blooded ones than in the coarser, cold-blooded types. Breed tells. Horses will often pick up distant sounds inaudible to the human ear, and they seem to distinguish between friendly and, to them, hostile sounds. The cry of hounds, however far away, will strike a responsive chord in any horse, but another sound will frighten him. Perhaps this hearing of odd sounds may explain otherwise inexplicable shying or bolting; a sudden echo of his prehistoric past. There are few horsemen who have not been bolted with and it is a terrifying experience; but usually the horse stops or slows down, presumably when he thinks he has got far enough away from the unseen danger. It is necessary of course to have plenty of space ahead when a horse does bolt with you. Many years ago I was riding a small pony mare, and we turned into the drive of the house where I was living which was off the road halfway up a steep hill. There may have been something coming, either up or down that hill, but it was certainly not in sight. Suddenly, without warning, she put her ears back and bolted along the drive, and I mean *bolted*. She seemed to be impelled by sheer ungovernable panic, and nothing on earth could stop her. The drive was about 200 yards long, and I had time to wonder in quite a detached way what would happen when we got to a bend at the end of it, when equally suddenly she stopped, and walked calmly back to the stables. I never told anybody about it for fear I would not be allowed to ride her any more. Up to then she had been a hundred per cent safety ride, and she was again after it.

Apart from that, horses seem to understand the nuances of the human voice, and obey words of command according to the way in which they are given. 'Whoah' is the universal sound for stopping, *à propos* of which I have always enjoyed this story. An old farmer, who had ploughed with horses for some forty years, at last gave in to modernism and bought a tractor. The first day he took it out he got to the end of the furrow and shouted 'Whoa!' and went on through the hedge.

But the human voice has a great effect on a horse, conveying as it does appreciation or anger; so to make it more difficult the regulations for dressage competitions ban the use of the voice, along with whip, martingales, blinkers and other extraneous aids. But, in private, riders talk a lot to their horses; show jumpers, for whom there are no restrictions, chatter regularly to their horses as they go along.

The eyesight of the horse is naturally very important; and it is regulated by its anatomy. With eyes at the sides of the head, not frontally placed, it can see well enough ahead at a distance, but has difficulty at close quarters; which is why, if you approach a horse from the front and hold out your hand to pat his nose, he will generally throw his head up as if to take avoiding action. Come up from the side, and he can see you quite well. He has good lateral and rearward vision.

When a horse comes up to a jump with his head in the normal position, he will be able to see the top of the jump but not the base line. To look at the latter he must lower his head, which is what all horses do before a fence, if they are allowed to. Then he is able to calculate the distance away, when he should take off, and how he should leap to get over it; and he does this instantaneously, usually making his decision before the rider gets round to it. This was the basis of Caprilli's thinking when he developed forward riding.

How far can a horse see? It is a moot point. Go to the gate of a field with horses in it at the far end from the gate, say 200 yards away. The chances are that they will notice you, whether you call out or not. A horse can probably see a good deal further than that; after all, in his wild incarnation he had to, for the plains on which he lived were wide open, the horizon a long way off. But it is probable that his vision was not very clear, or he would not be frightened of quite simple objects.

Can he see colours? It was long considered that the horse was colour blind, seeing everything in black and white. Grzimek, already mentioned, carried out a number of experiments on a group of horses and came to the conclusion that they could recognise the four primary colours, yellow, green, blue and red, the first two more clearly than the last two. (*Such Agreeable Friends.*) There are also authentic instances of a horse recognising a red-painted van. So it is not to be wondered at if horses introduced suddenly to red and white or blue and white poles on a fence are apt to take exception to them.

The sense of touch plays a major part in the training of the equine. The sensitivity varies with the breeding, but all will react to the human touch in some degree or other. There is the feel of the body in the saddle, of the legs, on the sides of the horse, of the bit in its mouth, of the whip and the spur. He is able to endure great pain, but is also extremely sensitive to it, witness immediate signs of lameness, and flinching when sore points are touched. Most horses seem to like being patted and stroked; gently pulling the ears is soothing for some, though quite a few horses are very chary of having them touched, due sometimes, no doubt, to ill-treatment. They have their special ticklish places, under the belly, inside the stifle and it is as well to respect them, but handling those parts delicately and gradually will usually eradicate most phobias of this kind. The horse will get used to practically anything, if you set about it gradually and with continual repetition.

A horse is an emotional being, and he usually shows his feelings very clearly, most often when he is disturbed. A swishing tail, rolling eyes, flat back ears, and restive feet betoken loss of temper or discomfort. Horses in a dressage test will often swish their tails, a sure sign of their disgust at the whole proceedings. However, a horse which goes along with his ears permanently pricked is not paying any attention to his rider. An attentive, intelligent horse will usually go along with ears flicking back and forwards alternatively. When both ears go back together, it is time for the rider to pay attention. On the other hand a horse at full gallop has both ears back. Not many horses have won the Derby with their ears pricked forward. A horse which lays its ears absolutely flat back and starts shaking its head is usually planning some devilment, so be prepared.

It is universally agreed, I think, that horses are very sensitive to atmosphere and to the state of mind of their human masters. A horse, more especially a pony, will try to 'old soldier' a nervous or weak rider. If the rider is frightened of an obstacle ahead – and who isn't some time or other? – the horse will know it at once and get frightened too. The courage of a horse is often a measure of the courage and determination of the rider and of the horse's trust in him.

This does not contradict the statement that the horse is a timid animal but underlines the courage that he shows in overcoming fears at the behest of the rider. Here also his docility and willingness to co-operate come into play. Such a horse will face any hazard and go on to the limit of his powers of endurance. Horse literature and tradition abounds in tales of the endurance of horses, which make Grand Nationals and three-day events look like child's play. Of course there are horses, as there are people, who are slugs and craven at heart, because while horses generally conform to a set pattern of rules and principles they are individuals too, widely differing in character and physical power.

The horse seems able, immediately, to detect and assess human character and reactions. He is also, I believe, affected by the wider atmosphere of group or environment, and has a sense of occasion. I had two polo ponies once, who were accustomed to playing first-class polo, not always ridden by me; their names were Sam and Santu; an Australian of good breeding and an Indian country-bred. Before a tournament match Sam would stand at the side of the ground trembling all over literally like a jelly; it was quite alarming to watch if you did not know him. The moment he was mounted and in the game the trembling ceased and he was ready for anything. Santu regarded station polo and practice games as waste of time; neither whip nor spur would get him to go faster than an unwilling slow gallop. In a tournament I carried neither, and he used to go like the wind. On the other hand, I had a charger, also a Waler, who was such a comfortable ride that he was known as Thunderbox; he was a most beautiful jumper – in private. Hopefully I entered him for show jumping competitions, but we never got beyond the second or third fences. No power on earth would make him jump in public. All horsemen will have similar experiences.

So we have this great, strong four-legged friend and servant of ours; a bundle of nerves, timid and fearful of the unexpected; sensitive to atmosphere, liable to suffer from nerves and to have off days; docile and obedient by nature, always in need of a leader and master; receptive to affection; I am sure that human love, if it is really given unstintingly and continuously, influences a horse very strongly indeed; and if the evidence of many people is true he can and does, respond to it in his own way. Relationships of this kind are rare, however; there are horses which are quite impervious to all signs of affection, unaffected by reward or punishment, I have known them too. For the most part horses are honest, down-to-earth creatures, who thrive on hard work and the right food, not playthings but servants and companions, who will always repay study. The better you understand the horse you ride the happier will be your riding.

6 Equipment and Accoutrements

The basic items are bridle; bit or bits; reins; saddle.

The bridle is the leather equipment on the horse's head for holding the bit and the reins. The principle part is the head-piece, a broadish strap which goes over the head behind the ears and merges into the narrower strap on either side of the head, called the cheekpiece, to which the bit is attached. The headpiece is kept in position by the front or browband, which goes horizontally round the forehead below the ears, and has a loop at each end through which passes the broad part of the headpiece. This bifurcates just below the browband into the cheekpieces, already mentioned, and a narrow strap which passes under the jaw, helping to keep the bridle in place. This is called the throat latch, always pronounced 'lash'. This should always be kept fairly loose, allowing two fingers to be inserted between it and the throat.

At the end of the cheekpiece is the bit in the horse's mouth, to which is attached the rein or reins, depending on the type of bridle and bit. Each rein is a single strap from three-quarters to one inch wide, attached to the bit either by sewing, buckles or studs. The cheekpieces are also attached to the bit in the same way, usually by buckles; few people have a bridle for each horse nowadays. The cheekpieces are divided into two with buckles for adjustment according to the size of the horse's head; and the throat latch has a buckle on the near side for the same purpose.

The simplest form of bridle is the snaffle bridle with only one bit attached to it and no noseband. This is a broad strap with a buckle for adjustment at the rear, and a head strap of its own, which also goes through the loops on the browband. The front strap should lie on the nasal bone a little below a point midway between the eyes and the nostrils. Its main use is for the attachment of martingales and other gadgets. It is commonly known as a cavesson noseband, but that is, strictly, the name given to a training noseband, which will be described later.

There is a variety of utility nosebands which have definite

purposes of their own for controlling the horse, usually for stopping it: drop noseband, flash, grakle, kineton, sheepskin, which are described below.

The snaffle bridle can also be used for a Pelham bit, which combines curb and snaffle effects in one. When two bits – bridoon (snaffle) and curb are used, another headstrap and

Fig. 5. Snaffle Bridle with drop noseband

cheekpiece are added to carry the extra bit, and you have the double bridle. The reins of a double bridle are usually rather narrower than the single one of a snaffle, for ease of holding. Once reins were always made of leather, either plain straight-forward straps, or, in the case of snaffle reins, for better grip plaited, partially covered with rubber, or made of a mixture of rubber and leather to make them more elastic; nowadays they are also made of webbing or nylon and similar materials. Some-times reins are made in two pieces, buckled at the ends. In Western tack they are not joined at all, so that they can immedi-ately be dropped to the ground when the rider dismounts, the American cow pony being trained to stay put when the reins hang like this. British and European horses never seem to be taught this useful trick.

It is convenient at this point to consider the bits. 'There is a bit for every horse,' is a common saying in the horse world, but I am not sure if it is not wishful thinking. The number of varieties of bit invented over the centuries is uncountable, and still horses pull and run away. It is always the hand at the other end of the rein that counts. But all these different bits have only been variations on two original themes, the snaffle and the curb.

The snaffle or bridoon, which is the 5,000-year-old prototype of all bits, simply consists of a mouthpiece and two rings. The most commonly used type is the jointed snaffle, which has the mouthpiece divided into two parts linked by welded rings in the middle. The two pieces broaden towards the ends, which are pierced to take the side rings. When the snaffle is used on its own, the side rings are large, often with a thick oval-shaped union to make it less likely to cut the horse's lips; it is known then from its appearance as an egg butt snaffle. Another variety with the same object is cut in the shape of the letter D, and called naturally a Dee snaffle. The mouthpiece of a single snaffle is thick, again to lessen the chance of cutting the tongue or the bars of the mouth. This is the part of the jaw between the horse's incisors or front teeth and molars or back teeth. When the bit is used in combination with a curb bit, it is much smaller and lighter, there being not so much direct pressure from it, and also it has to fit inside the mouth. The mouthpieces of a jointed snaffle are usually plain rounded smooth steel or stainless steel bars, do not use nickel or any other kind of metal for bits or stirrups, but occasionally the metal is twisted to make grooves and ridges, which can be very severe. This is known as a twisted snaffle. Other varieties of snaffle have straight bars, curved (halfmoon) mouthpieces, bars with ports (an arch in the middle of varying height), or chain mouthpieces – very severe and not to be used. For horses with very sensitive mouths, or for restraining, rubber or vulcanite mouthpieces are occasionally used.

The snaffle acts directly on the corners of the mouth with the object of raising the head. The jointed snaffle also has a nutcracker action on the mouth, which can be quite severe.

The curb bit is younger than the snaffle; the earliest of its kind known is a Celtic bit of the third century B.C. It was in general use in the Middle Ages in the days of the armoured knight. The mouthpiece is a single bar, usually with a port in the centre of it, with holes at each end through which go arms, short above the mouthpiece, longer below it. These are called cheekpieces, not to be confused with the leather straps of the bridle, upper and lower. The upper cheekpiece has a loop for attachment to the bridle and an open hook which takes the curb chain. The lower cheekpiece, which tapers nearly to a point, has a ring attached to take the rein. The proportions of the upper and lower cheekpieces determine the power of the

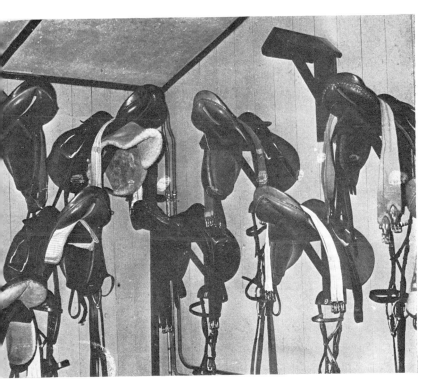

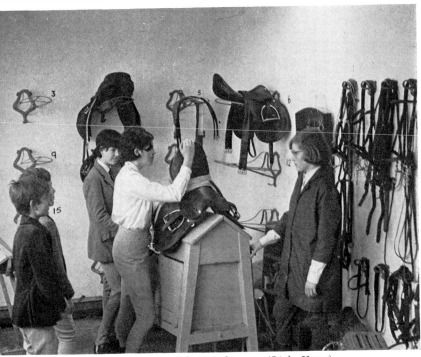

Two orderly and well-kept tack rooms (*Light Horse*)

GROOMING. The basic items of equipment for grooming a pony are as follows: *Top row (left to right).* Dandy brush (tail and mane), sweat scraper, curry-comb, body brush. *Bottom row. Water brush*, sponges (one for dock and sheath, and one for eyes and nose), hoof pick, wisp (made of straw) and below a comb. All these are laid out on a stable rubber, of which you should have a plentiful supply. A rubber curry-comb is a useful extra to use on thick and

action of the bit. The upper is, nowadays, more or less constant at about an inch; the lower can be anything from three

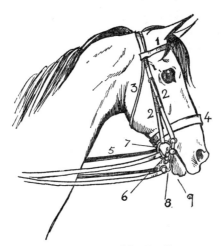

Fig. 6.   Double Bridle

1. *Browband*   2. *Cheekpieces*   3. *Throat Latch (pronounced 'lash')*   4. *Cavesson Noseband*   5. *Reins*   6. *Curb Chain*   7. *Lip Strap*   8. *Snaffle*   9. *Curb Bit*

inches upwards; the old medieval bits used to be twelve inches or more. In the case of a modern Weymouth or Ward Union bit used in a double bridle the length will not be less than three inches or more than five. Mouthpieces can also be plain straight bars, or curved (halfmoon), or made of vulcanite or rubber. To make it milder in the mouth the steel bar can be covered with leather.

The curb chain is made of a series of closely meshed steel links, about three-quarters of an inch broad and about eight inches long. The broad link exerts a more or less level pressure on the soft hollow behind the lower jaw known as the chin groove. It is put on by hooking one end over the off side hook, laying the links right-handed so that they are flat in the chin groove, and hooking the other end over the near side hook, Then the required length is found by taking up the requisite number of links, and looping the last one over the hook. Sometimes the chain can be covered with leather, or made of leather altogether, or elastic.

The curb has a lever action. The effect of a pull of the rein on the end of the lower cheekpiece is to pivot the mouthpiece in the horse's mouth and to move the top of the upper cheek- piece forward, which takes the curb chain with it and causes it to press on the chin groove. The effect of this is to induce the horse to open (flex) its lower jaw a little and bend its head from the poll: always provided that the training has been correctly done from the outset and the horse's conformation allows it.

Fig. 7.   Normal Curb Bit with moveable mouthpiece

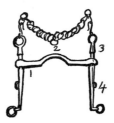

Fig. 8.   A Halfmoon Pelham Bit

1. *Mouthpiece*   2. *Port*   3. *Upper cheekpiece*   4. *Lower cheekpiece*

A horse with a thick neck and no play where the jowl and the throat meet is unable to flex properly and so is very difficult to control. So in the double bridle there are two different actions, the flexing and slight lowering of the head by the curb, and its raising by the snaffle, so that the carriage of the head is maintained at a normal level.

The mouthpiece of the curb bit can be either moveable (up and down) or fixed. In the normal double bridle, which only concerns us here, the bit with a moveable mouthpiece was known as the Ward Union, and with a fixed mouthpiece it is usually called a Weymouth. In dressage competitions the Weymouth bit with a fixed mouthpiece is *de rigueur*.

The Pelham bit is a curb bit which contrives to combine the functions of snaffle and curb in one bit. Rings at the ends of the lower cheekpieces take the curb rein, while side rings attached to the mouthpiece take the bridoon or snaffle rein. It is a compromise which does not quite come off; nevertheless it is a useful bit for many occasions, and it must on the whole be more comfortable for the horse to have only one bit in its mouth instead of two. Horses always seemed to go well in the Army bit, which is a variety of Pelham. It can be used either with one rein or two, but should never, repeat never, be used with a single double-ended rein, which has a completely deadening effect on the mouth.

The correct fitting of bit and bridle is of the utmost importance to all riding, so here are the points to look for when inspecting a horse before mounting.

The browband should be well clear of the ears and above the bony ridge which runs from the eye socket (orbit).

The leather cheekpieces should be the same length on either side of the head.

The noseband is two fingers' depth below the cheek bones, and loose enough to allow two fingers' breadth between it and the face of the horse.

The throat latch should allow at least two or three fingers' breadth between it and the back of the jaw.

The bit. (a) Snaffle. This should be high enough just to wrinkle the soft corners of the lips and no more. (b) Pelham. This is also a single bit, and it must be so placed that when the curb reins are pulled, and the upper cheekpiece goes forward, the curb chain should act on the chin groove and not above it on the bony jaw. (c) Double bridle. The snaffle must lie above the curb, fitting, as above, into the corners of the lips; the curb bit must be below it, resting on the bars of the mouth, again so placed that the curb chain acts in the correct place. The curb chain itself must not be too tight, and all the links must lie in the same direction.

All leather work must be clean, soft and pliable, all metal work bright and clean.

As a matter of interest, here are some of the different styles of bit most generally in use. Snaffle gag: There are holes in the rings of the snaffle, which are fairly large, and through them pass the reins, which with the headpiece make a single length of leather. When the reins are pulled they exert pressure on the poll at the same time as on the corners of the mouth, which is very effective with a puller. Many polo players, not to say show jumpers, use this bit. A variation is the Hitchcock gag, in which the cheekpiece (leather) goes from the bit to a ring on the headpiece, down again to a ring on the bit, and then to the reins, giving an extremely strong lifting effect. The Fulmer or Australian snaffle has a straight bar between the loose side ring and mouthpiece. In a ball-cheek snaffle the sidebar and ring are one rigid piece of metal. These sidebars or cheeks prevent the bit being drawn through the mouth, avoid pinching the lips, and by pressing against one side or other of the mouth help lateral movement, and so make good training bits. The loose ring type is to be preferred, because it allows movement of the bit in the mouth, promoting saliva, and encouraging the horse to play with the bit, which is an aid to obtaining a soft and yielding mouth. The cheeks can be kept in one position, if required, by a keeper attached to the leather cheekpiece.

The egg butt or Dee family of snaffles achieve the same objects, and are generally the most popular bit. Sometimes the rings of the egg butt snaffle have slots in them to maintain one position. A very popular snaffle is the German, which has a large hollow mouthpiece, making it very light in the mouth. It can be had either with a plain ring or an egg butt one.

The basic curb bit is the Weymouth fixed mouth or sliding mouth with a port. The variations on this theme are endless, mostly in the direction of longer cheekpieces and more complicated mouthpieces, all with the object of making the bit more severe and so giving it more stopping power. The cheekpieces are either straight or curved (swan-cheek). Mostly the mouthpieces and cheeks move together, but in the Banbury, which has a straight-bar mouthpiece slightly tapering from each end to the centre, the cheekpieces can revolve round the mouthpiece and also independently of each other. The movement facilitates mouthing, and the bit can be useful with very hard-mouthed or dry-mouthed animals. The Chifney, whose invention is attributed to the jockey, Sam Chifney, is a very powerful bit, but, in the right hands, effective and humane. The lower cheek pivots round the mouthpiece, while the upper cheekpiece is fixed, which helps to keep the curb chain in the correct position in the chin groove. A bit much in use at one time by polo players, but never seen now, is the Ninth Lancer, which had a straight mouthpiece and flat short lower cheekpieces, with two slots for reins, so that the strength of the action could be varied. The Western bit is an ordinary curb with curved cheekpieces and a variety of mouthpieces.

The Pelham bit most often seen is the halfmoon Pelham. The

military bit, the port-mouth universal, reversible, is an Angle-cheek Pelham; the snaffle rings are so made that the lower cheekpieces extend down not directly below the upper cheek-piece but a little way behind it. This tends to give quicker action of the curb chain; the lower cheek is provided with two slots, as in the Ninth Lancer, to give a wide range of curb effect. The mouthpiece has a port in it, and one side of it is smooth, the other serrated so that the bit can be reversed to use either way.

Other types of Pelham are: Globe cheek, in which all parts are fixed and the lower rings are part of the actual cheekpieces. Hanoverian, a high-port mouthpiece with rollers round the two arms on either side of the port. It is in effect a jointed bit, which with a high port can be very severe. This also was much used by polo players. A tendency of the normal Pelham to chafe the corners of the mouth is countered by the Scamperdale, popu-larised by Sam Marsh between the wars, in which the mouth-piece is angled forward so that the snaffle rings miss the corners. A similar result is obtained by the Rugby Pelham with a fixed cheekpiece but an independent linked snaffle ring. The Three-in-One (Swales) has the snaffle rings fixed to the mouthpiece inde-pendently of the cheekpieces and inside them. The bridle and bridoon reins are attached to this and not to the upper cheek-piece, so there is no displacement of the mouthpiece or the upper cheek before the curb chain begins to act, which is an

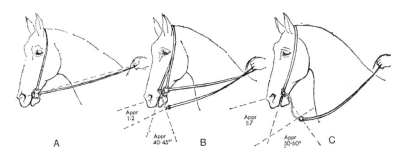

Fig. 9. Three different types of bits and their actions

a. *Modern Snaffle Bit*. No lifting, no pressing effects, only that in the corner of the mouth. The mildest possible effects.
b. *Modern Double Bridle*. Curb bit with straight lower cheek. Medium effects.
c. *Middle Age Curb Bit á la Guérinière*. Long 'S' shaped lower cheek with no bridoon. The possible strongest effects.

advantage; on the other hand the inside rings squeeze the mouth.

Included in the Pelham family is the Kimblewick, which was devised by the saddler, F. E. Gibson of Newmarket for Phil Oliver from a Spanish jumping bit, and so called from the village in Buckinghamshire where he lives. The essence of this is a short cheekpiece with a rather more than semi-circular ring which goes from the lower end of the cheekpiece to the upper cheek above the mouthpiece. The rein can move up and down the ring, so that when the hands are held low the rein slips down and the action is that of a mild curb; when the hand is held high, there is a snaffle effect. This bit has been popular with show jumpers, but needs skilful use.

Nosebands play an important part in the control of the horse, and the most widely used of them all, certainly since the war, is the drop noseband, a German invention for use with horses that throw their heads about and get their tongues over the bit. It consists of a front strap, which goes over the lower part of the nose, and a rear strap joined to it by a ring, which hangs nearly at right angles to it just in front of the rings of the snaffle. The front strap is adjustable so that it can be tightened round the nose, and it can also be placed up and down. The correct position is about two-thirds of the way down the face and clear of the nostrils. Used as a brake it is placed low down and used with a standing martingale, so that when pressure is exerted by the reins and by the horse trying to raise its head the nostrils are constricted and the breathing interfered with. In 1962 the British Show Jumping Association at last put an end to this unpleasant practice by banning the use of the standing martingale with a dropped noseband. Used with a running martingale the effect is less severe.

Other types of noseband are: Flash, an ordinary noseband with two straps attached to it which cross below it over the nose and are buckled at the rear. The object is to obtain something approximate to the effect of the drop noseband while having a standing martingale attached to the normal one. Grakle, named after the winner of the 1931 Grand National, consists of two straps crossing over the nose, one passing over the bit and one under it, and connected at the rear. The pressure on the nose is concentrated at the point of intersection, and it is a powerful instrument against a confirmed puller or a horse which crosses its jaws. The Kineton is a severe type of noseband, invented by Mr Puckle of Kineton, Warwickshire, which comprises a front piece of metal covered with leather, with adjustable buckles at each end attached to two open metal loops in contact with the bit. The action of the reins causes direct pressure on the nose. The sheepskin noseband is a bit of mystery, but people who use it must think that it does some good. It might be pleasant for a horse with very sensitive skin. It could act as a kind of blinker, preventing the horse from looking down at the ground and seeing sudden shadows or movement which might make him shy. The most practical suggestion that I have heard is that it makes a stargazer keep his head down. Raising his head up, he becomes temporarily blinded by the ridge of the sheepskin, and so has to lower his head to see where he is going.

Martingales: This word, of uncertain derivation, describes a small family of leather attachments between the girth of the saddle and the bridle for the purpose of correcting the horse's head carriage. The standing martingale is a direct connection between the girth, between the forelegs, by a loop, to the back of the noseband by a loop or buckle. It can also be made from a broad piece of cloth, adjusted by knotting, which has the advantage of being more resilient than leather. In the running martingale the strap is divided about a foot from the bridle end into two parts, each with a ring at the end through which the reins are passed. With a double bridle it is usually used with the curb rein. The bib martingale is a running martingale with flat piece of leather joining the two separate straps. The Cheshire martingale has the divided ends attached to the rings of the snaffle bit, and is best not used at all. A martingale with a very flexible sort of action, especially for lateral movement, is the pulley martingale. The strap, instead of being divided, ends with a ring, through which passes a cord with rings at each end, these taking the reins. A combined martingale incorporates the features of both the standing and running martingale, with the action of both. The Irish martingale, naturally, is not a martingale at all, but a short strap, six to eight inches, with a ring at each end through which the reins, the object being to keep them together.

Two special training martingales are the Market Harborough and the French Chambon. They both work on the principle of self-inflicted, and self-relieved, discomfort and pain. The first works through two strips of rawhide or rounded leather attached to rings on the main strap of the martingale, passing through the rings of the bit and then attached to the reins. If the horse throws its head up extreme pressure is brought to bear on the mouth, instantly relieved when the head is lowered

71

into its right position. The Chambon, used for dismounted work, has the martingale straps going through the rings of a strap over the poll and down to the bit. Resistance in the form of head raising exerts pressure on the poll.

The present form of the saddle has been set for nearly 1,000 years, and is not likely to change in the foreseeable future, except possibly as regards materials. The rigid inner framework of the tree consists of two waisted strips of wood, usually beechwood, united in front by a curved arch called the head or pommel, reinforced by a steel gullet plate. Below the arch two wings project downwards to fit on either side of

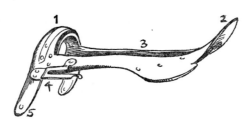

Fig. 10   Conventional Saddle Tree
1. *Head*   2. *Cantle*   3. *Panels*   4. *Stirrup leather bar*   5. *Point*

the withers, called points. The two waisted panels spread out to the rear to form a wide flattish arch called the back arch or cantle. Attached to the points on either side, just below the gullet, two slotted metal plates project backwards, the bars, which take the stirrup leathers. The slots are open at the rear but can be closed by a moveable catch (gate), a safety device to allow the stirrup leather to come away from the saddle in an emergency.

This type of tree has been replaced for specialist riding; show jumping, dressage, eventing; by a spring tree, the pommel of

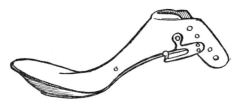

Fig. 11.   A Spring tree made of laminated sheets of wood

which is shaped more forward. The actual 'spring' is obtained from two pieces of light steel, one on either side, which connect the widest part of the panels to the waist. This gives resilience to the saddle seat, and so to the action of the rider in the saddle. The head of a spring tree is always set back at an angle of about 45 degrees. The panels are now often made of laminated sheets of wood, or of fibre glass.

The covering of the saddle is still made of leather-pigskin or cowhide, stretched on to the tree over a tightly strained webbing base. This is the seat. Welted on to the narrow part of the seat are the skirts, small flaps to cover the bars and protect the legs from the buckles of the stirrup leathers. Attached to the tree underneath the skirt is the flap, a large shaped piece of leather against which the knees and thighs of the rider are pressed when riding. The flap can be cut in various ways, from straight down in a showing saddle to well forward over the shoulders with knee rolls for jumping saddles. Fixed to the tree underneath the flaps are the girth straps.

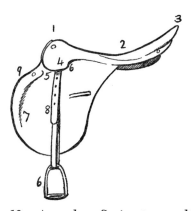

Fig. 12.   A modern Spring tree saddle

1. Head or Pommel   2. Seat   3. Cantle or Back Arch   4. Skirt   5. Stirrup leather Bar (under skirt)   6. Stirrup iron   7. Flap, with knee roll   8. Stirrup leather   9. Panel, inside flap

The under side of the saddle is covered with well stuffed panels lined with linen, serge or leather. These panels rest on the back on either side of the spine, leaving a central space well clear of it. The best lining is perhaps linen over serge. Leather is the strongest material, of course, but needs constant care to keep it soft and pliable. The panels are stuffed

with wool or thick felt. Underneath the outer flap is a sub-
sidiary, thin piece of leather (sweat flap), the same shape as the
outer one, slotted to receive the points of the tree. To the rear
of the outer flap is a slot to take the surcingle, a broad leather
strap which fits tightly over and round the saddle as a reinforce-
ment to the girths, for greater security in sports like racing,
show jumping and eventing. The pommel and cantle of the
saddle can have D-rings either side for attaching personal equipment, raincoats, rugs, etc. Rings on the forward edges of the
flaps are for use with draw reins or other gadgets. There are
always three girth straps on either side, two in use one in
reserve.

Attached to the saddle are girths and stirrup leathers, and,
on occasion, breast plate or crupper. Girths have two straps
and buckles at each end, and come in sizes from about thirty-
six inches to fifty-four inches and from three and a half to five
inches wide. The main varieties of girth are plain web or nylon,
used two together; Balding, double straps crossing over each
other at the middle so as to give plenty of clearance at the
elbows and to avoid chafing; Atherstone, which tapers to the
centre with the same object as the Balding; T-fold, a strip of
leather folded into three, with usually a piece of serge within
the fold so that the leather can be kept greased. I have always
found that this girth, if the leather is properly looked after,
is the best and strongest of them all and the least likely to cause
girth galls. Webbing and nylon girths must be kept scrupulously
clean and dry, and brushed carefully to remove dust and all
foreign bodies.

Stirrup leathers are thickish straps, five-eighths to one and one-
eighth inches wide, and from four to four feet six inches long
with a buckle at one end, made of cowhide, rawhide or buffalo
hide (red leathers), the latter being the toughest and also the
most expensive. Leathers go in pairs and are punched with
holes for adjustment. These start equal, but the leather stretches
unequally, so constant adjustment is necessary. Leathers are
like motor tyres; they should be changed the moment they
show signs of wear. Stirrup irons should be of steel of stainless
steel, heavy enough to hang down freely, and wide enough to
take the broad welt of the rider's boot easily, leaving a clearance
either side, but not so wide as to let the foot slip right through
and get caught. There are various patterns of stirrup iron on
the market, but the best is the conventional bell-shaped design,
with a good broad, serrated footplate. A 'safety' stirrup is made
with one side open and connected with a piece of elastic. Very

useful for young children is the box stirrup, which has a leather outer boot into which the toe of the rider's boot is inserted, automatically coming out if the rider falls off.

Breast plate and crupper speak for themselves. The former is fitted in front of the saddle to prevent it from slipping backwards on a high-withered horse; the latter has a rounded loop to go over the tail, and, attached to the rear of the saddle, it prevents it from going forward on a low-withered horse or, more usually, pony.

TWO

The Training of the Rider

7 Mounting, Dismounting and Position

The first act of riding is, naturally, to get on to the back of the horse, and there are various ways of doing it. Before mounting, however, one routine should never be omitted, the checking of the horse's tack, for its condition as well as its correct fitting. The correct fitting of the bridle has already been described on page 62. The parts of the saddle to be checked are all the straps and buckles of the girth (and to see that it is tight enough and that the skin lies flat underneath it) and the stirrup leathers. The approximate correct length for the rider is the length of his arm. Now you can proceed to mount.

The easiest way is from a mounting block. The horse is led alongside a platform on which the rider is standing. He takes the reins in his left hand and rests it on the pommel; puts his left foot in the stirrup, steps quietly over and settles gently into the saddle, finding the outside stirrup with his right foot.

The normal way of mounting is from the ground with stirrups. In the case of a beginner the horse should be held for him. The Army, which knows a lot about teaching, always does things by numbers, so we will follow suit.

1. Approach the horse from the near side and give him a pat.
2. Take the reins from the horseholder, and bring them over the horse's head.
3. Separate the reins for riding in the left hand. The beginner will always work with a snaffle bridle and a single rein, so the separation of the reins is as follows: Left rein outside the little finger; right rein between the first and second fingers, with the slack of the rein across the palm and between the first finger and thumb. Alternatively, the right rein can be held between the first finger and thumb; in which case the end of the right rein passes downwards across the palm and under the little finger, and the end of the left rein in the opposite direction and between the first finger and thumb. This method seems to give more flexible control when riding with one hand, playing polo or in gymkhana events, with less chance of the reins slipping.
4. Place the left hand on the horse's neck in front of the withers, or on the pommel, and turn your body so that it is level with

the horse's shoulder and facing partly to the rear. Rein contact should be enough to prevent the horse from moving forward, and even; unless the horse is fidgety, in which case have the near rein (left) slightly shorter than the off (right), so that if the horse does move about, it will turn inwards towards you and not away from you, which can be awkward.

5. Take the stirrup in the right hand and place the left foot in the stirrup, with the toe pointing well down so that it does not stick into the horse's side and make him move away.

6. Take hold of the waist or cantle of the saddle with the right hand.

7. Press the left knee into the saddle flap, and spring up from the right foot, still taking care to keep the left toe pointing downwards.

8. Pull and push the body up with hands and feet, until you are upright against the side of the horse, supported by the hands on the pommel and cantle of the saddle, mainly, and by the left foot in the stirrup. Pause momentarily here.

9. Bend the body forward and to the left, i.e. towards the horse's head, swing the right leg well over the back of the saddle, keeping the foot clear of the horse's croup, and shift the right hand from the cantle to the pommel.

10. As your right leg comes down the other side of the horse, support yourself on the left stirrup and with your hands on the pommel, and lower yourself *gently* into the saddle.

11. Sit quietly in the saddle and find the right stirrup with the toe of your right foot; if necessary hold the stirrup leather with the right hand. Make sure that both leathers are flat against the legs and not twisted.

12. Separate the reins with your hands, by slipping the little finger of the right hand inside the right rein and drawing the reins apart, securing the respective ends between the first finger and thumb of each hand. Some people prefer to have the reins between the third and little fingers. Hold the reins with enough contact to prevent the horse from moving forward (in this case there will be an assistant at the horse's head to do that, but it is a good habit to get into from the start).

The instructor should make the beginner practise this operation several times until he does it smoothly in one flowing movement. Then he should practise it from the opposite side, reversing the above instructions. Mounting can, in fact, be used as a valuable gymnastic exercise for the rider. The whole thing can be practised on a dummy horse. If the rider is small and the horse large, lower the stirrup leather by several holes on the mounting side, to be re-adjusted when mounted.

This leads to mounting without stirrups, another good physical exercise. Except with very small ponies, children should not be asked to do this.

1. With the reins in the left hand, face the horse opposite the saddle.

2. Place the left hand on the pommel, the right hand on the cantle.

3. Bend the knees and spring up smartly off both feet, and pull up with the arms until the body is straight, as in mounting with stirrups, but this time supported only by both arms.

4. Swing the right leg over the pommel and carry on as from No. 9 above.

A fourth method mounting is the leg-up.

1. The rider stands facing the saddle, reins in left hand, both hands on the pommel, or the right hand can be on the waist.

2. The assistant stands directly behind and close to the rider.

3. The rider lifts his left leg so that it is horizontal from the knee downwards.

4. The assistant cups the knee with his left hand and holds the ankle with his right.

5. When the rider says he is ready, the assistant gives a controlled hoist, smoothly and without violence, high enough to enable the rider's right leg to clear the horse's croup. The rider assists by springing lightly off the right foot. Then he carries on as before.

The beginner should practise this on both sides of the horse, and should also learn to take the part of the hoister. There is a happy medium about this procedure which takes a little learning. I have seen a rider thrown over the horse to the other side by a too-energetic hoister; and it has been known for a rider to lift the wrong leg.

The last method of getting on to the back of a horse is vaulting. This is really a gymnastic exercise, and also a prelude to circus riding. It is a recognised sport for young riders in Germany, for which there is an annual championship; and it has been taken up in the U.S.A. as well, in recent years.

From the halt: Stand beside the horse, level with his shoulder, both hands on the pommel. Swing the right leg forwards, then sharply back, and with the forearms and back muscles swing the body backwards and up over the saddle.

This exercise is of course much easier when done on the move. Run with the horse, holding the saddle pommel, or hand grips on either side of the withers, body facing forward and level with the shoulders. Jump *forward* so that you land with both feet on the ground *ahead* of the shoulders and forelegs, and make the spring from there. The momentum will help the spring, and the forward position will land you correctly into the saddle or on to the horse's back. If you do not get far enough forward for the spring, you will get left behind.

This exercise must be done with a quiet horse and under supervision, but it is a really good bit of equestrian gymnastics and helps to strengthen and supple the body and gives confidence to the rider.

Dismounting

The horse knows several ways of getting rid of you, but the quickest and safest way is to take the feet out of the stirrups, and quickly swing the right leg over the horse's back, again avoiding banging the croup, and land facing the horse with both feet on the ground together. *Don't* let go of the reins.

Position

'The normal position', wrote Gustav Steinbrecht in his *Das Gymnasium des Pferdes*, 'does not exist.' He qualified it by adding, 'if one means by that one single attitude which will suit the majority of occasions'. He goes on to explain how the position of the rider in the saddle depends on the movements of the horse and the shifting location of its centre of gravity, to which the rider must conform if he is to stay in balance with his mount.

Ideas about the normality of the seat have varied with the ages and with the tack available. In the days of no saddle or stirrups, the riders sat well back on their buttocks (ischia); the knight of the Middle Ages restricted by his armour rode straightlegged on his crutch, as did the early American cowboys; de la Guérinière, with a more suitable saddle, brought the rider back on to his buttocks in the precursor of the modern balanced seat; Caprilli insisted that the rider's buttocks should never 'come into brusque contact with the saddle'. The English hunting man and the Australian stockrider, defying all rules, sat well back on the broad part of the saddle seat, and the balanced brigade seldom saw anything but their heels.

Now there is no seat for all seasons; it entirely depends on what you are doing. Gregor de Romaszkan distinguishes four different kinds of seat: the full seat; the upper part of the body forward; the half-seat; the racing seat. The prime requirement of any position in the saddle is security, which is obtained principally from correct balance, combined with the gripping of the legs assisted by the design of the saddle and the support of the stirrups.

The ancient riders had no security except that which came from balance. The belted knight was kept in the saddle by its high pommel and cantle and, of course, the stirrups. The hunting man sat on a small flat saddle with superb suppleness and balance that seem to defy the laws of gravity and anything else. The cavalry soldier from the eighteenth century onwards has had the benefit of a deep saddle, hemmed in with kit front and back, and his seat at its best was approximately that of the balanced seat of de la Guérinière.* The show jumper follows the injunctions of Caprilli and tends to keep his seat off the saddle, resting on stirrup and knees tucked into supporting knee rolls.

The position of the soldier deteriorated in the nineteenth century into a stiff, backward straphanging, which is what caused Caprilli to rebel and reject it altogether. But with the teaching of Steinbrecht and others there came a return at the end of the century to the basic principles and to the recognition of the necessity for suppleness and adaptability. Now, apart from racing, there are two kinds of position, which we can call the balanced seat and the forward seat, though the latter is balanced too.

The forward seat was designed for outdoor riding – the *campagne* school – for going at speed over any kind of terrain and over fences on the way; Caprilli wanted the Italian cavalry to be able to go freely and straight across country, without interfering with their horses' mouths or putting any weight on their quarters. He limited the aids to their simplest form: forward movement of the hand and leg pressure to go forward. ('The leg,' he said, 'should never be brought into play without a corresponding forward movement of the hands.'); for turning, a pull on the direct rein and a corresponding relaxation of the opposite hand; it was immaterial to him which was the leading leg at the canter, arguing that 'a horse has never fallen because of galloping on the wrong lead'.

The position in the saddle he required was that the knees should be kept against the forward flaps of the saddle, stirrups short enough for the feet to press well down on the stirrup, toes pointing up and heels down; grip would be with the lower

---

*But Waldemar Zeunig (*Horsemanship*) says that the inventor of this seat was a German, Pinter von der Au, in his *Horse Treasury*, published in Frankfurt in 1688.

part of the thigh and the knee, the calves and heels never touching the horse except for good reason; the upper part of the body had to lean slightly forward, the seat just off the saddle. The trot is always a rising one. To achieve this a special saddle was necessary, with a low pommel, flaps cut well forward and with knee rolls, and a high pommel, which would tend to throw the body forward and into the lowest part of the saddle. The hand is held low, and bit, reins, hands, wrists and forearms make a straight line. This, with individual variations, is the position which was adopted all over Europe during the present century for show jumping and cross-country riding.

Piero Santini, Caprilli's pupil, has described it in detail in his two books, *Riding Reflections* and *The Forward Impulse*. Paul Rodzianko took it to Russia, and Vladimir Littauer took it from there to the New World – *Commonsense Horsemanship* and *Be a Better Horseman*. With it has come the new development in saddle making, already touched on above, which has spread not only to the outdoor school but to the indoor manège and dressage riding; the saddle has been adapted to place the rider in the correct position without effort, which could never be done by the old-fashioned flat saddle.

The forward seat has its limitations. It will not take the rider beyond the school of the open air, the cross-country course and the show jumping arena; but that is all its advocates required of it. The rider who is not content with this, who wants to penetrate the uttermost secrets of the control of the horse, must take a rather different standpoint. For Caprilli there was no meeting point for his system of forward riding and manège riding; collection and the curb were dirty words to him. Yet nowadays many riders combine the two in horse trials, the one-day and three-day events, where dressage riding and its skills always precedes the outdoor forward riding and its special requirements. They seem to make the transition without difficulty, as does the horse, and both seem all the better for the combination.

In the full, balanced seat, the rider rests on his seat bones in the lowest and narrowest part of the saddle, at least a hand's breadth in front of the cantle. Any modern type of saddle will help him into this position. The hips should be equally placed on either side, not one lower than the other, which is riding with a dropped hip and destroys balance and flexibility. The body should be upright, shoulders square and level, but no hollowing of the back. Neck and head should be erect, eyes looking to the front over and beyond the horse's ears. The head, shoulders, hips, and the heels should be in one vertical plane.

Below the hips, the thighs should slope gently forward in contact with the saddle, so that the insides of the knees are tucked into the flaps of the saddle. The lower leg is placed slightly behind the vertical (behind the girth), ball of the foot resting on the stirrup, toes pointing upwards and very slightly outwards, but never turned in. Heels are pressed down to keep the foot firm on the plate of the stirrup, with rather more pressure on the inside. Calves are in light contact with the sides of the horse.

The arms hang down naturally to the elbow, and the forearm, wrists, hands and reins to the bit should be in one straight line. The reins held in both hands as already described (page 79, 80), fingers turned inwards and the backs of the hands turned outwards.

Hands and wrists must be absolutely supple and relaxed. It is really the fingers which hold the reins and control the horse. In this there is no disagreement among any of the schools of thought. 'Nothing is quicker and stronger if properly applied than the fingers...' (Piero Santini – *Riding Reflections*.) 'The hand... must never turn into a cramped fist even when strong action is employed, which requires a fixed hand with firmly closed fingers. The fist makes the rider lose his "feel" for the horse's mouth and kills the "feel" in the horse's mouth.' (Waldemar Zeunig – *Horsemanship*.) The sensitive play of the fingers on the reins will make the horse in its turn 'play' with the bit, chew it and champ at it, and flex and unflex its jaw. To obtain these effects the reins must be lightly held, very slightly sagging rather than taut and tense. 'Lightness', 'softness', 'suppleness', are words used by every distinguished writer on equitation, and in the official manuals of the F.E.I., yet seldom are they seen in any dressage arena. All the more reason to cultivate these attributes at the outset.

Some lucky people are supposed to have been born with good hands, and this is often true. We have all met those people who, without any apparent effort, or even knowledge, on their part, have the most sensitive contact with any horse's mouth and seem able to control animals that would run away with riders of more common clay. But I have noticed that people with 'good hands' usually have perfect balance and security in the saddle, and I think that this is the key to lightness of control; the hand – fingers – must have behind them the support of a strong position in the saddle. 'The hand can be steady,'

Zeunig again, 'only if it finds support in the small of the back, which is flexed more or less for this purpose. But the small of the back can provide support at all times only if the seat is firm and independent. This is also a prerequisite for a soft hand, which promotes mouth activity and follows motion elastically.'

A term often found in instructional books is the 'fixed hand', which is death to all lightness. 'The completely closed hand used when the reins are tightened must never become hard and fixed.' For most of the time when riding the hands, and fingers, should always be in slight movement, following the motion, as Zeunig says above, of the mouth as it plays with the bit, and the nodding and stretching of the head. There are times, when changing to a slower gait or beginning collection, when the hand must be still, steady but not fixed or rigid.

Alas! The prerequisite for all this is a well-trained horse with a perfectly soft mouth. Too often the rider will find himself on a horse with a mouth that is dead or callous, which tries to support itself on the rider by leaning on the bit. The principle, however, remains the same, only the movements of the hand and the rein effects will have to be exaggerated. If a rider perseveres long enough with the soft movements of the hand and fingers, he will find it having an effect, even if slight, on the horse.

To return to the back, the muscles of the small of the back play a considerable part in all physical activity, and they are particularly important in riding. By bracing the small of the back, the rider's pelvis and hips are pressed forward and his seat bones forward and down into the saddle. This, combined with the pressure of the legs, pushes the horse forward up to his bit, so that it 'comes to hand'. 'Bracing the back' does not mean stiffness. If practised properly it should make the rider more supple, and becomes virtually an unconscious, reflex, action. The theory and practice of the braced back has been described in detail by Wilhelm Müseler in *Riding Logic*.

The lower part of the body – thighs and calves – remain in easy contact with the body, without any deliberate hard gripping. The leg from the knee downwards should normally be still, without flapping or niggling at the horse's sides, which only helps to blur the effect when leg aids are actually applied. Firm contact resides with the knees against the saddle, and the feet against the stirrup plates. These, with the seat bones, are the three main points of support of the rider, which should be maintained so far as possible in all circumstances. So far as possible, once movement begins and the pace quickens, adjustments forward, always forward, have to be made, so that the body always goes with the movement of the horse, which means harder contact with knees and feet and less with the seat, until at fast speeds it will be off the saddle altogether.

8 Riding on the Lunge

If the possession, or acquisition, of a firm position in the saddle, well balanced and independent of the reins, is the foundation of good riding, then the chief method of so acquiring it is that of riding without stirrups on a horse that is being lunged – riding on the lunge.

Caprilli was opposed to preliminary riding without stirrups, mainly because of the prevalent military practice of putting all cavalry recruits on stirrupless blankets and bumping them round the riding school for an hour or so a day for several weeks. They had their reins, however, and the net result was to produce a great many straphangers. Mainly for that reason, he did not permit the sitting trot in his curriculum, only the rising trot or posting; though he did allow periods of trotting without stirrups for gymnastic exercises 'to cause them (the pupils) to relax and prevent rigidity'.

Riding on the lunge as taught and practised by the Spanish Riding School of Vienna is very different from all this. It takes the form of a series of systematic and controlled exercises by the pupil sitting in the saddle on the back of a horse without stirrups or reins, while the horse is being driven on the lunge rein in a circle at varying speeds.

Properly carried out this kind of work makes great demands on both pupil and instructor; it is tiring and, at first, not a little frightening. The pupil must have courage, or at least trust in his instructor and the horse he is riding; above all he must have a genuine desire to ride well. He should set his sights high, even if he has no apparent hope of hitting the target. At whatever level of equitation he finally reaches he will be all the better for having ridden on the lunge. It is important, too, that he should be a willing pupil; the decision to take lessons on the lunge must be his and his alone. Civilian riding schools of the present day cannot force their pupils into difficult work as could a military riding master with all the authority of *King's* or *Queen's Regulations* behind him. So riding on the lunge must be voluntary.

On the other hand it is not essential, and no detriment, to

have ridden before; nor, within limits, is age any bar. I would not recommend children to start riding on the lunge before they are ten or eleven, but bareback riding before then on small ponies or donkeys is an excellent preparation for it. The danger that they will become too dependent on the reins can be overcome by insisting on the use of a neckstrap. Indeed the neckstrap should be an essential part of riding training equipment for young and old.

The most important person in this set-up is the horse. In the first place he must be quiet and thoroughly accustomed to this sort of work. He must be well trained and obedient to the correct aids. He must go forward freely and steadily without constant encouragement. His gaits must be level and comfortable, so as not to throw the rider up and down too violently in the saddle. He must be suitable in size for the rider, about 15 hands to 15.2 hands for an adult, and smaller, of course, for a child; narrow withers are an advantage.

The instructor must be competent with a lungeing rein so that he will not be busy handling that when he should be watching the rider. He must of course know his business as a teacher, with a clear idea of what he wants to achieve in the immediate lesson being given and as an ultimate objective. He must be able to assess the limitations and possibilities of the pupil and set his target accordingly. He must be quick at spotting faults and able to correct them, but he must also be able to distinguish the basic ones to be corrected from superficial bad habits which can be eradicated in time, so that the pupil is not under a continuous bombardment of corrections and commands. He must be able to inspire absolute confidence and trust in his pupil.

In all lunge work progress must be voluntary, so that a pupil should not be forced into any new position or exercise until he feels ready for it. No exercise should be carried on too long, and every exercise, indeed all work, should be done on both reins equally. Changing the rein gives a chance for a short rest. If the pupil appears to be tiring unduly the lesson should be stopped immediately, and some ordinary lessons with stirrups given instead. Sometimes lunge-riding is done with stirrups, but this loses the whole point of the exercise, which is to get the rider *down* in the saddle. If it is required to give some confidence and balance, a spell of normal lessons can be given, either individually or in a ride. The essence is to be flexible and adaptable, to be able to gear the work and the instruction to the capabilities of the pupil.

The work should be done in a quiet place away from distractions. A covered school is usually the first choice, but it is not at all necessary: an open manège will do just as well. In fact, I would recommend as much riding school work to be done in the open air as possible. The cult of the covered school is a little overdone, and sometimes I wonder whether there are not some riders who never emerge from its twilight security. It is of course useful in bad weather, for very novice riders and nervous young horses; but after all they must all come into the open sooner or later, so why not sooner? So, perhaps, a few sessions in the school for the beginner lunge rider and then out into the fresh air.

The equipment required is simple. For the horse: Snaffle bridle, with a cavesson lungeing noseband over it; the reins are knotted short enough to prevent them flapping or interfering with the horse's mouth; they are not necessary, but their presence gives confidence from the feeling that they are available in an emergency; neckstrap, also for the benefit of the rider; side reins, lightly adjusted so as to keep the horse evenly bent on the circle and restrained from going too fast; saddle; lungeing rein and whip.

The lungeing rein is attached to the front ring of the cavesson. One sees lungeing reins attached to sundry parts of the bit and bridle, a practice which should be avoided. The saddle, of course, must be a modern one, with a deep waist, high cantle and moderate pommel, forward-cut flaps and knee rolls, all to help the rider into the correct position.

For the rider: Breeches and riding boots, the latter giving better support and grip to the rider. Alternatively, jodhpurs or trousers with leather strappings and seat. Riding jacket, pullover, shirtsleeves, or whatever according to the weather. Riding cap or bowler. Jeans are better avoided for this work.

We now have the time, the place and horse and rider all together, so work can begin. An essential preliminary is for the instructor to ride the horse on the lunge himself for a few minutes on each rein, with an assistant holding the lunge rein, in the presence of the pupil. The objects of this are first to ride the horse in before the pupil mounts him; and secondly to show the pupil what it is all about and that it is really quite easy and safe. The instructor can demonstrate the various exercises. If the lunge horse is a pony, a lightweight assistant can do the demonstrating under orders from the instructor. Finally, on the ground before mounting the instructor will explain to the pupil the objects and scope of lunge riding. He will emphasise that the pupil will not be asked to do anything for which he does not feel quite ready, and that he should say when he is getting tired.

For most adult beginners the first lessons should not last longer than about twenty minutes, ten minutes on each rein, not counting short rest periods. As the muscles of the legs and back become attuned to the work the time can be increased to thirty minutes and then to a maximum of forty-five minutes. The longer the time that can be spent comfortably and without tiring the better, but the pupil must be the judge, although the instructor should be able soon to size up his ability to go on. There is no point, however, in going on if overtired, for there will be no value in the exercises.

With children the initial period should not be more than ten minutes, five minutes on each rein, and that can seem an age to a young mind. I recall a delightful book by Josephine Pullein-Thompson about children who, for various good reasons, ran their pony club themselves. They decided to do work on the lunge, and one of them was trotted round. After a few circles she asked how long she'd been doing it. 'One minute,' said the girl on the lunge. 'Only one minute!' screamed the other. 'It seems like *hours*.'

The rate of increase of riding time in ordinary civilian conditions will depend inevitably on the amount of time the pupil can give to riding, every day, two or three days a week, once a week or even less. The ideal of course is daily lessons.

First lessons on the lunge are at the halt. The instructor gives the pupil a leg-up on to the horse, which is being held by an assistant, and allows him to settle into a natural position, telling him to relax completely, letting his legs hang straight down naturally and loosely, with no attempt at gripping, hands resting on the thighs away from the saddle, body normally upright but unbraced. This is the moment to impress on the pupil that intensive gripping is not necessary for staying in the saddle; indeed that it will tend to push him out of the saddle instead of deep into it. The working of the muscles of the small of the back can be explained now, and the pupil can use them himself and feel the effect.

Then the instructor can start building up the riding position which has been described in the last chapter. Allowing the hands to hang loosely down on each side, the pupil will gradually straighten his back and square his shoulders, holding his head up and eyes to the front. If he really feels it necessary to keep his balance, he can touch the pommel of the saddle with the finger tips of one hand, not holding on to it tightly, nor leaning forward: but he should be encouraged to do without that support for the present.

Then a squeezing of the knees forwards, with accompanying pressure of the inside thigh muscles, will bring the knees forward into their more or less normal position behind the knee rolls. Pressure should be just firm enough to hold them there, but not excessive. The lower leg will now hang vertically below the knee.

The heels are pressed down, and the toes raised, which will bring the toes in a line with the knees, and the heels in the same vertical plane as the hips and shoulders.

When the pupil is comfortable in his position, he can raise his hands as if holding the reins: elbows lightly to the sides, forearms nearly horizontal, wrists in a line with them and supple, backs of the hands outwards, fingers flexed, hands four or five inches apart. The interval between the hands is of course variable, depending on the movements of the horse and needs of the rider.

Having been, as it were, fitted into this position, the pupil should fall back into his original relaxed position and start the process over again. Doing this several times is a useful exercise in itself. The pupil should be encouraged to ask questions and to record his impressions and sensations during this and other stages of the lessons.

The main faults to look for are: tenseness and excessive gripping with knees and calves; stiffness of the joints – ankles, knees, wrists and elbows, and of the back and neck; a tendency to crouch forward with rounded shoulders and to get a perched position in the saddle; not sitting level, with one hip lower than the other; looking down; lower leg too far back, or too far forward; body leaning back; a tendency to let the toes droop; turning the toes out, or in; all signs of stiffness and tension.

When the rider's position at the halt is fairly stable, the assistant leads the horse round in a circle at the walk, and the positioning exercises are repeated while the horse is circling. The pupil can make use of a hand on the pommel to preserve his balance, but should try to manage without it. As a preliminary exercise, the rider, holding the pommel with one hand, is asked to 'push' his seat and weight down into the saddle. After a few turns, the horse is halted, and the instructor explains the various suppling and muscle-building exercises.

These are ordinary physical training exercises, and they can be divided into basic and advanced.

The basic ones are: Hands on hips; arms stretching sideways; arms swinging; body turning sideways; legs swinging forwards and backwards.

The advanced ones are: Arms stretching upwards; head turning; touching the toes; bending forwards and backwards.

The difference between the basic and advanced exercises is that the former do not interfere with the position of the rider in the saddle, while the latter tend to raise the seat, which has to be counteracted, so these are really tests of the stability of the rider's position.

The exercises are self-explanatory, and should be done in a regular sequence:

Hands on hips: Palms over and round the hip bones, thumbs to the rear, bracing the loins, elbows out and in the same plane as the body. There should be a strong downward pressure. This exercise helps to straighten the shoulders and encourage an upright position. On the command 'hands down' the hands are dropped smartly to the sides. This can be repeated several times.

Arms stretching sideways: The arms are raised slowly outwards from the hands down position until they are level with the shoulders, where they are held for a few seconds then lowered slowly to the sides. This is an aid to balance, and enables the instructor to check the pupil's position in the saddle. This exercise can be varied by raising the arms forward and stretching them in front of the body. It is important that the shoulders should remain braced and not follow the arms forward. A variation of this is to start with the hands touching in front of the chest, arms held horizontal, then fling the hands outwards briskly so that the arms end stretched to right and left as before. This is good for chest expansion and suppling of the shoulders.

Arms swinging: First swing the right arm round and round, keeping the other arm hanging down to the side. Repeat with the left arm. Then swing both arms together the same way, first of all forwards, then backwards; then swing them in opposite directions. There must be no shifting of the position of the rest of the body while this is being done. Done smoothly and rhythmically these exercises improve balance, increase suppleness and strengthen the body position. Faults to avoid are moving the head and neck, swinging the body out of the saddle with the movement of the arms, swinging the legs and letting the toes drop, and moving the body sideways with the arms.

Body turning sideways: This can be done from the hips firm position and with the arms stretched. The body is turned from the waist, first to the left then to the right. The whole of the upper part of the body – shoulders, neck and head – turn, but the hips and the lower part of the body should remain facing to the front in the same plane as the shoulders of the horse. This strengthens and supples the muscles of the waist and back. The rider should not be allowed to overdo the turning, i.e. too much movement of the shoulders and too little of the waist; the whole upper part of the body must move together and in the same plane. As in all these exercises, a little movement correctly done is worth all the excessive but incorrect movement.

The above exercises tend either to help the body downwards into a deep central position in the saddle or to maintain it there. The following advanced exercises should not be asked for until the instructor is satisfied that the rider's position has been well established. They are really tests of the rider's ability to stay in the saddle in spite of the contrary influences.

Arms stretching upwards: Carried out in the same way as the other stretching exercises, helps to straighten the back and correct crouching.

Head turning: The body remains facing to the front as the head is turned slowly from side to side, first to the left then to the right, keeping erect without any bending forwards or sideways. At first the head should stop between turns in each direction, but with practice the full turn from left to right can be made in one movement. The hands can be in the riding position, on the hips, down to the sides, or stretched sideways. The objects are to loosen and supple the neck muscles and improve balance. This is a difficult exercise and three or four turns at a time are ample. More than six are liable to cause dizziness. It should not be performed on the move until the rider has done a good deal of lunge riding and really established his position.

Touching the toes, body bending forwards and backwards, body turning in the saddle, legs swinging forwards and backwards from the knees are more in the nature of test exercises and games in the saddle to show the rider's control over himself and his position in the saddle. They should never form part of elementary exercises, whether on the lunge or during ordinary riding lessons. Too often they are recommended in books at this stage or given to young novice riders long before they are ready for them.

When the pupil has learnt the basic exercises and done them

94

at the halt, regular work on the move can be started. These preliminaries take a long time to describe, but they can be got through quite easily in the first lesson.

The pupil can, if he wishes, balance himself to begin with by his hand lightly on the pommel, quickly reducing to a mere finger touch, but he should be encouraged to do it without keeping the hands in the riding position and letting the muscles of the small of the back and the thighs get to work.

The first tendencies will be either to crouch forward with excessive grip with the consequent raising of the knees, or to get left behind with the legs going forward. Halt and correct these faults, repeating as often as necessary. Another tendency will be for the legs to start swinging with the movement of the horse, especially at the trot, and a lowering of the toes. The movement being on a circle the inner leg may stretch downwards and the body lean inwards, causing a collapsing of the hip. These are initial faults which must be corrected at the outset, otherwise a good deal of the time on the lunge will be wasted.

The exercises should be done first at the walk, but with intervals of trotting to get the rider used to the faster pace. At first there should be frequent pauses for rest and relaxation, which should become fewer and fewer as progress is made and all the riding muscles are strengthened. Not all the exercises will be carried out in a single lesson, but two or three at a time, with a short revision at the beginning of each new session.

At the trot, and later, the canter, another reaction of the rider by putting more weight on his outside leg and buttock and leaning outwards. Often it will be found that this and other tendencies will be more pronounced to one side than the other, which is the reason why all work, whether with riders or horses, should be done more or less equally on each rein.

In the early stages the same horse should be used all the time, but as progress is made a change of mount is a good thing to prevent the rider's reactions from becoming stereotyped.

Progress in these lessons depends on the skill and understanding of the instructor and the determination of the pupil. Their duration depends on circumstances. For the riders of the Spanish Riding School, riding on the lunge goes on for about a year, and does not entirely stop even then; as a concert pianist continually does scales to keep his fingers in trim so must the horseman continually exercise himself in this basic way. The actual lunge-riding session is about forty-five minutes daily. Few civilian riders can afford the time or money for such concentrated basic equitation, but the more they can do of it the better. Even the rider who does not aspire to the higher flights of advanced riding but only to jump and have fun across country in the hunting field and in hunter trials will benefit from it, and it will certainly not interfere with forward riding. If he wants to excel in horse trials, where a dressage test is part of the exercise, he will find this experience all the more helpful.

The reason for all this labour is of course perfection. 'Perfect self-control is the stipulation for every rider; he must have not only his body in hand but must be able to control his own temperament at any moment, because only then will he be able to subordinate the other living creature, and help it to develop the talents given to it by nature.' (Colonel Alois Podhajsky in *The Spanish Riding School*.)

Above (and overleaf): a variety of exercises in indoor riding establishments
(*Light Horse*)

9 The Language of Riding

A sensitive and skilled horseman communicates with his mount by all the means at his disposal; his mind, his voice, his whole body, but principally his legs and hands. This, so far as the horse is concerned, is the language of riding; commonly called the *aids*. The term is not wholly accurate, because in general they do not actually help the horse but tell it what to do.

It will have been noticed that all through the work on the lunge described in the previous chapter the rider has been completely passive in his relations with the horse, which has just been a vehicle to carry him round while he worked his own body into a fit state to be able to talk to the horse accurately and intelligibly on all occasions. That is where riding on the lunge contrasts with the old military habit of bumming around on a blanket, hanging on with the reins and trying to apply leg aids at the same time.

If lunge-riding cannot be carried out, owing perhaps to there being a lack of time or facilities for individual tuition of this kind, a ride of say three or four pupils can be led by a mounted assistant round the manège while they carry out as near as possible the same procedure without reins and stirrups for a preliminary period in each lesson. The time that be given even to this will not be wasted.

As soon as the pupil is on a free horse, reins in his hands, feet in the stirrups, he will start using 'aids', however elementary. He must use his legs to keep an old soldier of a school horse in his proper place in the line, or restrain him with the reins to prevent him closing up on the horse in front of him; he must stop him, make him go on or faster, and change direction. He will be asked to feel the reins with one hand while relaxing with the other – to make a turn or a circle – and to support it with more pressure from one leg than from the other; and more often than not the school horse will know the answers before the rider. These will be simple signals, but the prelude to a whole gamut of effects which will vary with every individual horse and with the skill and sensitivity of the rider, who at this early stage will discover that the aids, that is to say the means by which the signals are given, have three different ways of making themselves felt by the horse. They can *act*; they can *resist;* they can *yield.*

The hands, through the reins, act when they increase the tension of the reins. Extreme cases of this are when the reins are pulled sharply backwards to stop a galloping horse, as in polo, or when one rein is used to make a jibber turn smartly round and round.

The legs act when they are used decisively against the horse's flanks to stimulate movement, forward, lateral or back.

The hands resist when they are used passively, held steady, to keep the horse's head in position.

The legs resist when they too act passively but firmly to prevent unauthorised movements – swinging of quarters – of the horse's body.

The hands yield when, after acting or resisting, they relax the tension on the reins, as when a horse has halted in obedience to the signals. The immediate giving of the rein is an immediate sign to the horse that he has done correctly, and usually a sufficient reward. A single hand can yield, while the other hand is acting or resisting, as in the case of a turn.

The legs yield in the same way by relaxing pressure as soon as the horse has obeyed the signal.

The body, by altering the position of the seat, supports the actions of the reins. A shifting of the weight to one side or the other will have the effect of pinning down one hindleg while releasing the other. Normally, shifting the weight forward will make the horse lengthen its stride; shifting it back towards the quarters will shorten it. But in the case of an extended trot, for example, the 'pushing' of the seat will induce the horse to lengthen its stride.

It is an axiom that all movement starts from the hindquarters, and that the signals to the horse begin with the leg aids. These are simple enough to apply, and usually go in stages according to the sensitiveness and submissiveness of the horse. They begin with a squeeze of the legs against the flaps, a drawing back of the lower leg and the direct contact of the calf with the flanks of the horse, a stronger action with the heels, and finally the added support of spur and whip. Books are very keen on soft, subtle aids, but not every horse is responsive to such refinements, as every horseman well knows. Too often the imperceptible squeeze is replaced by a succession of banging heels before the required result can be obtained. The principle is the same, but the performance is less elegant. Particularly is this the case with children, who seldom have the strength to make any impression on their thick-skinned little ponies. The same condition applies to the hands and reins. The steady and yielding hands, the supple fingers, have very little effect on mouths which have become deadened from a long succession of straphanging riders and owners. The action must be sharp not to say violent. However, even this must never be sustained, but intermittent, conforming to the principle of take and give which is at the heart of all riding at whatever level.

Still, we must have our ideals, and all instruction in this book will aim at perfection and presuppose a reasonable horse, while remembering that different circumstances and problems require different, or rather variations of the same, solutions.

The progress of the horse is conducted by a series of transitions. Dressage test jargon has given this word a somewhat esoteric significance, but it is, quite simply, a change from one gait, including the halt, to another. Thus, we can have a transition from the halt to the walk, trot or canter, and to the rein back; from the walk to the trot or canter, and to the halt; from the trot to the canter, and back to the walk and halt; from the canter to the gallop, and back to the trot and halt; from the gallop to the canter and halt; from the trot to the walk or halt; from the walk to the halt. Transitions from a slow to a faster gait are upward, and from a fast to a slower gait downward. There are other transitions, too, from forward to lateral movement, which will be considered in their proper place.

The object of applied aids is to translate the will of the rider into a language that a horse can understand and obey, and so carry out these various transitions and movements as instantly and as smoothly as possible. It is not fair to take the horse by surprise with a sudden command; he should be physically and mentally prepared for any change from his present state.

So, you are at the halt, relaxed, standing easy as it were. You warn the horse of impending action by an easy closing of the legs with steady contact of the reins and a slight vibration of the fingers. This alerts the horse and brings him to attention. To go forward, the leg pressure is increased firmly but moderately, the hands still steady, so that the horse starts to stretch his head forward as he starts to move. The hands must not lose contact but must go forward with the movement of the head, while at the same time restraining that movement from becoming excessive. The moment the horse walks steadily forward the action of the legs is reduced to normal contact with the sides, and the hands remain steady. The legs first of all acted, then yielded; the hands have yielded slightly and then remained passive.

The horse should walk briskly with a long, level stride, which will be described in more detail in Part III. If he tends to slow down or to get unbalanced, by one pair of diagonals coming closer together than the other pair, leg pressure must be applied to correct it, the legs signalling actively, the hands remaining steady, resisting. To halt, still holding the hands steady press the horse up to the bit with the legs. If the horse does not respond, the hands must act more decisively, first by a backward vibration of the fingers, then, more drastically, by short sharp pull, instantly relaxed. Once halted the horse should stand evenly balanced on all four feet, placed foursquare underneath him. Any taking up of tension by the hands should be relaxed, so that there is the lightest possible contact with the mouth, the head held up so that the poll should be about level with the rider's chest, the head at an angle of 45 degrees to the ground.

To digress slightly, every horseman and horse owner likes to be photographed on a horse or to have his horse photographed, but the halt position described is no good for photography, as the resultant picture will make it appear that the horse has only two legs, one in front one behind. So the horse has to get used to standing with the legs furthest from the camera slightly inside the nearer pair, the outer foreleg *behind* the inner one, the outer hindleg *in front* of the inner one. It takes a great deal of adjustment and experience to get this position just right, but the trouble is worth taking in order to get a really pleasing picture.

Returning to the riding lesson, the pupil may now try a reinback. This movement is not taught at this early stage to a young horse, but the rider is, or should be, on a fully trained horse. As before prepare the horse for a movement by alerting him with the legs and hands. Then, as with all movement, apply the legs smoothly and firmly to push him forward up to the bit, which is in firm contact with steady hands. The horse will understand that some movement is required of him; it is obviously not remaining at the halt, and the hands prevent him from going forward, so the only alternative is to go back. Once more, it will often be necessary to support the leg action with more positive action of the hands. The horse should step back diagonally – near fore, off hind, off fore, near hind, or the opposite pairs. One or two strides are sufficient, then stop the horse by yielding with the hands, and go forward at once. (See page 98)

Now move forward at the walk, and prepare the horse for the trot. The signal for the change of pace is the same as for the halt to the walk. Preliminary work on the lunge or in a ride should have accustomed the rider to sitting easily at the trot. If the rider is relaxed and supple at the sitting trot, he should have no difficulty in rising at the trot, or posting, as the Continentals first called it from seeing English postillion riders using it.

The horse trots in two-time by using his diagonal pairs of legs alternately, off fore, near hind, near fore, off hind. In fact the pairs of feet do not come to the ground exactly together, but in succession, though so close together that only high-speed photography can detect it; for practical riding purposes the movement of the diagonals can be regarded as instantaneous. There is a moment of suspension between each diagonal when all four feet are in the air. The ancient Egyptians depicted this several thousand years ago, but they were not believed until Muybridge's photography again revealed it in 1882. When the horse moves with lateral instead of diagonal pairs – off fore, off hind, near fore, near hind – he is said to be pacing or ambling, a gait which does not concern us here.

To rise at the trot, the rider must raise his seat, using his back and thigh muscles while keeping his knees and legs against the saddle, for one diagonal and lower it back on to the saddle for the next, and so on. A common tendency is to rise up too high and to make a jerky movement of it, coming down into the saddle with a bump. Rise up just enough to clear the waist of the saddle, and sink down easily and quietly without bumping. Knees should be pressed against the saddle and the lower legs in sufficient contact with the sides of the horse to keep them still. The legs should neither flap outwards nor move forwards and backwards. The hands remain independent of the up-and-down movement of the body, and the body from the waist upwards should keep with the forward movement of the horse, that is the weight of the body should be placed slightly more forward than at the halt and the walk.

The hands should be in light and sensitive contact all the time with the mouth, the fingers playing with the reins to make the horse in its turn play with the bit, chewing it, nodding its head and yielding its jaw, while keeping a steady, regular speed of about eight to ten miles an hour. The legs maintain the speed, and make the horse use his hindlegs and engage them underneath the quarters, not letting them drag behind; while the hands regulate the speed.

The description of the diagonal is determined by the foreleg; thus off fore and near hind make a right diagonal, near fore and off hind the left. When riding in a manège it is more convenient at all times to speak of outside (the side nearest to the wall or outer edge of the school) and inside (the side nearest to the centre of the school). These diagonals should be changed regularly whether in the school or in the open. It is easy to tell when this has not been done, for a horse that has become used to being ridden on the same diagonal all the time will not readily take to a change, throwing back to the accustomed one a rider who tries to make a change. Riding on the right diagonal (when the rider's weight is on the saddle) tends to overburden the horse's near hind, and *vice versa*.

When riding the rising trot in a manège or on a circle, which diagonal should one choose? There are two schools of thought about this. The first, and majority opinion says the rider should post on the outside diagonal, i.e. if on the right rein, the near (left) fore and off (right) hindleg. Thus the weight of the rider burdens the inside (off) hind, and, it is claimed, achieves 'an increased and energetic engagement of the inside hock by the driving aids of the rider'. (Richard L. Wätjen, *Dressage Riding*.)

The opposite opinion is that the rider should go on the inside diagonal, i.e. (again on the right rein) the off (right) fore and near (left) hindleg. The object again is the full engagement of the inside hindleg to support the weight of horse and rider and to maintain equilibrium. It is maintained, however, that the horse can better do this by having this inside leg free and not overburdened, because of the increased flexion caused by the weight, which it will try to counteract by reducing the engagement of that hindleg. It is maintained that it will be much easier for the driving aids to encourage the movement of the inside hindleg under the horse, if it is in the air to start with and not on the ground. However, in competitions the rider can use whichever diagonal he prefers, provided that he is consistent throughout the movement. Of course the diagonal must be changed with the changing of the rein, as smoothly as possible and without interfering with the cadence of the trot. The diagonal is changed by simply sitting down in the saddle for one stride, reducing the bump to a minimum.

The transitions up to the trot and down to the halt and the rein-back should be practised frequently in the first lessons, until the signals are given smoothly and precisely. The response of the horse will be the best guide to progress.

So far we have been theoretically on a straight line, but, the manège not being limitless, it regularly becomes necessary to change direction, to turn at the corners and to change the rein diagonally across the school, which brings into action the lateral aids. The simplest signal is the rein acting on one side of the mouth to make the horse turn his head in the required direction. If this action is continued alone, the horse may follow the indication of the rein and move round in the direction of the aid, to right or left, but the unsupported hindquarters will tend to swing out in the opposite direction. Or the horse may just bend his head round and continue going forward. So supporting action is necessary with the legs, combined aids. If the turn is to be to the right, the right leg will remain passive, merely assisting forward movement while the left leg increases pressure behind the girth to keep the quarters from swinging to the left and to urge the horse to move to the right, using his hindquarters as the pivot. The signal is the same for both turns and circles. When the movement is completed the hand and leg are relaxed to go forward again.

This action, like every other phrase in the language of horsemanship, can have many variations, nuances of meaning, according to the state of training of both horse and rider. Assuming that we are on the right rein, the hand can be moved away from the side of the horse outwards to the right, called by Blacque Belair (*Cavalry Horsemanship*) the direct opening rein. First the head bends to the right, then the neck, and the shoulders follow the neck. This would be used on a very green horse in its first lessons, or to intensify the normal direct lateral signal. The hand can be drawn straight back, when it has an opposing effect on the shoulders and quarters, moving the latter to the left. This has been called the direct rein of opposition.

A further action of the same rein will be across to the left. This will turn the head to the right but shifts the weight of the neck on to the left shoulder. More movement of the hand to the left will make the horse turn in that direction. This is an indirect rein, and it will be used in lateral movement on two tracks, and in neck reining. The effect is varied by moving the hands in front of and behind the withers. To turn to the right the right direct and left indirect reins are used, combined with the right leg regulating the movement forward and the left leg supporting the movement to the right.

A final refinement of these signals is not to activate the right direct rein, i.e. to move it back, but to hold it steady and at

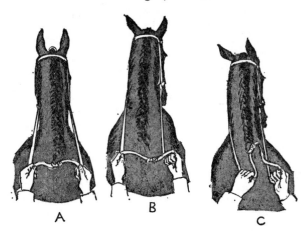

Fig. 13.   *The Actions of the Reins*

A. Direct: reins acting equally on either side. B. Lateral: for simple turns to left or right. C. Indirect: the opposite rein is used to support the other for turns or other movements sideways. This is also called neck reining.

the same time yield with the left rein by moving the left hand forward. The relaxation of contact on the left side of the mouth will intensify the contact on the right side, and, supported again by the legs, will indicate to the horse that a movement to the right is required. Further emphasis can be given by the shifting weight of the body, and, in the last resort, by spur and whip, and the voice.

This is the simple grammar of the language of riding. It will be interpreted by the horse according to the context in which it is given, i.e. its gait, pace and direction, and by the standard of its training. Its transmission to the horse by the rider must also be adapted to circumstances, and again to the individual horse and its level of education. If a horse holds its head too low, it is corrected by extra drive of the legs combined with a light upward action of the hands. Excessive raising of the head is a definite resistance. To counter this, first of all slow down the pace by applying the normal aids; then with the driving action of the legs and a yielding of the hands encourage the horse to lengthen its stride, to do which he will have to lower his neck and head. Repeat the action as often as is necessary, but do not try to hold the horse's head down by lowering the hands, which will only increase the resistance. Whatever the position of the horse's head, the rider's hands must still be in a straight line from the elbow to the horse's mouth. It is the art of equitation to understand the horse you are riding, its individual idiosyncrasies and limitations, and to be able to apply the signals in harmony, clearly, and sufficient for the purpose required.

Learning to ride is the practising of this application so that it becomes instinctive. Regular work in the manège is like doing scales in music. An obvious proviso here is that the 'scales' must be done correctly. It is not *what* is done that matters but *how*. As William Steinkraus, horseman and musician, says, 'There is nothing beneficial at all in the mechanical repetition of wrong movements, no matter how interminably prolonged. A bad scale becomes a good one not by repeating it, but by correcting the causes of its badness.'

10 Balance, Impulsion, Flexion and Collection

Balance

Basically there is no mystery about balance. Any object at rest is in balance so long as it is able to stay at rest without altering its position. A table on four legs is in balance; so is a horse on four legs, so long as it remains in that position. The difference between the two is that the horse is alive, has muscles, and is seldom, if ever, really motionless.

A horse on its own may stay with his weight evenly distributed on all four feet for a short time, but before long he will shift his position, take the weight off (rest) one hindleg, which will entail a muscular adjustment of his whole body by taking more weight on the other three legs in order to remain in balance. The point is that he will see to it that he remains in a comfortable balanced position whatever the distribution of the weight. Of course, with each change of position there is a slight shifting of the centre of gravity, which has to remain within the base of support, inside the oblong made by the four feet on the ground. In riding, all movement results from a loss and recovery of balance.

Whether at rest or on the move a horse on its own has little trouble about balance. Anybody who has watched riderless horses in a steeplechase will note that they jump much better than their still burdened colleagues. A horse galloping normally will extend himself, his centre of gravity well forward. When a horse is excited, or suspicious, he will collect himself, raise his neck and do something like a passage or a piaffe, his centre of gravity shifted to the rear.

In turns and circles, the horse naturally places more weight on the inside legs, principally in front, and the centre of gravity shifts accordingly. To counteract centrifugal forces, he tends to lean inwards. This is slight at slow paces, but when done at a gallop, as when playing polo, or in the case of a hunter going all out round a show ring, or a cutting horse baulking a steer, the inward list is extreme, perhaps at an angle of 50 degrees

106

to the ground. The horse is then strictly not in balance, because his centre of gravity could be outside the base of support – the four feet; the only things which keep him from falling are the grip of the ground and his own power to resist the centripetal forces. It is not a problem which arises in *haute école,* but a very real one in hunting and outdoor riding of all kinds.

The presence of a rider on his back naturally makes things harder for the horse; a great deal depends on the tact and skill of the rider, but more on the strength and natural balance of the horse. The problem for the rider is to make his own centre of gravity coincide with that of the horse. The value of the central seat is manifest as a starting point for all sorts of movement.

At a normal halt position, with the rider upright in the lowest part of the saddle, the two will be in perfect balance. If the rider is sitting nearer the cantle, or leaning back, his centre of gravity will be behind that of the horse, and the balance will not be perfect. The centre of gravity of the combined weight will be somewhere between those two points, and as a result of this shifting of the weight to the rear the horse will have to make a greater effort to move forward than before.

A man on a horse galloping must lean forward in order to keep his centre of gravity with that of the horse; if he leans back, he is not in harmony with the movement and the true balance is disturbed, again requiring unnecessary effort on the part of the horse. On the other hand, if the rider collects a horse at the walk or trot and maintains his correct position, the horse will adjust his weight to the rear to conform with the lowering of the hocks and the redistribution of the rider's own weight. In one case the extension of the horse requires the rider to adapt his posture to the horse's equilibrium; in the other the shortening of the horse requires the horse to adapt its equilibrium to the burdening of the rider (de Romaszkan, *Horse and Rider in Equilibrium*).

The same kind of adjustments have to be made in lateral movements and in jumping. The situation is entirely fluid; every instant horse and rider have to make adjustments of weight (of the rider's position) in order to preserve true balance. Part of equestrian tact is the rider's feeling for the movement and balance of the horse, so that he conforms to it or controls it as the case may be. These are the feels of riding, which can only come from experience and knowledge and the riding of many horses.

The balance of the rider has already been achieved by his

work on the lunge, with which he should refresh himself and re-practise himself as often as possible. The natural balance of the horse can also be improved, first by his initial training on the lunge, and then by balancing exercises in the school, consisting of turns, circles, halts, half-halts, which constitute the ordinary riding school exercises. (See Part III)

Impulsion

Very few of the great equestrian writers mention impulsion; it is something that seems to be taken for granted. Yet it is the essence of that forward movement which is the basis of all training and all horsemanship. Here are three definitions:

'A forward urge manifested by the energetic use of the hocks.' (*Summerhays' Encyclopaedia for Horsemen.*)

'Impulsion is forward movement made use of under the exact discipline of the aids, in accordance with the end desired. It is the basis of training. Its seat is in the hindquarters, which push the weight forward, or at any rate ought always to be ready to do so.' (Blacque Belair, *Cavalry Horsemanship.*)

'Impulsion varies greatly in individuals, and primarily relates to *the manner in which the horse moves.* Excellent natural impulsion is characterised by that ample, supple and springy action of the joints which gives an appearance of great momentum generated with but little effort.' (Harry D. Chamberlain, *Training Hunters, Jumpers and Hacks.*)

Impulsion has no connection with speed. A galloping horse may well lack impulsion, as is often manifest when he comes up against an obstacle. On the other hand a horse at an alert halt may be full of it; like a compressed spring full of latent power. Impulsion comes from the hocks and is controlled by the reins, and is one of the results of the correct gymnastic training of the horse.

Flexion

The yielding of the jaw and the bending of the head from the poll are the prerequisites of collection and control. Flexion begins with the lower jaw of the horse giving to the action of the curb bit and curb chain. The bending of the head from the poll follows after that, and can be distinguished from the incorrect bending of the head from the neck by the fact that from the latter the head is lowered and drawn back beyond the perpendicular, so that the horse becomes behind the bit. For the beginner rider to experience the effects of flexion he must use a double bridle.

Successful flexion depends, apart from the skill of the rider and trainer, on the horse's conformation (pages 46–53). A horse with a short thick neck and a too-closely coupled lower jaw, giving no room for play backwards, will never be able to flex easily, if at all. Even if he has a good neck, he will not be able to flex unless there is room between the jaw and the top of the neck. Many ponies suffer from this fault of conformation, and so are very difficult for children to control.

Collection

'The collection and proper head carriage of a well-trained riding horse cannot be mechanically determined, but must always be adapted to the conformation and individuality of the horse.' (Richard L. Wätjen, *Dressage Riding*.)

In English, 'collection' is a portmanteau word covering a wide range of effects, for which French and German have different names. The term is apt, however, because one does really collect, or unite the horse, bringing together its forehand and quarters, so that the forehand is lightened (the centre of gravity shifts back) and the hocks are engaged underneath the quarters, with a flexing of the hip, stifle and hock joints. The horse has the appearance of being shortened (*raccourci*).

The first degree of collection is merely being at attention, in fact the positioning or preparation of the horse for other movements (pages 84–7). There should be slight engagement of the quarters, and the head should be raised so that the muzzle is about level with the rider's knees, the angle of the head in front of the vertical, at an angle of about 30 degrees to the ground. The action for collection of any kind is first the legs and a bracing of the back, then the restraining action of the hands. The horse is thus collected from rear to front and receives an urge to go forward.

More complete collection is produced by the engagement of the quarters followed by more active action of the hands to flex the head from the poll, so that it comes nearer the vertical (*ramener*). As collection becomes more extreme the head will be vertical, but it should never be allowed to go behind the vertical. Total collection for high school airs is *rassembler*.

Collected movements must be energetic and full of impulsion, rather more elevated than ordinary gaits. The official dressage definition makes it clear. At the collected trot 'the neck is raised, thus enabling the shoulders to move with greater ease in all directions, the hocks being well engaged and maintaining energetic impulsion, notwithstanding the slower movement. The horse's steps are shorter but he is lighter and more mobile.' (F.E.I. *Rules for Dressage Competitions*, Section 404.) The actual rate of progression is slow, not from any slackness of movement but from the shorter steps, whether at walk, trot or canter.

For ordinary riding school and outdoor work (the *campagne* school), only elementary collection is necessary. Collected movements were taken out of one-day and some three-day event dressage tests some years ago. But some collection is necessary for all forms of riding.

One thing leads to another, and the novice rider may want to move beyond just galloping across country and jumping, to taste the fascination of a highly trained and responsive horse, a rare thing. The one thing to remember is that collection should never be forced. The horse must really lead the way, responding to the tentative suggestions of the rider through his legs and hands; and the rider must know enough about his horse to appreciate when he has gone far enough.

Here are the official (F.E.I.) descriptions of the collected walk and canter.

> *Walk*. The horse moves resolutely forward, with his neck raised and arched. The head approaches the vertical position, the light contact with the mouth being maintained. The hindlegs are engaged with good hock action. The pace should remain marching and vigorous, the legs being placed in regular sequence. Each step covers less ground and is higher than at the ordinary walk because all the joints bend more markedly. The hind feet touch the ground behind the footprints of the forefeet. In order not to become hurried or irregular the collected walk is slightly shorter than the ordinary walk, although showing greater mobility. (*Rules for Dressage Competitions*, Section 403 (b).)
>
> *Canter*. At the collected canter, the shoulders are supple, free and mobile and the quarters very active. The horse's mobility is increased without any loss of impulsion. (*Rules for Dressage Competitions*, Section 405 (b).)

The word 'cadence', usually applied to high school work, means the rhythmical succession of measured beats of the feet in movement; four at a walk, two at a trot, three at a canter, and every rider, whatever his standard, should try to ensure that his horse moves with an even, level cadence, particularly marked, of course, in collected movements.

11 The Canter and Gallop, Turns and Lateral Work

The Canter and Gallop

The canter, as we have already observed, is a three-time gait, which differs from the trot through the breaking of the beat of one of the diagonal pairs of legs, so that the leading foreleg and following hindleg will be on the same side during one complete canter stride. Both the canter and the gallop are springing gaits, with an obvious moment of complete suspension, and the taking of the weight by one (leading) foreleg. One hindleg also carries the weight for an instant during a stride.

Canter is an English word and usually indicates variations of speed up to about twelve miles an hour, after which it is considered to merge into the gallop, which can be any speed up to and over thirty miles an hour. A very slow canter can become a four-time gait, with little or no suspension. In America this is called a *lope*, and it is an exceedingly comfortable pace for both horse and rider, which can be maintained for long periods without tiring. It is, of course, not a school gait, and regarded as faulty in the dressage arena, where the three-beat movement must be clearly marked. This three-time gait is also known as a *hand-gallop*.

In the gallop the horse reaches out his leading foreleg and takes a much longer stride than at the canter, and it really seems to leap from the hindlegs to the forelegs, as the old artists portrayed it before rapid photography and slow motion cinematography revealed the true situation. The length of stride of the ordinary canter is about ten to twelve feet, and of the gallop from fifteen to twenty-four feet. The school gaits are assessed at eight feet for ordinary canter, five feet for collected, and twelve feet for extended canter.

The riding pupil will have experienced the canter during work on the lunge, or at an early stage in the riding school, when it is a welcome change from the trot. At this stage the horse will act on the command of the instructor; the use of the aids and the correctness or otherwise of the canter will be

immaterial. Turning the corners at the canter will help to give balance and confidence. Mistakes of the horse in cantering are:
1. Going on the right rein with the left leg leading and *vice versa* (false canter). But this can be done deliberately as a school movement (counter canter).
2. The leading leg followed by the opposite hindleg (disunited).

The school canter is ridden with the seat in the saddle, activated downwards by the muscles of the small of the back. The rider should strive to go smoothly with the movement without being rocked up and down and swaying the upper part of his body backwards and forwards, or going up and down in the saddle. The ideal is a smooth flowing motion forwards in harmony with the advance of the horse.

For outdoor riding, jumping, cross-country, hunting, the body should lean moderately forwards, the seat out of the saddle, hands going forward to release the head, and body going easily with the movement. In the first case the horse will adjust its balance to the position and movement of the rider; in the latter the pace and extension of the horse will dictate the forward position to the rider.

The faster the movement, up to a full gallop, the more forward will be the rider's position – and the stirrup leathers will be shortened according to the purpose of the outing until the extreme position of the jockey on a racehorse is reached.

There are several ways of obtaining the canter, according to the state of training of the horse, amounting really to a 'convention between horse and rider' (Jean Froissard, 'The Departure at the Canter', *Light Horse*, July, 1969); but the pupil rider will only be concerned with a trained horse. So the transition from the trot to the canter is produced by the application of the same principles as for the walk and trot. In a canter to the right the horse leads with his off fore, and to the left with his near fore, and he will tend to bend his head in the direction of the canter. An untrained horse will tend to go crooked, almost on two separate tracks of the fore and hind feet; a trained horse will go straight, but in the preparation for the transition his spine will be flexed longitudinally from front to rear.

The first intimation of a change will be a half-halt, after which the sequence for a canter to the right (off fore leading) will be as follows: feel the right rein to move the horse's head slightly to the right, and support with the left rein to keep him going straight on the track; left leg behind the girth to stimulate the near hindleg which will start the movement; right against the girth to maintain straightness and impulsion; shift of the body weight to the left to free the off hindleg. The hands must continue to act directly to control the pace, so that the horse will not try to make the canter by increasing its trotting rate or extending its trot stride. If a horse (ponies are more prone to it, however) persists in doing this, halt and start again. As in all leaping movements, the horse will want to stretch his neck and head forward, and the moment he does this after receiving the signal, the hands should yield accordingly. During the canter, the right hand should continue to act gently to keep the bend of the head to the right; and the right leg should act to keep the horse straight and prevent the hindquarters from moving inwards off the track. (See pages 117–20.)

The signal for the gallop is simply strong pressure of the legs, with a forward bending of the body and steady hands, which will yield to the natural extension of the head and neck. Contact must normally be maintained, and with most horses it is likely to be pretty strong. Some riders like their horses to take a good hold at the gallop, but the idea sometimes expressed that a horse will fall down if the contact is relaxed at the gallop is entirely disproved by the polo pony, the ideal for which is a full gallop ('sixteen annas' as they used to say) on a loose rein. And, as a matter of fact, Gordon Richards used to ride many of his finishes on a light or loose rein. In the long run it all depends on the horse.

At this point it is as well to stress the value of riding with one hand. Every horseman should be able to ride confidently with the reins in either the left (usually) or the right hand, leaving the other free. For the soldier it was a necessity, and still is for the polo player, hunt staff, or gymkhana rider; it used to be *de rigueur* in hack classes. Now the influence of the dressage arena is making it almost a lost art. A concomitant of this of course is that the horse or pony must be bridle wise. I have seen courageous riders with the arms in slings in the jumping phase of a three-day event struggling round with most bewildered though willing horses who could not understand what was happening to them. Ted Edgar, the show jumper, once performed a *tour de force* by completing the Hickstead jumping 'Derby' course in just this way. So in all instruction periods and at all paces there should be spells of riding with one hand.

Turns

Turns at the Halt: Simple turns are changes of direction on the move, either at right angles or diagonally (French *la* *conversion*, German *die Wendung*). The volte and half-volte are small circles or half circles, usually at the corners of the manège. Circle (*cercle; Zirkel*) is a larger round with the short side of the manège as diameter. Turns on the quarters and forehand, apart from their practical applications, are training exercises for both rider and horse, teaching the one how to apply aids correctly and the other to understand and obey them. A turn on the quarters on the move is a pirouette, half (180 degrees) or complete (360 degrees). Turns at the halt usually begin with a quarter-turn (90 degrees), and progress to half and complete turns. The same applies to the turn on the forehand.

Turn on the forehand: With the main weight of his body in front a horse usually finds it all too easy to turn on its forehand, although it requires precise aids to perform it as a schooling exercise. For this reason it should be practised sparingly whether by rider or horse. It has a practical value for the opening of gates, or when a quick change of direction is required.

In this case the horse pivots on its foreleg, the off one in the case of a right turn, when the quarters go to the left but the horse ends up facing to the right. The rider's body weight is concentrated on the off shoulder. The right rein turns the head slightly to the right, left rein supporting as before. The right leg behind the girth moves the quarters over to the left and round the pivot of the off fore, while the left leg maintains impulsion and prevents the quarters from swinging outwards. (See pages 106–10.)

Turn on the quarters at the halt: Let us assume that the turn is to the right. Reverse the aids for the left turn. Halt about midway on one or other of the long sides of the manège, going on the right rein. Steady the horse by slight collection. With the right (direct) rein invite the horse to move his head to the right. At the same time the left leg applied behind the girth encourages the body to follow the direction of the head and neck. The left rein yields slightly and acts on the neck, making the horse step to the right with the off fore. The right leg on the girth holds the quarters in position and maintains impulsion. The weight of the body to the right rear pins the off hind-leg and foot to the ground to make that the pivot of the movement. With continued impulses from the reins and legs the horse takes the next step with the near fore and hind, which should go in front of the off fore and off hind respectively. And so the movement proceeds, step by step. The end of a half-turn places the horse facing the way he originally advanced, thus changing the rein. For a beginner a quarter-turn will be enough, and then he can practise the reverse turn to the left, using the opposite aids.

Except to shift his weight the rider should not change his normal position throughout the movement; and he should endeavour to make the turn as rhythmical and cadenced as possible. To make a good turn the horse must be light in hand and on his hocks, with the head perhaps raised a little during the movement.

In both cases, the movement is made a step at a time, pausing after each step. In both cases also, movement forwards or backwards must be avoided as far as possible.

Turning on the quarters on the move is really a school movement and comes into more advanced training of the rider. The essence of it is that the same aids are used but there is no preliminary halt, the horse, at the walk, going straight into the movement. At the trot and canter it becomes a pirouette, half and full, which will be considered later. (Pages 176–82.)

Changing the leading leg at the canter: It is noticeable that even a very young and untrained horse will change his leading legs at the canter smoothly and effortlessly, and without change of gait, the flying change in fact, for which so much thought and preparation will be given later on when he is mounted. A normally trained horse will also do it automatically to keep its balance when changing direction suddenly, for example during a show jumping round. Neither then, nor at polo, has the rider time to give carefully prepared aids. Caprilli did not care which leg was leading when his pupils' horses started to gallop, remarking that 'a horse has never fallen because of galloping on the wrong lead'.

For practical purposes, however, in the riding school, the horse should always be asked to lead with the inside leg, or the same as the rein on which he is going, i.e. off fore for right rein, near fore for left rein. In advanced riding making a horse canter with the opposite lead, or counter-canter, is a demonstration of its training and obedience. Otherwise, at every change of rein the lead must also be changed, and it is a good thing for a pupil to learn fairly early both the simple change of leg and the flying change. These exercises are best done on a circle to start with.

For a simple change of leg, the rider is, say, on a right-handed circle of half the manège, cantering with the off fore leading. On approaching the centre of the school, he will slow down to a trot, straighten up and prepare the horse for a change of movement, then give the aids for the canter on the near fore leading, and turn into the left circle in the other half of the school. Ultimately only two or three intermediate steps will be necessary. In due course the pupil, whether on his own or in a ride, will do the same on the straight on the long sides of the manège. Going into the canter and also the simple change should be done from the halt as well as from the trot. Indeed, for a horse that is impetuous at the trot, starting from the walk will be beneficial.

The flying change done under command is most satisfying for the rider. Once a rider has become well accustomed to the rhythm of the canter, and can obtain the leading leg at will on the straight, and perform simple changes smoothly and correctly, and can feel which leg his horse is leading with without looking down, there is no reason why he should not start learning the flying change.

The actual change from one pair of leading legs to the other must obviously happen when the horse is in a state of suspension with all four legs in the air. So the rider's signal must be given just before that instant, when the leading foreleg is about to strike the ground, having previously prepared the horse with a half-halt. The signal for a change from off fore to near fore will be the same as for a strike off on the near fore, left rein, right leg. If the signal has been correctly timed, the near hind and forelegs will be felt to move forward in a new rhythm. Of course the aids must be given as smoothly as possible.

Turns, voltes and circles are preliminaries to lateral work, and a word about riding them is appropriate here. When a horse makes a turn of any kind, the main force which acts on him is centrifugal, pulling him outwards, to counteract which he tends to place more weight on his inside legs and to lean inwards, to the right, if on a right rein, and *vice versa*. At slow paces, walk and trot, this is hardly noticeable, but becomes very obvious when circling at the gallop. In a circular movement, also, the inner legs have a shorter distance to cover at each stride than the outer legs; though the difference is virtually imperceptible. A horse going on a circle is rather like a four-wheeled railway coach with fixed wheels, only of course the body and spine are far more flexible than the chassis of the coach.

The position of the rider in a turn or circle should remain upright in the same plane as the body of the horse, i.e. at walk and trot it should be as near upright as makes no difference, and his chest and shoulders should be square to the front of the horse all the way through the movement. As with the horse, the rider will find an outward pull which has the effect of lowering his outside leg, which he will adjust by an extra pressure of the inside foot on the stirrup iron. If the pace is faster – canter or gallop – or the turn sharper, volte, he must adjust his position accordingly, so that the above conditions are fulfilled.

When turning, the horse's head will, of course, be flexed slightly in the direction of the movement, the spine also bending as much as it can, which is slight, in the same direction. The inside leg on the girth will control the body and keep it moving forward, while the outside leg will keep the quarters from swinging outwards; and the horse will keep on a single track, the hind feet stepping in the same line as the tracks of the fore feet.

Lateral work

Practising turns at the halt and in turns and circles will have prepared the rider for moving sideways. There are two kinds of lateral movements. 1. Those in which the head is flexed (bent) opposite to the direction of movement. 2. Those in which the horse bends his head in the same direction as the movement.

The first is a training and suppling exercise in the school known as the shoulder-in. This exercise was invented by the French master, François de la Guérinière, and he regarded it as the 'first and last of all the lessons we can give the horse in order to obtain complete suppleness and perfect freedom in all parts of his body . . .', and it has remained a basic exercise in all equestrian schools ever since. 'The object of this movement,' wrote Richard Wätjen, 'is to increase the lightness and suppleness of the horse, and to obtain a higher degree of obedience. These exercises improve the activity of the hindlegs, and the horse becomes more responsive to the rider's leg and rein aids.' (*Dressage Riding.*)

The shoulder-in is usually performed or practised on the tracks on the long side of the manège, so that there is a wall or guiding line to keep the direction straight; but of course it can be done on any straight line anywhere. In this exercise the horse continues to go forward in its original direction, it is positioned at an angle made by the shifting of the forehand off the track, the fore feet making their own separate track parallel to the original one, on which the hindquarters are still moving. So it is an exercise on two tracks.

The head is flexed slightly inwards, as in every turn or sideways motion, that is away from the direction of movement. The body is at an angle of about 30 degrees to 45 degrees to the main track, the horse goes forward with a side-stepping movement, inside fore and hind feet crossing in front of the outside ones. So, on the right rein, in a right shoulder-in, the horse's head is flexed to the right, the horse moves forward, and the right fore and hind feet cross in front of the left (outside) ones.

A preliminary lesson for the rider is the wall to the wall movement. On the right rein: the rider changes direction to the right, with right rein and left leg, at an angle of about 30 degrees, continuing the movement until the horse is just clear of the track, then straightening up for three or four strides, then bearing left on to the track. As the horse departs from the track it is in position for the shoulder-in.

After a little practise at this, the rider can ask the horse for the shoulder-in. The right rein, left rein supporting, flex the head to the right, and the left leg turns the forehand just off the track to the right. The trained horse can carry on the movement for the length of the school, but normally a few steps at a time are sufficient. Then the horse is straightened up by the outside rein and inside leg bringing the forehand on to the track again. A yielding of the aids for a few steps forward brings relief and is a reward for carrying out the movement.

The opposite position to the shoulder-in is the quarters-in, known also as head to the wall or travers. On the right rein, the left leg will move the quarters off the track to the right, while the reins, with a slightly increased action of the right rein, will keep the forehand on the track, and the head flexed to the right. So, in this case, the bend of the horse is in the direction of movement not against it as in the shoulder-in. The horse will continue to move forward, on two tracks, the outside (left) fore and hindlegs crossing in front of the inside (right) fore and hind.

The exact opposite to the travers is the renvers, also called quarters-out, or tail to the wall. The hindquarters remain on the track, while the forehand is moved off it, but this time the bend of the head is to the left, *with* the direction of movement. The outside leg (left when on the right rein) and the outside indirect rein move the forehand inwards while keeping the head flexed outwards or forwards.

The shoulder-in and its variations are not asked for in dressage tests; they are solely training exercises for the horse, and also for the rider in improving his aid application and general at-homeness in the saddle. The aids should be applied on the principle of minimum force, smoothly and, in time, imperceptibly, or as much so as the training of the horse will allow.

118

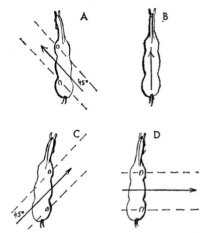

Fig. 14. Lateral Movements

(a) Half-pass (left) or left half-pass (b) Straight position for one length of horse before changing the flexion to the left (c) Half-pass (right) or right half-pass (d) Full pass (right) or right full pass

The second type of lateral movement is when the horse moves sideways with his body straight and head flexed in the direction of the movement. The movement can be straight across at right angles to the original direction, full pass, or diagonally at an angle to the original direction, half-pass.

The full pass has disappeared from the normal school curriculum, and is never asked for in a dressage test, but in moderation it is a most useful movement and an excellent training exercise for rider and horse. I remember once seeing a line of about twenty mounted policemen formed up at the old Richmond Show to receive their awards after a competition. The stewards decided they were in the wrong place and asked them to move over several yards to the right. An ordinary group of present-day riders would have had to do a great deal of manoeuvring, going forward and turning, or going back and turning, and there would have been a good deal of milling around before they got safely into the new position. The policemen merely did a full pass to the right, moving altogether with amazing precision, and were in position in a few seconds. It was a most impressive sight. The danger to be avoided is a tendency to get behind the bit.

There are many occasions out hunting when a change of position can be most quickly effected by doing a full pass.

So the ability to obtain, or perform, a full pass smoothly and without fuss is a most practical accomplishment for any outdoor rider and horse, and I would strongly recommend its practice in the school.

First of all, however, we will consider the half-pass. The horse moves diagonally across the school at an angle of 45 degrees to the side track, keeping its body as near parallel to it as possible. The head is flexed in the direction it is going, and the outer legs cross over the inner legs, in a half-pass to the right the head is flexed to the right, and the left fore and hindleg cross over their right opposite numbers. The horse makes progress sideways and forwards across the school.

This, like the shoulder-in, is always a collected movement, and the horse must be prepared beforehand by being collected, with a preliminary half-halt and lengthways flexing of the body. The degree of collection need not be very great, but sufficient to give it an energetic and slightly elevated gait. The half-pass must be a well cadenced movement, the feet stepping in a lively manner, with lots of impulsion.

The active aids are the inside rein and outside leg. For a half-pass to the right, the right rein, kept close to the neck, flexes the horse lightly to the right, so that he merely looks in the required direction, and the left leg on the girth moves the body to the right. The right leg maintains impulsion and forward movement, while the left rein supports the forward impulse of the legs.

To begin with half a dozen or so diagonal steps will be enough, the rider then going forward about the same distance and then making the movement across in the opposite direction back to the track. Eventually the rider will cross to the centre of the school, which is the limit of the movement in any one direction in dressage tests. Finally the half-pass can be done right across to the other side of the school, when the rider will straighten up, go round the short side of the school and on the other long side repeat the exercise across the school in the opposite direction.

An advanced two-track exercise is the *zig-zag*, in which the horse is asked to change direction without stopping the two-track movement, i.e. direct from right half-pass to left half-pass and *vice versa*. In dressage terms this is the counter-change of hand. The action of the rider in half-pass is called *tenir les hanches,* holding the quarters, in German *das Pferd stellen.*

All these exercises are done at the walk, trot and canter, and are always collected movements.

12 Riding Exercises and Games

There is always a debate whether it is better to learn to ride solo or in a class. The horsemen of my generation mostly began their riding solo with a groom or other mentor running on foot beside them, and I always admired the fitness and willingness of these not so young men, or taking them mounted on a leading rein. The classical schools of the past, so far as we know, gave their instruction solo. In the army numbers enforced training by classes, and most of the great military riders must have been through this mill. Today the bulk of instruction is given by civilian riding schools in classes; if you want individual attention, you pay extra.

There is a place, I think for both in the training of a horseman. The pupil in this book began solo on the lunge, and I am confident that, if it can be achieved, that is the best of all foundations for whatever progress in horsemanship the pupil wishes to make. Every rider has his ceiling, but the grounding given by that work on the lunge will probably make that ceiling higher and increase his proficiency at whatever level he finally reaches.

After that, riding in a class has many advantages: companionship and a spirit of emulation and competition; practice in considering and adjusting to the horses and riders in front of and behind you; experience in riding other horses in the class, for changing horses should be a regular exercise in a riding lesson. If riding on the lunge has been impracticable, then I would advocate beginning work in a class, if it is not too big, four for absolute beginners, with a maximum of eight after further progress. Solo instruction can be given periodically at later stages, perhaps to correct bad habits that may creep in unchecked in a class, or to bring the pupil on to more advanced work. When the pupil has mastered the simple aid applications sufficiently, he can be allowed spells of completely solo work on a programme provided by the instructor, say for more practice at canter transitions or lateral work, which cannot be conveniently done in a ride.

Class instruction takes the form of various permutations and combinations of the regular school movements, transitions, turns, voltes, circles, walk, trot, canter, rein back, and lateral work. The whole object of these for the rider, is to practise him in applying the aids for the various occasions, to give him balance, flexibility of control, experience of the reactions of his horse to aids, especially when wrongly given, knowledge of different horses, and generally the acquisition of a whole range of experiences which we call the feels of riding. Keeping one horse length behind the rider in front is in itself a constant exercise in the interplay of driving and restraining aids.

The first exercise of all is the turn at the corners of the school. This is, of course, inevitable, and the horses know it; so they try to cut the corner. The pupil should make every effort to keep the horse going forward right up to the actual corner, then apply the aids for the turn.

The next exercise is the change of rein, when the horse is moved off the track just after the turn on to one long side of the school and directed on a diagonal path to the opposite corner. The pupil learns to modulate his aids for the exact limits of the change of direction, to keep the horse straight along the diagonal path, and to bring it exactly to the same spot relatively on the other side of the school as the one he has left.

The change of rein is also effected by turning inwards at any point on the long side, going straight across, and making the opposite turn on the other long side. In all these descriptions we will assume that the ride starts on the right rein, so the above mentioned turns will be right and then left. The class can first of all follow the leader in single file, and the essence of the exercise is for the followers to turn exactly at the point taken by the leader. When the class turns together, the riders must endeavour to keep their horses in perfect alignment.

There can be a great many variations of these simple movements. The ride divides itself into two by going down the centre, then odd numbers turning to the right, even numbers to the left, turning in the same direction at the long sides, and so passing each other – always right hand to right hand – in opposite directions. They can unite by turning down the centre in pairs – half sections. They can also change the rein at opposite corners and cross on the diagonal at the centre of the school. And it will be noticed that these and other movements can all figure in the evolutions of a quadrille or musical ride. Piped music is a mixed blessing, but it can be used with advantage in a riding school; most horses seem to go better under its influence, and it gives rhythm to all the work.

Circles should begin in single file using the width of the school as diameter. The ride can then make circles together of half the width diameter. Here again the benefits of the exercise spring from aid applications to maintain impulsion, keep alignment all through the circle, and to preserve balance.

Voltes, and half-voltes are carried individually, starting at the corners with a maximum diameter of six and a half yards, which can be gradually reduced until it is almost a pirouette.

The serpentine is a first-class exercise for practising aid application and preservation of balance, which is good for the horse as well as the rider, as of course all these exercises are. Usually three loops are made, the first starting at the centre of one short side, the third ending at the centre of the opposite short side. The loops should be sharp so that the horse goes straight across the school at the end of each loop.

A useful and entertaining variation of the circle exercises is reducing and enlarging the circle. Starting from a circle of half the school, the class in single file gradually reduces the radius of the circle until the leader reaches the very centre, when he starts to enlarge again. It can be a preparation for the pirouette, and of course is a spectacular item in any musical ride.

For the ladies chain the ride must separate to intervals of eight to ten yards. The leader circles about, a tight half-volte – and zig-zags between the rider from front to rear, passing on the right and left hands alternately. At the end he turns again and takes position at the rear of the ride, and the next rider follows suit, and the others in succession. All this will be done at the same pace. In the same movement from rear to front, the overtaking rider must move at the next faster pace to the rest of the ride.

Other exercises teaching independent action are the leading rider trotting or cantering ahead to join the rear of the ride, and leaving the ranks singly when lined up in the centre of the school, both by going forward and reining back.

Games on horseback all help to produce suppleness, balance and muscular strength, gaining as it were complete freedom of the horse. Examples are vaulting, changing horses on the move, bending, and jumping exercises without reins or stirrups. For the latter, a series of three or four cavalletti are laid on the long sides of the school. First of all the riders become proficient at going down simply without reins or stirrups. Then they try other concurrent actions such as taking off their jackets; then taking them off and putting them on again; then ungirthing and removing the saddles from underneath them as they go down.

All these performances vary the monotony of learning, keep riders and horses mentally and physically alert and supple; they make riding fun.

There is a tendency now to do too much work in the covered school, which nearly every up-to-date riding school now possesses. Of course it has great advantages, especially in bad weather, and enabling instruction to be given after normal working hours at night. But there is no substitute for riding out of doors.

So outdoor manèges should be used as much as possible, the school work combined with riding across country, not necessarily over a lot of jumps at the start, but over uneven and unexpected terrain. Practice should be given at opening and shutting gates. The horseman of today may never have to open and shut a gate but the operation exercises all his aid-applying powers, as well as the steadiness of the horse. I remember once watching a girl groom at Cowdray Park, before polo, riding one horse and leading three others, come up to a gate, open it, get all four horses through, and shut it, without the slightest hitch or fuss. In its way it was a perfect piece of horsemanship.

Jumping has not been mentioned yet, as it is more convenient to deal with it in a separate chapter, but of course it will be part of all the training just described.

13 Jumping

Like nearly everything that we try to teach the horse, he can, on his own, jump just as well as after months of effort trying to teach him, if he wants to. A case in point is an Australian remount at the Indian Army Equitation School, Saugor, in the Central Provinces. A thoroughly unwilling horse, he had only been in training a week or two, and certainly had never jumped, when he was admitted to the veterinary hospital for some reason or other. He stayed there a few days, then one day his stable was found empty. It was the usual Indian type with bars across the opening, the top one being about five feet three inches high, with a gap of three feet to the top.

He had taken a very skilful and accurate standing jump without any apparent trouble at all. That was the last to be seen of him until about a year later he was discovered in the jungle not very far from Saugor, woolly as a bear, fat as butter, having maintained himself successfully against every predator in the jungle. So a horse is not a bad jumper at any time; it is the man on his back who complicates matters.

In the 'Thirties in New York, Captain Vladimir Littauer and Captain S. Kournakoff carried out a series of photographic experiments to show how a horse jumped and how its movement was affected by the way people rode. The object then was to prove the advantage, to the horse, of the forward seat, which the results did do very conclusively. The whole experiment was described in *The Defense of the Forward Seat*, a book which is now out of print; but a summary is given in Vladimir Littauer's *Commonsense Horsemanship*. Nobody denies the value of the forward seat for jumping now, but the photographs taken of the movement of light bulbs attached to various parts of the body, such as the withers and the croup, showed that under the best conditions – of horsemanship, the path of the two spots coincided in a fairly shallow parabola, while the whole body of the horse altered its position continually during the leap. These pictures have been confirmed recently by more sophisticated photography, published and described in *The Kingdom of the Horse* by Hans-Heinrich Isenbart and Emil Martin Buhrer.

125

However, the idea often expressed that a horse 'arches' its back over a jump is not correct. I have taken many photographs of horses in every phase of the leap (See *Riding Technique in Pictures*, by C. E. G. Hope and Charles Harris), and they show a number of interesting things. In the approach, the horse carries his head normally high, but gradually lowers it in the last three strides. Then at the last stride it flexes its hocks and, practically simultaneously, raised its forehand – the skeleton drawing on page 35 shows this conclusively. The hindlegs straighten out to give the push forward and upwards, so that the forehand is raised enough to clear the jump. The hindquarters follow the forehand up until the whole body is over the obstacle at its highest point and roughly parallel with the ground. This is the instant when horse and, sometimes, rider look their best while jumping, and is much favoured by photographers. In this fraction of a second also the movement is at its slowest.

But the motion of the leap is continuous, of course, and immediately the forehand of the horse begins to descend, while the hindquarters continue the upward movement, following the arc made by the withers. The forelegs, which have been curled up over the top of the fence, stretch forward and down to meet the ground. The head and neck are raised to adjust the balance. The hindlegs are flexed upwards to avoid the top of the fence.

The fore feet meet the ground, with a terrific flattening of the pasterns to take the shock, the leading foot of the take-off being still in the lead. The hind feet come to the ground almost on the same spot as the fore feet, the hocks are flexed again to propel the horse forward.

It will be seen from this that the body of the horse has swung upwards, and then downwards like a see-saw, which is exactly how the French describe it, *bascule*. If the bascule is correct and smooth, then the leap will be good.

Of course, all sorts of things can happen to spoil the regular flow of this action. The horse can get too close, when he will either go through the fence, jump like a cat off all four legs – demonstrating once again the extraordinary strength and agility of the creature – or refuse. He can take off too far away from the fence, in which case he will either hit it with his fore feet, or drag his hindquarters into it. A very powerful horse will sometimes be able to make an extra effort at the last minute to make the extra spread necessary to clear the obstacle; clever, agile horses will discover a fifth leg in an amazing way to get themselves and their riders out of trouble. Never forget that the rider can get himself and his horse into trouble, only the horse can get them out of it.

It follows from all this that the rider must do as much as he possibly can to help the horse during a leap, which means doing as *little* as possible. Once the horse has started to take off the rider can do nothing more about it; the horse is in charge and generally, like an airline, will look after him. So the rider should first of all keep his weight off the horse's hindquarters until he lands, which he does by leaning forward and keeping his seat in the air and off the saddle throughout the leap. He should keep his hands forward to give the greatest possible freedom to the horse's head and neck. His position should be such as to keep his weight concentrated behind the withers, which is the point of oscillation of the bascule. The rider will grip, without excessive tension, from the lower part of his thighs downwards to the calf, and keep as still as possible without changing position throughout the leap.

There is probably, in the whole range of horsemanship, no thrill like that of a big leap on a good horse performed in complete harmony. Certainly, at the present time, there are more people riding who find this to be so than those who gain their peak thrill from some other activity, dressage, polo, racing or whatever. There are more people, too, who enjoy watching it, witness the millions of television viewers. The great thing is to achieve this harmony from the outset.

The rider's jumping training can begin as soon as he has acquired reasonable security in the saddle and maintain his position at all paces. It is desirable that the horse should be a willing jumper, going forward freely and smoothly.

The first jump will be over a low bar or *cavalletto*. This last piece of equipment, usually referred to in the plural – *cavalletti* – is an Italian word for trestle, and it is a pole attached at each end of an X-shaped support, which enables the pole to be placed at three levels – close to the ground, about six inches high, and twelve inches high. The use of this equipment for jumping training was invented by Captain Ubertalli – later to become a General – of the Italian Army between the wars, and has been adopted by schools of instruction all over the world.

So the ride is formed up in the centre of the school, the trestle is laid across the track at its lowest level, and each rider goes over it in turn at the trot. The horses' reactions will vary; some just stepping over, others making a great fuss to clear it, another will hesitate and inspect the fearsome object most closely, and yet another will rush at it. The rider's task is to remain steady in the saddle, pivot slightly forward from the knees to raise the seat just off it, and let his hands go forward with the movement. If desired he can put one hand on the pommel or hold the neckstrap. An assistant should give a lead to the first horse over. It should not be necessary to shorten stirrup leathers at this stage.

Progress to higher obstacles should be quite quick. The cavalletti can be used successively at their next two heights, up to twelve inches. The emphasis all through should be on the rider's position and timing over the fence, so that he learns to go with the horse and to adjust his position forward as much as is necessary. The final practice at this point should be going over the jump without holding on to the reins; the arms folded in front.

Special points to note are: smoothness of body movement, no sudden flopping on to the horse's neck, or crouching with rounded shoulders; no resting of the hands on the neck or making a bridge of the reins; stillness of the legs; no slipping or leaning backwards; seat off the saddle.

The next stage is practise over two or more fences. Go back to the lowest level of jump, this time with two placed two strides apart. The jumps can be raised progressively up to twelve inches, and the interval reduced to five feet. From there the instruction moves on to cavalletti in series of three, following the same procedure as above.

Higher jumps up to two feet can then be tackled. Two cavalletti, one on top of the other, will provide the height, or a post and rails with adjustable heights can be used. The stirrup leathers should be shortened by one or two holes.

If possible, there should now follow work in a jumping lane. A jumping lane is really a most essential item of equipment for training both horse and rider. In fact there should be two; one a straightforward series of obstacles, mainly post-and-rails type, on the flat; the other a cross-country type over uneven ground.

The first type can be either in a straight line, or circular, or, better, oval. The former requires more staff to operate it, and considerable mobility on the part of the instructor. The latter facilitates control, can be worked singlehanded, and is more economical.

The late Colonel Jack Talbot-Ponsonby, three times winner of the King George V Cup, was a strong advocate of the jump-

Exercising over the cavalletti in an indoor arena (*Light Horse*)

Exercising over the cavalletti in a jumping lane at Porlock Vale Riding School (*Light Horse*)

Dressage

A perfectly turned-out horse and rider (*Light Horse*)

ing lane, and describes one in his book, *Harmony in Horse-manship*. The dimensions he gives are seventy-two feet long by thirty-five feet wide, with a track nine feet wide, the length of the straight on either side being forty-nine feet, with a semi-circle at each end. The jumping track is enclosed with open timber fencing, and the centre area is free for the instructor. The basic fences are four, one on each side, one at each end on the curve. There is room on the straight sides for a combination (double), and, of course, spread fences. A screen of hurdles or close fencing on the outside is a desirable refinement, shutting out possible distractions, but not absolutely essential. The fences in the lane must be adjustable upwards from one foot to four foot six inches, and for the provision of spreads (parallels) up to five feet. All obstacles in a lane should be fixed, and jumpable in both directions, the ideal being a pole that cannot be knocked down but which has a slight play horizontally. This can be achieved by fixing the poles between two pairs of uprights. Additional variations can be introduced by the use of brush fences, cavalletti, and so on.

Usually the entrance and exit to the lane are at the same point on the curve at one end; but there is a case for having them separate, which anyway would happen if the lane were a straight one. The chief point is that the horse must always receive a reward of some corn or other tit-bit at the end of the circuit, and he will grow to appreciate this fact and so be all the more eager to get to the other end.

Another point about the lane is that it should be used sparingly, especially for the horse. For the rider it is first of all a safe introduction to higher obstacles than those first encountered in the school, practice in negotiating a series of jumps, under direct and close observation and control of the instructor, and, later on, a challenge when the jumps are four feet and over.

Before work in the lane, the rider can be practised in various combinations of cavalletti and twelve-inch jumps, one, two, then three cavalletti preceding the higher fence; and in spread jumps, two twelve-inch cavalletti placed one foot, then two feet, apart.

The fences are then raised, eighteen inches, two feet, two and a half feet, taken singly, and then in various combinations as before. The rider can practise 'doubles', the fences being placed first about twenty-two feet apart to allow one full non-jumping stride in between, then closed to half that distance for a definite in-and-out. Hitherto all work has been at the trot, but now it can be done over the higher fences at the canter.

Whenever convenient at this stage the lane can be tackled.

E   129

The ride goes out into the open field and makes a large circle close to the lane at a walk, continuing to do this all through the lesson. As a preliminary, the horses should be sent down the lane free. Each rider in turn dismounts, tucks the stirrup irons to the top of the leathers, knots the reins, leads the horse into the lane and sends it on its way, being ready to meet it at the exit with a handful of corn. The riders then mount and go in one by one.

For this first run, the fences are at their lowest – one foot – and the riders leave the reins knotted and go round holding the neckstrap or pommel. The second time they go round without holding on to anything, arms folded in front of them. The instructor in the centre keeps the horses moving by a show of the lungeing whip, and watches the positions of the riders, who should also use their legs to maintain impulsion if their horses show any hesitation. The circular ends test their balance and grip. In due course they will go round with reins in their hands.

Up to now the approach and placing before the jump has been left to the horse, but for higher fences and jumping in the open the rider will start to take control to some extent. This does not mean interference but a greater control of pace and stride before the jump is reached.

To interfere or not to interfere used to be the subject of furious debate, which seems to have died down of late. There were the 'let the horse do it' school, *à la* Caprilli, and the 'give him the office' brigade, signally exemplified by the Mexicans and Spaniards after World War II. The latter enforced strict control right up to the final pre-jump stride, often finishing off with a jerk upwards of the reins to 'raise' the horse. As the horse must have made his own arrangements long before that instant, I very much doubt if it affected the issue in any way, but there is no doubt that this method achieved many successes. However, as Littauer has pointed out (*Commonsense Horsemanship*) the exponents of this method were highly specialised and expert riders on highly trained horses in a particularly exacting sport, show jumping. For the open air rider, hunting, racing, horse trials, far less exact not to say risky control is needed. Even in show jumping the tendency is much more for freedom of movement all through, with only such steadying and control of stride as may be necessary in special situations. This inevitably involves a good deal of yanking about, but it does not alter the principle.

The great problem, whatever the method of jumping, is timing – the timing of the approach to the fence and of the take-off. For the timing to be right, the rider must first of all acquire a feeling for pace and stride, which is one of the objects of the preliminary lessons; then he must be able to judge quickly the distance in front of the fence known as the take-off zone.

It is universally recognised that a horse is likely to be in difficulty if he takes off closer to the fence than the horizontal distance equal to the height of the jump, i.e. for a fence four feet high the closest take-off point is four feet away from the base of the fence. In front of this point there is an interval, varying in depth, within which an optimum jump can be obtained. It is hard to be exact about this, for every horse's stride and power varies to some extent, but roughly it is the length of a normal stride over a fence less twice its height. Taking the scope of a leap over a four-foot fence as about eleven feet, the extent of the take-off zone will be eleven feet minus eight feet equals three feet. The optimum take-off point would then be about halfway between the inner and outer limits of the take-off zone. For lower fences the take-off zone is extended, and for higher ones it is reduced. These measurements refer to upright fences, which are always the most difficult to jump accurately.

Spread fences present different problems, but on the whole, until they become really big, they are less difficult to negotiate cleanly. So far the pupil has only been dealing with small upright fences, but henceforward he will be tackling a greater variety of obstacles, including the spreads. These fall into four categories: parallel, staircase, pyramid (this is the nomenclature of the late Jack Talbot-Ponsonby) and water.

The true parallel has two upright fences of the same height at a given distance apart, which can be anything up to five feet. Most parallels, however, have the first element slightly lower than the rear one, which makes it easier. The horse has to jump both high and wide, and so the take-off point will be further away than for an upright.

The staircase is one of three elements which rise up in steps, best known as a triple bar. The spread from the lowest to the highest pole can be anything up to six feet, and, the highest being the furthest away, the take-off point will be close to the first and lowest element, which acts as a guide to both horse and rider. In fact, it is one of the easiest of fences.

The pyramid has its highest point in the middle with a lower element on either side, again at varying spreads. It can take many forms, the most usual being the double oxer. The rules about take-off are the same as for an upright, and this again

131

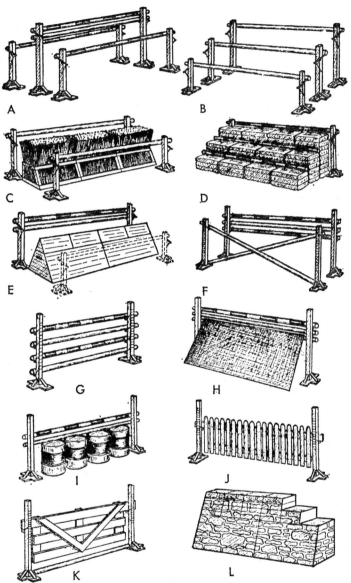

Fig. 15. A selection of fences

(a) Hog Back (b) Triple Bar (c) Double Oxer (d) Triple Bar with Straw Bales (e) Oxer with Chicken Coop (f) Rails with crossed poles (g) Plain rails (h) Rails with Panel (i) Rails over Oil Drums (j) Picket Fence (k) Gate (l) Stone Wall

in its straightforward form is a comparatively easy fence to jump.

Water always seems to present the most difficulties, horses and riders often making a great fuss over it. The width of water can be from ten to sixteen feet, and it is usually presented with a small brush fence on the take-off side, which acts as a sort of ground line. The timing here is to make the take-off just in front of the brush fence, or the edge of the water if there isn't one. Judging by performance, not even the world's champions are quite decided on how best to tackle it, whether at speed or steadily and well collected. Whatever else is lacking, there must be maximum impulsion, and perfect timing. What is nearly always useless is a furious uncontrolled gallop. A horse can often be encouraged to jump water by placing a rail across the middle of it, but it should not be more than eighteen inches high, otherwise it will make the horse jump too high and lose length. A lot depends on the horse; one will soar over it, another go very flat. The rider's own part in the affair is, as always, to keep still with the body forward and seat off the saddle, to give the hindquarters every chance to clear the far edge of the jump.

Once the basic work has been done, the rest of the rider's training will be to ride over as many different kinds of obstacle as possible, with steadily increasing heights up to four feet, and to practise the timing of the approach. It can be begun in the school over, say, three-foot fences. The horse should be steadied five strides from the jump, and for the last three the instructor should count out loud: 'One – two – three – squeeze,' (or 'up' or 'off'). The rider will already be using his legs during the three strides but will give a final pressure (squeeze) for the take-off. In time he should do the counting for himself. Only practice can make perfect.

A useful training aid is to have a low cavalletti placed in front of the main jump at the five stride point. This steadies an impetuous horse, and should ensure the correct timing of the approach. The legs should act progressively more strongly with every stride up to the last so as to produce the maximum impulsion in the horse. The main fence can be raised up to four feet, and it can be varied, an upright to begin with, then a triple bar, a pyramid, and a parallel.

Some instructors insist that the rider should sit down in the saddle for the approach, only leaving it to go forward at the take-off. The Caprilli school is opposed to this, requiring that the horse's quarters should be free all the time. There is no certainty as to which is the more effective. The followers of Caprilli achieved some wonderful jumping feats with their method; so have the 'sit-down' school. It is really a matter of individual choice, governed as much by the horse you are riding as by any other consideration. The essence is correct timing and not being left behind during the approach.

The next stage is work in the open paddock with a laid-out course of jumps of various kinds. They should all be numbered, and the instructor will name the numbers of the fences to be jumped in succession. At first two fences in a straight line, then the second fence coming after a circle, or one set diagonally to the first one. Then the rider will be required to take three and later four in one run, involving change of direction and of the leading leg. This practises him in control and approach, and in thinking, and looking, ahead to the next fence. Finally the complete course can be jumped. If the rider is 75 per cent sure of his timing and can maintain his position consistently, he will be doing very well.

A further exercise is riding against time. This involves taking fences at a faster speed than normal, and also taking them at an angle. All competition jumping, except puissance or nations cup types, is either wholly or in part against the clock. Time is saved by greater speed and by shortening the distance to be covered, by sharp turns – for which you need a very handy horse – and by jumping obliquely. Some horses can go a consistently fast speed over the whole course, others need to be steadied before each fence, and will often be presented at a big fence from barely two strides away. In the last resort everything depends on the horse, who will do his best and often achieve the impossible. Apart from guiding him, the only help the rider can give is to keep his own point of balance well forward and to give the horse impulsion through his legs. This of course goes back to the preliminary training of the rider for the acquisition of a firm and independent seat and the strength and ability to apply the aids.

Practice in this particular art is simple. Go back to the cavalletto, and approach it first on a fairly wide circle, gradually shortening it until it is just a sharp turn in front of the fence. Another exercise is to ride towards the cavalletto on a parallel line, first three or four strides from the fence and gradually reducing the distance, then turn sharply towards it when it comes opposite. In the same way practise jumping obliquely, first at an angle of about 30 degrees off the straight, increasing to 45 degrees. Do this, of course, to right and left, and both ways over the fence. The jumps are raised progressively, and their type varied. Finally, practise a double combination, taking the first part at one edge of it, crossing over in the interval to take the second part over the opposite edge. All this will be done slowly at first but with increasing speed.

Concurrently with this work on a flat surface, the pupil rider should be practised in going across country, over uneven, undulating ground and odd unsuspected obstacles such as ditches, logs, brush fences and so on. The work should be done at a steady canter, following the instructor as leader, and the forward position, seat off the saddle, should be maintained all the time. If the means and land are available, a cross-country jumping course with a circuit of half to three-quarters of a mile should be built. This should contain twelve to fifteen cross-country type fences, with adjustable heights or alternate fences, of the kind likely to be met out hunting, in hunter trials or in horse trials (one-day and three-day events). Used with circumspection, say a run over it once a week or once a fortnight, this kind of course is the finest instruction for both horse and rider in cross-country riding, in particular accustoming the horse to meet strange fences and to ride alone, which is the essence of this particular sport. The late Stewart Goodfellow, an enthusiastic and dedicated supporter of the horse trials sport, was the originator of this kind of lane, building it on his own land near Wokingham, Berkshire, and making it available free to any rider who wished to use it. Many leading riders did with great advantage to their horses.

Again, if means permit, it is useful to have a couple of steeplechase fences in a big field which can be taken at real speed. They need not be full-scale obstacles but approximate to them. Once again the work must be progressive, starting with a twelve to fifteen mile-an-hour gallop, finishing at twenty to twenty-five m.p.h. The rider's position before the fence will be that of a normal racing seat, short stirrups, body and hands well forward, seat high off the saddle. The horse will be allowed to make his own arrangements about the take-off; trying to steady him or position him when going at speed only unbalances him. So leave it to the horse and concentrate on going with him. Once in the air we part company with principles and allow nature to take its course. It is not impossible to maintain the forward seat throughout the leap, but improbable. The best steeplechase jockeys in the world will be seen invariably sitting, even lying, well back on the landing side of a fence, especially at top speed and over big ones. What they do not do, however, is to interfere with the horse's mouth; they allow the reins to slip through their fingers, if necessary to the fullest extent. That is really the essence of steeplechasing – non-interference. At slower paces the beginner should try to ride forward from take-off to landing, but as the speed increases it is a matter for his own judgement and dynamics.

The word 'style' has not been mentioned so far, although in fact we have been talking about nothing else. Style in any sport is the correct placing of the performer to enable him to get the best results. Obviously there is a position of feet, body, eyes in all ball games which will ensure the most efficient use of whatever implement is used. The result of correct style also happens to be pleasing to the eye. True, all sorts of other factors operate all the time, and players, when they reach a certain level, develop their own individual styles and methods; but every good player has been taught the basics first. The same applies to riding.

Good style in riding stems from the position and techniques of the use of hands and legs that have been taught from the outset, based on the principle of always being in balance with the horse. So the signs of good style will be recognisable: straight head, neck, shoulders and trunk, upright or leaning forward according to the gait and nature of the exercise; knees and thighs to the saddle, lower legs close to the girth, slightly to the rear, heels down and toes up, hands in light contact with the horse's mouth, making a straight line with wrist and forearm: the whole effect elegant and firm. The rider who moves on to higher things in top-class show jumping or eventing may adapt his style to circumstances, but he will always benefit from the discipline of the basic training, and will always show it.

There are two kinds of obstacle which a rider will seldom encounter except in competitions, banks (and in Ireland of course) and drop fences or slides.

A bank is a solid earthwork, grass covered, usually four to five feet high, and of varying width. A training bank will be about three to three and a half feet high, and five to six feet wide. The approach and take-off is the same as for an upright jump, but there is no descent; the horse lands on the platform, takes a stride, or not, according to the width of the platform, and then jumps down. A variation is to have a post-and-rails on the far side of the bank to make the horse jump big and wide. The most famous of show jumping banks proper is the big double bank at Dublin; and there used to be a tremendous bank at Aachen. The Jumping Derby bank of Hamburg, Hickstead and other places, is not so much a bank as a long steep slide after a gradual climb up by steps.

This brings us to the slide or steep descent, about which there are different ideas. The final verdict of Caprilli and his followers was that the rider should adopt the forward seat all the way down, on the theory that this released the quarters and also took the weight off the forehand. The climax of this teaching was the descent by Colonel Francesco Forquet, Commandant of the slide of the Tor di Quinto Cavalry School of Italy between the wars, without reins and leaning forward. Lesser mortals may prefer to lean back. It is doubtful whether the horse is materially affected by either method. Perhaps for short distances a forward position is all right. The nastiest slide that I ever met personally was the one at the Indian Army Equitation School, Saugor, from which all the earth and dust had long since been rubbed off leaving very literally a slide of almost virgin rock, of about ten feet. It was taken sitting forward, and I never heard of anybody coming to grief on it. The most dangerous and impressive slide is the famous *Cortoduras* at the Madrid Cavalry School, which is a cliff some forty to fifty feet high, the first part of it being almost vertical; but it is all soft sand, which helps. This is invariably negotiated leaning back.

The essence of tackling both banks and slides is strong impulsion, and, for the slide, keeping absolutely straight all the way down. Deviation from the straight and narrow leads most truly to perdition. Considerable control of the position and strength of leg is necessary to keep the right contact or even to give the horse's mouth complete freedom while negotiating these obstacles. The pupil should not take on these jumps until his seat is well stabilised and he is able to jump four-foot fences of all kinds successfully.

This brings us to the parting of the ways, the end of what can be called the intermediate stage of horsemanship. The rider should be ready to make his choice for the future: high school riding; show jumping; outdoor riding, which includes horse trials and hunter trials. (I do not include hunting in this, because it is more than likely that, whenever possible, hunting will have been added to the formal part of the training.) All these advances will involve competition, for there are few people who are content with art for its own sake, at least in the horse world, so they will be considered in a later part of this book.

It may be realised by now that the basic test and criterion of horsemanship at any stage is the ability to give the right signals to the horse at the right time; in other words a full understanding of the language of horsemanship. It sounds easy, but only constant practice aided by the muscular power that comes from riding exercises can produce results. In thinking on this I was reminded by Mrs Lorna Johnstone of the story told by the great French horseman, General L'Hotte, in his *Souvenirs*.

A great nobleman of France took his son to the most celebrated riding master of his time, Monsieur Duplessis, and said: ' "I am not bringing my son to you to make him an *ecuyer*. All I ask is that you will be so good as to teach him to co-ordinate his legs and his hands with the thought of what he wishes his horse to do."

"Monseigneur," replied Duplessis, "that is the height of my own ambition, and what I have been striving to achieve myself for about sixty years." '

THREE

The Training of the Horse

14 Kindergarten

The education of a horse begins at birth. Or it should. Horses that have been allowed to run wild can be difficult to break in when they come to three or four years old. This was particularly the case with Australian remounts, who mostly did not take kindly to that sort of thing at all. Bad education of a foal is even worse in its effects, because the horse will have acquired a built-in hatred or fear of the human race; or, in cases where he has been weakly handled and surfeited with tit-bits, he has developed into a bully.

This happens especially to children, whose well-meaning parents have allowed them to buy foals with the idea of their 'growing up together', in fact the height of folly. It is most disturbing to see advertisements, not in horsy papers, of yearlings for sale for that purpose and declared to be quiet to ride.

However, it is everybody's dream to breed, break in and train a young horse and win glittering prizes on him in the jumping ring, dressage arena or whatever. There is no harm in dreaming. Yet, if the conditions are right, proper facilities of land, stabling and equipment, time, and experienced advice, the training of a foal, even if not of your own breeding, can be a very satisfying experience.

Every foal is an individual with its own special characteristics, its own virtues and vices; but in common with every other young animal, it is particularly a compound of curiosity and timidity. If you have the foal from birth, its curiosity can be stimulated and its timidity overcome by growing familiar with its surroundings and its confidence in man. This confidence, once won, is a priceless asset in the future education of the foal.

First impressions are all important. Right handling at the beginning makes the foal appreciate human contacts and also impresses it with the power of human authority. 'I teach my foals,' said the late Henry Wynmalen (*Horse Breeding and Stud Management*), 'to lead from the first time they go out ... it is the easiest thing in the world, and quite an enchanting pastime, to teach a little foal to lead; if left till later, it becomes

141

a much more difficult matter and the results are hardly ever quite so good.'

So, at the very first opportunity, in the box, with somebody holding the mare, put your arms round the foal, one round his breast, the other round the quarters. Stay passive while he struggles, but do not let go. At this stage, for the first and only time in his life, you are stronger than he is and he will recognise the fact remarkably quickly; so the first battle has been won without it being fought. It will take a lot of bad treatment to make him forget this lesson.

After that a soft halter can be put on, and the foal is led about with the mare, from and back to the loose box for the first few days, and afterwards every day in the field. These leading lessons should not be long, but they must be regular and systematic. At the same time the foal should become accustomed to being handled all over, to having its feet picked up, its hoofs cleaned out, and to the presence of the farrier and his tools. It is common sense that all the things that will be happening to him in the future should, as far as possible, be made to appear perfectly normal to him in these early days. It is wise, too, that the foal should become used to being handled and led by as many different people as possible. It is very gratifying to the human ego to think that you are the only person who can do anything with a foal, but very bad for those who will have to follow you. The properly trained horse is one which will obey anybody who gives the correct signals.

All this is very ideal, however. Most acquire a young horse for training at a much later stage, after weaning at the earliest, preferably as a yearling, more probably at two or three. You are no longer dealing with a blank page, but one on which all sorts of marks have been made, good and bad, and in invisible ink. You will try to discover from the previous owner as much as you can about the treatment and character of the foal to date, but no one is going to tell you if he has made mistakes or beaten up the youngster or whatever. You have got to get your information, as far as you can, from the foal itself.

Whatever its background and short past may be, the mere fact of being uprooted from its birthplace and familiar surroundings will be a traumatic experience in itself. Once again its first impressions will affect his future outlook on man. Quietness should be the keynote of the reception, produced by preparedness and the absence of fuss. A loose box well bedded down should be ready for the new arrival, with water and hay available. Arrange for the youngster to arrive at the end of the day, and lead him straightaway from the horse box to the stable and let it loose. Chat to it, and, if it is not too obviously nervous, give it a pat. If it looks nervous, one can always tell, and keeps its distance from you, do not attempt to touch it. Talk to it for a minute or two in reassuring tones, then leave it for the night.

In the morning a good test of its reactions will be whether it has eaten its hay or not. It may be friendly but wary, or it may still view the whole human race with deep suspicion; whichever it may be do not force yourself upon it. Carry on with the routine chores of mucking out, spreading fresh bedding, filling up the water bucket, which should be fixed to the wall, and so on; make everything appear as normal as possible. Leave it again and go to breakfast.

After breakfast, come back with a chair and a book. Put some corn mixed with some sliced carrots and chaff in the manger, but on no account offer it tit-bits in the hand. Put the chair in the middle of the box and sit down with your book, apparently ignoring the creature altogether, but keeping an eye on it all the same. It had better be an interesting book and a comfortable chair, for the treatment may take a little while. It may be an hour, perhaps less, or it may take several sessions before the youngster settles down. But sooner or later he will settle down, curiosity will overcome fear and distrust, and true confidence will be born. Don't react to the first tentative sniff; stay quiet, then get up and leave him for a spell. When you come back he may even be pleased to see you.

Before long he will allow himself to be patted gently and stroked on the neck and back; but leave his head and ears and legs to the last. Some people will reward him with a piece of sugar or something when he allows himself to be handled, but it is much better not to do so. The foal can become very greedy for such tit-bits, will expect them every time he sees you, and get quite angry if nothing is forthcoming, nipping and kicking with his fore feet. The young horse can easily grow into a bully, and I have known of inexperienced people being terrorised by one small foal. Start as you mean to go on: quietly, gently, but firmly.

The next stage is to slip a halter on to his head, and once he is used to that, lead him out of doors. If he hangs back, get someone to push him from behind. Once in the field let him go and leave him to explore and play on his own. If no other horses are available for company, get a donkey or a goat; the great thing is a companion of some kind.

All this may seem an unnecessarily complicated procedure, a superfluity of fuss and caution, but it is worth it in the end, if only for gaining the full trust of the youngster from the outset. Why have unnecessary battles in the future, if a little present patience will avoid them?

Home-bred foals which have been born in a loose box should be accustomed gradually to being out of doors, until in a few weeks they can stay out altogether with their dams, if necessary coming in at night. Although left free to play and enjoy their foalhood, there is no reason why their education should not continue quietly, with regular contacts with people, leading, and handling, particularly of the feet. Nothing is so maddening as a horse or pony which will not allow its feet to be picked up; and care of the feet is also all important. The foal should be regularly visited by the blacksmith to have his hooves rasped and kept in good condition, which will prepare him for shoeing later on. The object of all training is to produce a well-mannered, well-schooled and obedient horse, and at this stage manners and obedience are paramount.

Another valuable lesson which can be taught during this first year of the foal's life is to enter a horse box or trailer without fuss or resistance. The obvious way is to leave a horse box, ramp down and all partitions removed, in the field or stable yard, and put the foal's food and water inside it. If he can be persuaded to go in on his own, and associates it inevitably with food, there should be no more trouble in the future. If this is not feasible, he can be practised at leading up the ramp and into the box, enticed by food at frequent intervals. It is all simple common sense plus a little forethought.

Soon you have a yearling: either one that you have brought up or one that you may have bought. In the case of a colt, unless it is to be kept especially for stud purposes, gelding will be necessary. This can be done in his second spring, i.e. while still a yearling, or you can wait until he is two years old, but not much longer than that. Choose a mild spell in the spring, if possible without an east wind, to avoid the risk of chill.

More serious leading lessons can now begin. If you intend showing the yearling, and even if you do not, it is essential that the youngster should learn to walk freely forward and straight. The basis of all horse training is free forward movement, and like so much else it can begin now.

All the equipment required is a head-collar on the horse, a long leading rein attached to it, and a long switch. Show him the latter, scratch his neck and tickle his nose with it, so that he has no fear of it. It is not, and should never be during training, an instrument of punishment, but the first aid, a substitute for the future leg aids, and a stimulator of impulsion. If you are dealing with the home-bred product, there should be no trouble at all. The newly-purchased animal may make a fuss, dancing away from you. Let him go to the end of the leading rein and have his fling, playing him quietly like a fish; gradually he will come back to you, perhaps all the better for the demonstration.

Take up the leading rein leaving three or four feet slack, and start walking forward beside the pupil, encouraging him to go forward with the command 'Walk,' and clicking with the tongue. If he hangs back, flick him on the quarters with the switch, held in the left hand. In difficult cases it may be necessary to have someone behind to shoo him on; but it is better, if possible, to work quietly on your own.

After a short walk, give the command 'Whoa', and bring him to a halt. In this way he soon learns the meaning of the different sounds. After one or two halts practise standing him up correctly as if before a judge. Directly he has stopped step round in front of him, hold the head-collar with a hand on either side, and manoeuvre him quietly into position, square on all four legs, head up and alert. Some horses will show lively energy at the halt, others contrive to look like dead ducks; a bit of sugar in your hands will often work the miracle.

After the walk, the trot, when he should trot freely forward at the end of the lead rein three feet or so from the leader running beside him. Remember to repeat the lessons on the off side as well as the near; the more the young horse becomes used to working from both sides the better. As well as the display halt, there is also, as already mentioned above (page 100) the photographic stance, which it is worth while teaching the horse also. If you win a class at a show, someone will want to take a picture, or you will want a good photograph for your own record or for selling purposes. The object is to get one pair of legs showing inside the other, the inside ones being those furthest away from the photographer. The technique is to make the horse step backwards diagonally, starting from the pair nearest the photographer in the hope that the outside legs will then fall into place. Sometimes they will, but usually a good deal of manoeuvring forwards and backwards has to be done before the horse gets into the right position. As in the display position the feet must be placed directly under the horse, not splayed out or crossing one in front of the other; the body must be quite straight, there being sometimes a tendency for the quarters to be out of alignment with the forehand.

In the actual photography there is a lot more to it than that: the head must be placed right, ears pricked and alert, not the hangdog expression that many horses and ponies seem to take delight in assuming, mainly, I suppose, through boredom. The ears of even the most stubborn horse can be made to prick forward, if the operation is carefully planned. Usually the act of bending down to pick up a handful of grass will interest the subject, but it must be done at the right moment. An assistant should stand a little way from the pony slightly to one side of the holder and on the same side as the photographer, so that the horse's attention will be focused in that direction. When the camera-man is ready, and not before, the assistant starts to pick up the grass. If this fails, the same assistant, again under orders from the photographer, walks in front of the subject at right angles to his position and carrying a rug or coat or something large. As he crosses the line of vision of the horse he throws the rug up into the air, and there are very few case-hardened characters which can resist that. At the same time the other end of the model, the tail, must be right, not tucked in between the legs or swishing about. Always face the horse into the wind if possible when having a picture taken.

It can be objected that teaching two ways of standing will be confusing for the youngster. Perhaps so, but provided the basic display position is taught first, I have never known the other exercise worry them overmuch. Yearlings, foals even, are photographed at every show during the season, as well as privately, and one exercise does not seem to affect the other. The ones presenting the greatest difficulty are hackneys, Welsh mountain ponies, Welsh cobs, and heavy horses, who are trained to place their feet so that they cover the maximum amount of ground.

Is all this unnecessary waste of time? I do not think so. Photography is part of the modern equestrian scene, and preparation for it is all part of the training and discipline of the horse. One thing it will do is to introduce the young horse to the rein back, which can save a lot of time and trouble later on when one comes to do it mounted.

From leading at the walk and trot it is quite simple to proceed to the next stage, lungeing. All this, it must be emphasised again is quiet preliminary training and nothing to do with the serious work to follow later on, but a valuable and lasting preparation for it. You already have the leading rein attached to the head-collar, under the chin, and the switch or lungeing whip with which the horse will already be familiar. From the straight line forward gradually change to a circle, wide at first and gradually narrowing to the diameter of the leading or lungeing rein. The leader then moves away from the horse, progressively lengthening the rein, until the horse is on its own. Holding the rein in the left hand, the trainer will show the pupil the lungeing whip, flicking it along the ground behind it. This should be enough to get the horse moving round after some preliminary hesitation; if not, touch his hocks lightly with the whip to stimulate him to go forward. A few circles will be enough, then repeat the lesson on the opposite rein. All that is required at this stage is for the horse to go round quietly and freely and stop at the word of command.

None of these lessons should last more than twenty minutes, and need only be continued until the horse has acquired the necessary confidence, obedience and free forward action. After that, except for regular contact and occasional refreshers, the youngster can be left until the time comes for serious training and backing.

15 Lungeing and Backing

Finance rather than science dictates the age at which a horse should be backed and put to work. The Derby and other classic races are for three-year-olds, which means that thoroughbreds are raced as two-year-olds and broken in and backed as yearlings. How many of them remain sound?

The horse is a big and enormously strong animal and is backed by lightweight riders, by contrast with ponies who are asked at equally early ages to carry proportionately heavier weights and suffer more in consequence. The fact is that backing and working a yearling or two-year-old is like making five-year-old children work in the mines, and all veterinary opinion that I know of is against it. But horses and ponies are expensive to keep and owners and breeders want to see their money back as soon as possible; so it goes on.

However, these breeders and owners might reflect that a sound horse at four or five years is worth more than one already gone in the legs at three. The prospect too of a longer working life might encourage buyers to go for the older horse. Moreover, we are not concerned here with breaking in racehorses but training good riding horses to be hunters, hacks, show jumpers, event horses and high school performers. For them the programme should start not earlier than three years old, with lungeing and backing, and then no serious riding until the age of four years, coming into full work at five.

Henry Wynmalen preferred to wait a year longer than that: 'As a rule, I break them as four-year-olds, and get them to ride nicely and quietly, mostly at the walk, with a little trotting and cantering later on. But I do no strenuous work with them. At five years old, I take them into regular hacking exercise, I may send them to a few shows, and I may take them cub hunting; but I still give them no real hard work, no long days, no big jumping, and no heavy going. Then at six they are ready for anything. . . . We may well be lucky with a four-year-old in hard work, but the chances of unsoundness occurring in such a youngster are at least ten times greater than in the mature horse.' (*Horse Breeding and Stud Management.*) The Lipizzaners

148

come into training at four years and the process lasts for three years. De la Guérinière preferred to wait until six years at the earliest.

People have invented all sorts of short cuts for the breaking and training of horses. The Red Indians used to do the job in an hour or so by first tying the captured mustang so that it could not resist. As Chenevix Trench makes clear in *A History of Horsemanship* the horses were under-sized ponies of about thirteen hands, so it was really no problem. The Argentine gauchos throw the unbroken horse with a *bola* (three ropes joined starwise with a small heavy ball at the each free end) or with a lariat, tie it to a strong post and leave it to exhaust itself, then fit a rawhide thing (*bocado*) round the lower jaw and wait until it gets used to that; finally a saddle is put on and the horse is ridden. Another method suggested to us in India, as Argentinian and humane for dealing with a stubborn remount, is to tie one foreleg up and lunge the horse round on soft going until it collapses from exhaustion. Then you sit on it, gentle it all over, and generally try to make friends with it. We tried it out on a very unwilling, not to say malicious, Australian remount of about five years, with negative results.

Another wild Waler, which I was supposed to train at Saugor, went through the preliminary lungeing lessons quietly enough, though with a marked lack of enthusiasm, but there was no joy when it came to backing. I spent several back-jerking days riding his prodigious bucks in an Australian buck-jumping saddle, while he was only prevented from rubbing me off on the walls of the covered school where the operation took place by the equally prodigious power of Regimental Sergeant Major Hefferman of the 17/21 Lancers hanging on to the lungeing rein. The horse settled down eventually but he never really gave up the fight and was never safe. The last day of the Saugor course he threw himself over backwards, and I watched him gallop back to the horse lines with no regret.

The course of horse breaking does not necessarily run smooth, but a good deal of trouble, if not all of it, can be avoided by careful and humane preliminary training of the very young horse. And the long way is the surest and quickest in the end. Whether you go the short cut or the long way round, the basic task is to con the horse into thinking he has not the power to disobey, and then to keep on until obedience is a habit. If this can be achieved without a fight, so much the better. Another theory is that you should provoke a fight at an early stage and win it. To make victory certain the French use the Chambon tackle already described (pages 71–2). However, the great majority of English and European horses have the habit of obedience ingrained in them by generations of domesticity, and they respond well to the process to be described.

Choosing three years as the earliest to start serious training, the preliminary work will be to introduce the pupil to the bit, and practise him in being led in a straight line. If he has been with you since he was a yearling or earlier, there should be no problem. If he comes fresh as a three-year-old, then time will have to be spent on this preliminary stage, gaining confidence, and so on.

Bridling and bitting should be done with care. The bit will be a light jointed snaffle attached to a simple bridle without a noseband. Warm the bit beforehand, and rub it over with sugar. Let the horse have a sniff and lick at it, so that he will almost welcome it into his mouth, making a pleasant fuss of him at the same time. He will already be used to wearing a head-collar, so he will not mind the bridle being put over his head and ears, and then a pressure on the corners of his lips will make him open his mouth and accept the bit. The pleasant taste will occupy his attention while the bridle is adjusted and the throat latch is buckled up. Walk him about for about ten minutes with the bit in his mouth, then take it out; and be as careful taking it out as when putting it in. Frequent short lessons like this will soon get him used to the bit in his mouth, and the sweet taste will induce him to play with it and chew it. Let him have it in his mouth for one of his daily feeds.

Later on he can be left alone with the bit in his mouth for about an hour at a time, without side reins. Henry Wynmalen had little use for side reins at any time, and he is a good guide. If used they should be long enough not to interfere with the natural head carriage of the horse. Some people advocate special mouthing bits, and they do no harm if used in the manner prescribed above. It is the sensitive handling of the reins which really do the mouthing in time to come.

This is a good time also to introduce the horse to a body-roller and surcingle and pads, as a foretaste of the saddle. Place the pads quietly on the horse's back, and loosely do up the strap, talking to him the while. An assistant is useful here to hold his head and keep his attention fixed on a bowl of corn. Gradually over a couple of days the girthing can be tightened, until he is quite used to the process.

Lungeing

Side by side with this goes lungeing. This time a proper caves-son noseband is put on over the snaffle bridle, and the lunge-ing rein is clipped or buckled to the ring in the centre of the front of the noseband. An assistant is useful now, but if none is available it must just be done singlehanded.

The trainer gets into the leading position, holding the rein about three feet from the horse; the assistant takes the rest of the rein and stands in the centre of a circle of twenty-five feet radius. Assuming the movement is left-handed, he will hold the rein in the left hand with the remaining slack in the right, coiled up. If the horse should play up and try to get away, there is then some play in the rein to break the force of the pull, and the horse should be allowed to move away, trainer and assistant following him, until he subsides. The effect of the rein on the cavesson ring will tend to turn the horse's head inward facing the humans.

At first the trainer will lead the horse forward as usual, the assistant keeping pace with him; then almost imperceptibly the horse is led on to a circle, and kept going on it for a round or two, with halts and walks-on. Then the trainer gradually moves away from the horse, until he is about halfway between him and the assistant. Stay there for a while, walking round with the horse. If the latter tries to turn inwards to follow him, show him the whip, pointing it at his nose or his flanks. Then a flick of the whip on the ground behind his hindquarters should make him move on. If the horse still turns inward, take a firm step towards him – never move back – speak the word of command to 'walk on', and touch his hocks. There is no idea of punishment in this, nor should it ever enter into the training period, but an aid or signal to be obeyed. This half-way position of the trainer gives him close control of the pupil while it is at the same time on the full length of the lungeing rein.

Working by himself, the trainer must combine both functions, holding the lungeing rein coiled in his left hand, and the whip in the right. When working on the opposite rein the positions are of course reversed. As before, start on a straight line, then merge it into a circle, and start moving away from the horse, pointing the whip at its shoulder if the horse tries to follow. If the horse tries to get away, let the rein run out until nearly its full length then take the strain with the right hand, holding the whip across as in driving, the slack still in the left hand. When the horse has settled down, shorten the rein to the required length of about twenty-five feet and show him the whip behind his quarters to start him moving on the circle again. However often the horse may play up, quietly repeat the process with a kind of inexorable firmness which will have its effect in the end.

Opinions are divided about the method of attachment of the lungeing rein. Some prefer it attached to the ring behind the jaw instead of the front ring on the nose. Others lunge off the snaffle bit direct; others with the rein attached to the far ring and running through the near ring. It is said that the rein on the front ring causes discomfort and pain to the sensitive nose; but with a well-padded noseband it should not be too upsetting, and there is the important element of better control. With the rein on the bit or to the rear of the jaw, if the horse wants to get away, he will only have to gallop on and pull you along, unless you are exceptionally strong. I only knew one man who could hold an unwilling horse this way – the aforementioned R.S.M. Hefferman.

What is the point of lungeing? It has, in fact, a number of advantages. First, it exercises the horse helping to make it fit and to tone up the muscles, it is basic gymnastics for the horse. Next, it inculcates the habit of obedience. It teaches free forward movement, and it improves the action at all gaits. It helps to supple the spine on the circle and to balance the horse. It is also a sure method of retraining a badly made horse or one that has got into bad habits.

The venue of this lungeing work has to be considered. Whenever possible trainers use a covered school, for obvious reasons; but it is not absolutely necessary. In fact there is a lot to be said for doing as much work as possible out of doors. There is a growing tendency nowadays to confine the horse, and rider for that matter, cosily in a somewhat twilight covered building far from the madding crowd, which seems unnatural. The horse is an outdoor creature, and he can learn just as well in the open as indoors. Of course his 'schoolroom' needs to be quiet and undisturbed, to start with at any rate; but even this can be overdone. The horse is a gregarious creature and loves company, and anyway he has got to do most of his work in later years in public, so why not get him used to it at an early date. Sheila Willcox used to school all her horses at one time in a manège situated next door to the entrance to the Clitheroe Golf Club, and nothing ever shook their self-possession in the dressage arena. Police horses learn very soon to cope with crowds and noises. Anyway, not every private owner and trainer has a covered school.

A nicely prepared manège, sixty yards by forty yards, is a nice thing to have, but a fenced off corner of a field will do equally well, provided it is level, quiet and not too far from the stables, where the young horse will be tacked up for the great adventure. One must always adapt methods to the means available; on the other hand no one should attempt the training of a horse without adequate facilities and assistance ready to hand and without experience. For instance, do not start wielding a lungeing whip without first practising with it in private, so that you learn to handle it moderately and with maximum control.

Once the horse settles down and begins to move freely forward on the circle, the words of command which he should have already learnt in the leading sessions can be given: 'Walk', 'Trot on', 'Halt' or 'Whoa', and so on. Commands for movement or increase of pace will be given in a sharper more high-pitched tone, for slowing down and stopping at a lower pitch and more drawn out. If the horse does not respond immediately to a retarding order, repeat, and vibrate the lungeing rein slightly.

The rein should be changed frequently, and this is an opportunity to teach the horse to come to the centre of the circle on the word of command. Draw him in with the lungeing rein, and at the same time trail the lungeing whip along the ground in front of him, so that he associates it with the inward movement. Make much of him and give him a small reward, then – at first – lead him to the circumference of the circle facing the other way. In time he will go there himself on being turned round to face outwards and given a touch on the quarters with the lungeing whip.

During all the work on the lunge the trainer must bear in mind the principle objects, namely to improve action and stabilise the gaits, to produce balance and correct head carriage, and to make the horse supple and his back flexible. He cannot bend his rib-cage, that is the body between the withers and the lumbar vertebrae, but the bones of the spine can become flexible and enable him to move freely on a circle and balance himself with greater ease. So the trainer should plan each lesson beforehand, so that no time is wasted in the horse aimlessly bumming round and round. After one or two steadying circles, changes of pace, stop and go, change of rein, should happen in regular succession, equally on either rein, so that the horse is always kept on the alert. Of course things will not always go according to plan, so the trainer must be flexible in his handling of situations, modifying the programme if necessary, but always returning to it as closely as possible. Lessons for the first week or so should not last longer than fifteen to twenty minutes.

When the horse is steady and obedient at the walk and trot, he can be asked to take-off at the canter. Have the horse going at a smart, energetic trot; with the lunge rein turning him slightly inwards, then yield immediately so that he turns outward again on to the original circle and at the same time give the command 'Canter' and apply the whip aid. This is described by Waldemar Zeunig as 'the most favourable position for a gallop depart'. Repeat the aids until he complies. If on the other hand he dashes off into an uncontrolled gallop – usually from sheer exuberance – signal down to a trot again, helped by a vibration of the lunge rein, taking your time about it, and start again. You may have to do this several times before he finally gets the message. Do the same thing if he should strike off with the outer leg leading.

The trainer must watch the action of the horse all the time, and check any tendency to sloppy movement in any of the gaits. There will be no collection, but the trainer can bear in mind the F.E.I. definitions of the ordinary gaits (*Rules for Dressage Competitions*, Sections 403, 404, 405).

> '*Walk.* A free, regular and unconstrained walk of moderate extension. The horse should walk energetically but calmly, with even and determined step, distinctly marking four equally spaced beats.'

The longer the walk stride the better, and the hind feet should be well into the prints of the fore feet. A horse with a short, tipputy walk stride will seldom be a good galloper, and frustrating to ride.

> '*Trot.* The horse goes forward freely and straight, engaging his hindlegs with good hock action ... his position being balanced and unconstrained. The steps should be as even as possible. The hind feet touch the ground in the footprints of the fore feet.'

Dragging the hind feet is a common fault in many horses. The horse may hang his head on account of the weight of the lunge rein, in which case raise it at the centre, and stimulate the quarters with the lungeing whip. Use the whip whenever necessary to maintain the energy of the movement and regularity of cadence.

> '*Canter.* The horse ... moves freely, with a natural balance. The strides are long, even, and the pace well cadenced. The quarters develop an increasing impulsion.'

With a normal eager horse the problem will be always to restrain him from going too fast, and so swinging his quarters outwards on the circle. Try to reduce the inward drag on the head to the centre by walking round on a small inner circle and giving a bit with the rein. Slow him down with retarding sounds and a vibration of the rein, at the same time showing the whip to maintain the gait. A slug will have to be pushed forward with the whip on the hocks.

Backing

Before these lessons the horse will have become accustomed to a body-roller and girth, as already described (page 150); during them he can be introduced to the saddle. Begin with a light numnah pad, which can be kept on with a surcingle. Put it on before taking him to wherever the lungeing lessons are taking place, and he will soon get used to being lunged with this on his back. Repeat this process with the saddle. The first time have an assistant at his head with the usual bowl of corn, and there should be no trouble. Make sure from the outset that the saddle is put on gently and correctly, a little in front of the withers and then slid quietly back into place so that the hairs of his coat are smoothed down with the grain and not against it.

The horse can be backed any time the trainer chooses, after he has got used to being lunged with a saddle on his back, and to having it girthed up. No one can predict with certainty how a spirited young horse of three years old and upwards will react to having a man on his back for the first time. He may accept it quietly, or he may explode. In the latter case the battle is on, and it must be won by the rider. To make certain of this I would recommend the use of an Australian buck-jumping saddle, which has a deep seat, wide cantle and two knee flaps in front. To sit it correctly the rider must depart from the accepted canons of modern horsemanship and sit well back in the saddle, with his legs forward and his knees under the flaps. Every movement of the horse will then press the knees more firmly and safely up to the flaps. There are not many horses who will dislodge you. This would ensure victory in the shortest time. Failing this, use a show-jumping saddle with good knee rolls and hope for the best.

Helpers are needed for this backing business: somebody at the horse's head with the corn bowl; the backer; and somebody to lift him up. The sudden appearance of these auxiliaries on the lungeing scene could make the horse suspicious and nervous, thinking, rightly, that something must be up. Let the extras appear a few times before the backing is to begin, perhaps checking the saddle and making much of him in the intervals of lungeing. All this will help to reassure him and calm him on the day.

Do not fix a definite day in your mind – such decisions cause a slight anxiety, which has a way of communicating itself to the horse – but choose the right moment during a lesson, perhaps at a change of rein and the horse has been brought into the centre, when everything has gone well, and horse and trainer are calm and happy. If either is hot and bothered postpone the operation to a more propitious moment.

The horseholder takes the lungeing rein, coils it up in one hand so that it can easily be let out if necessary, and interests the horse in the bowl of oats. The horseholder must keep his mind concentrated on the horse, not letting his attention wander by watching the proceedings behind the withers. Without any delay the trainer will give the backer a leg up far enough for him to lay the upper part of his body across the saddle. He stays there a moment, then slips back to the ground, and the holder makes much of the horse. Repeat this several times, and that may be enough for one lesson. It all depends on the attitude of the horse and the insight of the trainer. However, it is always better to proceed slowly rather than hurrying things.

The next day the backer can stay across the saddle for a longer time, patting and stroking the opposite flanks of the horse while he does so. If he gets fidgety, slip off his back before he can think of taking more violent action, and start again. If all has gone well, the backer puts his right leg over the saddle and actually sits astride on the horse's back. The holder should make the horse keep his head up, which will lessen the chance of his trying to buck or plunge about; few English or European horses really buck, at least not with the technical skill of the Australian or the mustang. Reward at this stage should be lavish; much patting and gentling and plentiful oats. After a few minutes in the saddle, the backer dismounts, and the ordinary lunge lesson is carried on, or the horse is led back to its stable, according to when the backing took place.

Finally, stirrups are put on the saddle and the backer mounts carefully with them, but he will not handle the reins at this stage. A few steps forward can be taken, and in a few days it should be possible to do a few circles on the lunge with the rider in the saddle, and then to walk about independently.

There should be a short backing lesson like this every day,

but this should be the limit of the ridden work for several months, until the horse is rising four at the earliest.

The length of the lungeing period is a variable one, depending on the receptivity and aptitude of the pupil, bearing in mind always the principle of never rushing the horse but letting it assimilate the lessons slowly but surely. Three months is about the average, and the trainer should plan his work ahead on that basis, always keeping his mind flexible and ready to modify the plan according to circumstances. The following suggested programme is taken from *Riding Technique in Pictures*, by C. E. G. Hope and Charles Harris:

First month. Exercise approximately fifteen to twenty minutes. First fortnight. (Commence with left rein.) Twice on each rein at walk and trot for about two to three minutes – mainly trot. During the first two days, horse should be led at the beginning of each rein change. *Second fortnight.* (Commence with the right rein.) Twice on each rein for about two to three minutes at walk and trot – mainly trot.

Second month. Exercise approximately thirty minutes. Third fortnight. (Commence with left rein.) Twice on each rein for about four to five minutes with walk and trot variations during each period. *Fourth fortnight.* (Commence with right rein.) Twice on each rein for about four to five minutes with walk and trot variations during each period. If the horse breaks into a canter during any part of these lessons do not immediately suppress the gait.

Third month. Exercise approximately forty-five minutes. Fifth fortnight. (Commence with left rein.) About four five minutes each rein. First time both reins: walk-trot variations; second time both reins: canter trot variations; third time both reins: walk-trot variations. At the end of the daily school during the fifth fortnight – mounting and dismounting at the halt. *Sixth fortnight.* (Commence with right rein.) Same work as above. During the third, and last, rein period in the sixth fortnight rider mounted (being led first time round on each rein).

16 Forward Movement and Balance

After all this going round in circles we come back to straight lines. The young horse has learnt certain signals given by the voice and by the whip and indirectly on the mouth by the leader when going in hand. Now he must translate them into the language of leg and hand, assisted by the body. These aids and their application has already been described previously in Chapter 8 and need not be repeated. Then we were considering a beginner rider in charge of an experienced horse; now we have the young horse in the hands of a skilled and understanding horseman.

The youngster will have been ridden for a few lessons while on the lunge; now, with the trainer on his back he should be led up and down in straight lines, making fairly wide turns at each end of the manège. The verbal orders to walk on, halt, and the touching with the whip will be accompanied by the appropriate leg and hand actions, very gently applied at first, but quite definitely. In a very short time the horse should be interpreting the simple aids correctly, but this initial instruction must continue until he does thoroughly understand the new language. There is no need for this work to be confined to a manège or indoor school. Take the young horse into an open field, so that he does not get the idea that there is a special place for lessons. It does not matter if the ground is uneven in places or on a slope; the pupil will have already spent three months, perhaps more on a level surface, now the occasional variation will alert him mentally, make him pick his feet up, and start the process of muscling him up and opening his lungs.

As soon as the horse has assimilated this new lesson, the leader's job is done and the youngster is finally out of leading strings. He is now alone with his rider to be made – or marred. If all this apparently pernickety preliminary work has been carefully and patiently done, there should be no question of marring. The horse will be well prepared mentally and physically for all that is to follow; what he needs from the trainer is skill combined with patience and perseverance: the skill to know what is wrong and to apply the remedies; the patience to keep calm on all occasions; and the perseverance to go on and on until the right answer is obtained. It always will be obtained up to the limits of any particular horse's understanding and capability. Every horse, like every man, has his ceiling of intelligence and ability to learn and perform and the trainer must be able to recognise when this top limit has been reached.

The first job is to go forward freely in straight lines, and to move straight. Use the wall of a school, a fence or hedge, or a spitlocked line in the open field. At first, with the new weight on his back, the horse may be unbalanced; he may take uneven strides, which can be corrected by a slight check of the pace and then firmly pushing the horse forward into a long easy stride on a free rein.

The primary task of the rider of a young horse doing mounted work for the first time is to gain contact with the horse's mouth. The bit used is of course a snaffle, with a good thick mouthpiece and large rings of the egg butt type. Reins are held in both hands, which should be more widely separated than normal so as to give more lightness and flexibility to the handling of the reins. A long switch should be carried to supplement the leg aids when necessary; spurs need not be worn at first, but should be added later when the horse is going freely and quietly. They should be used very lightly at first but always definitely. With a free-going eager horse they should not be necessary, but with an unresponsive, sluggish animal they will have to be used sharply. Only the trainer can decide on their use.

The search for contact is slow and gradual. Let the horse walk forward on its own, pushed forward by the legs. Hold the reins loosely, then carefully increase the tension so that there is a feel on the mouth, then instantly relax. Driven by the legs the horse will tend to reach forward with his head and neck until he makes contact of his own accord. A gentle vibration of the reins will make the bit move in his mouth and encourage him to play with it and chew it. After a few steps make much of him, relax the reins and let him go on a loose rein, which he will appreciate as freedom after the slight constraint.

Remember always at this stage to have the reins relaxed when the legs signal him to go forward. Halting the horse should be carried out from a position of contact; the legs act to make the horse go forward, accompanied by the downward action of the back muscles, and the hands then pull back slightly. When the horse comes to a halt make much of him and relax the reins.

The transitions from walk to halt, halt to walk and back again are an excellent and necessary preliminary suppling exercise, and help to achieve the correct head carriage. At first the tendency is to hold the head low, with the neck stretched out; but gradually the increase of the soft – always soft – contact will raise the head and flex the neck. When the horse comes to the end of the school, outdoor manège or field, he can be turned with a simple direct rein aid to right or left, quietly assisted by the outer leg. There will be, of course, no deliberate attempt at flexion or collection, but the horse will achieve a sort of natural collection as he responds to the gentle actions of the hands on the bit, and as he learns to engage his quarters and thrust forward from obeying the actions of the legs.

These lessons should be short, fifteen to twenty minutes, only at the walk. It will take several sessions to achieve true soft contact, and the process should on no account be hurried, no matter how willing the horse may appear to be. To have a horse with a soft mouth is the ambition, perhaps only a dream, of every horseman, so it is worth taking time at the beginning to increase the chances of achieving it.

Once the horse is going freely, not fast, on a light contact he can be encouraged to lengthen his stride into what will eventually become an extended walk. 'A horseman should make continuous effort throughout the career of his horse to develop and maintain a long, low-striding walk.' (Harry D. Chamberlain, *Training Hunters, Jumpers and Hacks.*) To this end he practises obtaining extension.

Begin this work in a manège or covered school, and continue it in the open. The rider should have a slightly forward position, and will use his legs and hands alternately to combine with the natural roll of the horse. The left leg is applied and the left hand goes forward to follow the movement of the horse's head, when the horse is swinging leftwards, and with the next stride the right leg and hand act in the same way. The hands must of course be well separated. The horse is allowed to extend his head and neck as much as he likes, and the stride of the hindleg is gradually lengthened. Three or four strides at a time are ample, but the exercise can be practised several times in a lesson.

The actual requirements of an extended walk under the F.E.I.

Negotiating a Derby Bank; notice the rider
leaning well back (*Light Horse*)

Mrs L. Bates' John Blandon ridden over a fence at Wylye by Lorna
Sutherland

The approach to the jump at a trot. The rider is sitting down in the saddle, quite relaxed, keeping the horse lightly in hand but pushing forward with the legs

The take-off. The rider has pivoted forward slightly from her knees and lowered her hands in order to give complete freedom to the horse's head and neck, keeping the weight of her body over the forehand. This has freed the quarters to do the work of propelling the horse over the jump. Compare the steady position of the legs with those in the above picture

A later stage of the take-off over a higher obstacle. The body is rather more forward than in the centre picture, but the basic position is exactly the same; note again the easing forward of the hands and the firm position of the leg from the knee downward

Rules for Dressage Competitions, Section 403 (c) are as follow:

> The horse should cover as much ground as possible, without haste and without losing the regularity of his steps. The hind feet touch the ground clearly beyond the footprints of the fore feet. The rider lets the horse stretch out his head and neck without, however, losing contact, the head being carried in front of the vertical.

The formal lessons can be varied by walks across country in company with a quiet trained horse as auxiliary instructor. Practice can also be given in getting the young horse used to traffic.

This can well begin at an early age within the confines of the training area. The horse should become accustomed to the sight of as many different sorts of vehicles as possible, a man riding a bicycle to begin with. Let somebody lead a bicycle beside the trainer and his horse on some of their leading rein lessons; then let him meet the horse and pass him. Progress from there to a mounted cyclist; at some stage the horse should allow a mounted cyclist to lead him.

Let him then become inured to the appearance of a scooter and motorcycle and to the sound of the engine running. Do not suddenly start the engine up behind him, but let him hear it from a distance at first and then gradually approaching. Common sense will dictate the kind and progress of instruction from then on. The principle is quiet progression from one thing to another. By the same token use should be made of music in the riding school, because it undoubtedly has a soothing effect and promotes good rhythm.

The horse can be got used to flags waving, clothes hanging on a line, people moving about. Once the preliminary lessons are over, the more company he has the better. He can work in the school with another horse, either a pupil the same as himself or a trained horse. After he has got used to sights and sounds on his home ground, he can be taken for walks, dismounted at first, on roads, progressing from quiet to busy. When doing this put on knee caps in case of accidents. Great care must be taken all the time to avoid these, and the trainer must be alert to give clear signals to traffic, and be prepared to have them disregarded. If there is a response, do not let your preoccupation with the horse prevent you from acknowledging it with a smile, a wave or some sign of gratitude. Some other horseman on the road will benefit from it somewhere sometime. As for the horse, the voice, the petting, the material reward, and above all the quiet confidence of the trainer whom he knows, will increase his present trust in him and encourage him to accept the unknown.

After two or three weeks of walking exercise trotting can start, still on straight lines. The signals for the trot (already described in Chapter 8) are given during an ordinary walk with rein contact. The experts are silent on whether the first mounted trotting lessons should be given sitting or posting, but I would suggest a sitting trot to begin with, for the main reason that it is easier to restrain the horse from trotting too fast. The object is a lively energetic gait, rather slower than normal. If the horse persists in trying to go faster than you wish, halt him, and start again. Repetition is the answer to nearly all resistances.

Ring the changes of transitions – walk, halt; walk, trot; trot, walk, halt – and so on, so that the horse becomes continually more alert and supple, mentally as well as physically. There is no reason why you should not try a rein back at this stage; the horse already having learnt something about it during his dismounted training (pages 148–57). It is all part of forward movement, for the horse is given the leg signals to go forward, the impetus being transmitted to the rear by the reins.

The first lessons are best done on the ground, thus avoiding any danger of rough handling of the horse's mouth. Stand the horse alongside a hedge or wall, hold the reins close to the bit on either side of the mouth and quietly manoeuvre the horse to stand up to attention, squarely balanced on all four feet. Gently move the hands forward (backward from the point of view of the horse), saying 'Back'. Holding the reins in one hand and tapping the horse on the breast with the butt of the whip, will help to make it understand what is required. If the horse is reluctant to lift a foot, tap it with the toe of your boot below the fetlock joint while using the reins and voice aids, and it will usually comply. The moment one foot has moved backwards, relax and make much of the horse, then move him forward a step. Gradually progress from this to one full step, then two, making sure that he moves diagonally, the opposite hindleg moving with the foreleg. After that carry on with the work mounted.

Begin the first lessons in front of a school wall, or a hedge or fence, to impress on him that he cannot go forward. Press the horse forward into the bit, holding it steady but gently vibrating backwards to make quite clear what is wanted. The rider's body should be just a little forward so as to free the hindquarters. One foreleg will go back first, followed by the opposite hindleg and that will be enough for the first lesson. Make much of him and let him go forward on a light rein. Some equines, ponies more than horses, can be very obstinate about going backwards. One reason is that they are not ready for it, not supple enough; so do not make an issue of it at this stage. When you do try again, have an assistant to stand at his head and tap one of his forelegs to make him lift it up. But if the early training has been done correctly there should be no trouble.

The most important element of all this preliminary stage is the handling of the reins and the establishment of the right relations between hand and mouth. The rider's hands must follow the movements of the horse's head, allowing him to stretch his neck, and by constant give and take encourage him to play with the bit in his mouth, to chew it. 'Letting the horse chew the bit is an indispensable aid of training, for it makes the horse's trusting contact with the bit while stretching its back and neck as comfortably as possible for the horse and turns it into a habit.' So says Waldemar Zeunig (*Horsemanship*); and he adds, 'It is also an infallible indication of correct dressage of riding horses, besides being very important in evaluating previous training.'

The position of the hands can be flexible, not rigidly fixed in one posture. They should be fairly wide apart, ready to be adapted to the requirements of the situation. If the horse tends to be too strong to one side, the opposite hand will remain low and firm, while the hand on the same side can be light and yielding and placed rather higher. Constant opening and closing of the fingers will give a vibratory action on the bit via the reins, without any pulling back or tightening of the reins. It is impossible to translate these reactions into words, but the experienced trainer, with his firmly acquired seat independent of the reins will *feel* it, so that there is a continuous back and forth flow of dialogue between horse and man along the reins and from the legs and body of the rider – which is *equestrian tact.*

The sitting trot can be alternated with the rising, and the horse accustomed to the regular change of diagonal, and soon he will be ready for balancing exercises. These are turns and circles on the move and at the halt; they have already been described in relation to the pupil rider (Chapters 10 and 11). The young horse has already worked on a circle when on the lunge; now he has a rider on his back, and so has to use himself to adjust his position and centre of gravity. The axis of all this effort is the spine which must be kept straight along the line of movement and made supple by the effort of conforming to the circular movements. The spine can only bend, slightly, in front of and behind the rib-cage, but the vertebrae which compose it can become flexible with exercise and have a small play in them, preventing complete stiffness and ramrod rigidity.

In a turn or a circle the horse has to resist the inward, centripetal, pull of gravity, and the outward centrifugal, force, which tends to throw a circling body outwards. In this he is helped by the rider, who will first prepare him for the turn or circle by flexing him longitudinally with a half-halt, and then by giving him the right aids and by his, the rider's, weight adjustment.

The half-halt is a very subtle instrument in the education of the horse. It is a momentary checking of forward movement, to alert him for a change of plan and to loosen the muscles of his neck and shoulders. It is obtained by a closing of the legs and a quick acting and immediate yielding of the hands, so that the horse will flex his head slightly and engage his hindquarters. This, as it were, *positions* the horse for whatever is to come. The half-halt can begin to be taught during the straight line period, and its use continues all through the horse's career. It is the basic means of retraining and resuppling horses which have become stiff and of curing hard mouths.

The first turns have already been performed, on a widish circle and with simple aids. Now the pupil goes back to the manège or riding school. Do not push him into the corners yet, but let him take a wide turn, using the inside rein and action of both legs to maintain impulsion, with additional pressure of the outside leg to impart extra energy to the horse's outside legs, which have just a little bit further to go than the inner ones and must not be allowed to lag behind. The left hand yields and at the same time the indirect rein on the neck, but not brought across the withers, supports the turning movement.

About now a useful exercise for teaching the aids to a horse and gaining quick response to them, especially making him obedient to the leg, is the turn on the forehand at the halt.

Halt the horse somewhere on the long side of the manège, alert it with a half-halt, and proceed as follows for a right turn, which is accomplished by moving the hindquarters to the left, the horse being on the left rein.

Keep the horse steady and facing straight to its front by light and even contact with the reins. Apply extra pressure with the right leg, and shift the weight of the body to the left, which will start the hindquarters moving to the left, by the raising of the right hindleg and its shifting to the left in front of the left hindleg. The rider's left leg is close to the girth to maintain impulsion and prevent a step backwards. In this movement the horse should pivot on his left fore foot, moving neither forwards nor backwards.

After one step relax the aids and make much of the horse. Continue step by step until one eighth of a full turn (45 degrees) has been made, which will be enough for the first lesson. This can be repeated later on in the same session, but no more for that day. As I have said already, most horses find that this is an easy movement to make, so that their co-operation is more or less assured, which makes it a valuable educational exercise. A few lessons will enable the lesson to be completed in full, and it can be repeated occasionally as a refresher, but it should not be overdone. It is not recognised by the F.E.I. as a test movement, though it was once included in the B.H.S. novice tests, but fortunately abandoned some years ago.

Balancing exercises, which also supple the spine and forehand of the horse, preparing it for collection and advanced work, can be carried on concurrently with the above lessons. The are simply a variety of circles of progressively diminishing radius, from half the width of the school, say ten yards, to three yards or less.

The essential thing is to vary the work as much as possible. Alternate circles with straight lines, frequent transitions, and also changes of tempo in each gait. Intersperse half-halts at walk and trot, on the straight as well as on the circle. Make sure the action in each gait is regular and evenly cadenced. Count the beats out loud and see that the horse conforms to them. Suitable music is conducive to rhythmic movement, and a tape player is very much part of the modern training equipment. A cine-camera is not quite a luxury these days; better if it has an ultra-fast speed so that the resulting films can be shown in slow motion. Better than nothing is a robot-type camera. The great thing is to be able to see yourself as the camera sees you, so that you can check the errors.

Change the rein frequently, sometimes by going diagonally across the school, or going straight across, or by a large figure of eight. Progress to smaller circles, and serpentines, and lateral changes of direction, from the wall to the wall; and by half circles in the corners of the school, returning diagonally back to the track in the opposite direction.

Gradually the head carriage will become stabilised, the horse's poll being about level with the rider's chest, and the head at an angle of 30 degrees to 45 degrees to the vertical. Frequent relaxations for free-going walks and trots will reward the horse for his labours and prevent him from stiffening up.

This work done over some three to six months will prepare the horse for more exciting things – the canter and the gallop. As explained in Chapter 11, only the English have separate words for the different speeds of the gallop gait, and the canter or hand gallop is the first gait that is now asked of the horse. He will have cantered already under orders while on the lunge, and, of course, freely whenever let out on his own; the youngest of horses can change quite effortlessly from trot to canter, but with a rider they have the problems of weight and balance to overcome. The task now is to teach the young horse to move into the canter from the trot, and later from the walk and halt, at command and on the required leg.

The generally accepted method is to start from the trot, at a corner of the school or on a circle, preferably on the less favoured side, all horses tending to be one-sided, to the left more usually, or to the right. Assuming that our horse is biased to the left, let us consider the canter depart with the off fore leading.

The main phases of the canter on the right, off fore leading, are: suspension (all four legs in the air); near hind on the ground; off hind, near hind, near fore; off hind, near fore (diagonal); off hind, near fore, off fore, off fore (leading leg); suspension.

Start in the manège or covered school, towards the end of a normal schooling session, when everything has gone well, the horse quiet and relaxed. Get into a slightly collected but energetic trot, ridden sitting on the right rein. On the long side of the school, approaching the corner, position the horse with a half-halt, and then, as the horse enters the corner, and when he is on the left diagonal (off hind, near fore), feel the right rein lightly, supporting with the left to control the speed, and at the same time apply both legs, the right against the girth, the left (outer leg) more strongly behind the girth, and shift the body weight slightly to the left.

The legs activate the hindlegs and push him up to the bit. The hands restrain the movement, preventing the horse from trying to go into a fast trot, and bend the horse's head gently to the right. The activated near hind will be accompanied by the leading of the off fore, followed by the off hind, thus breaking the rhythm of the trot and starting the canter.

Do not allow the horse to try to make the canter depart by

speeding up his trot, which many are inclined to do. At the first sign of that relax the aids, bring him quietly back to a walk and halt. Calm him down with a few walk-trot, trot-walk transitions, then start again. An increase of speed *at the start* of the canter is permissible for a few strides, after which steady him down.

A few departures at the corners should be sufficient to get the idea into his head, when you can practise on a large circle (half the manège), following with lessons on the straight. When the horse is confirmed on the off fore leading, repeat the whole process for the near fore leading. At a later stage, he can be practised in the canter depart from the walk, and then from the halt.

The aids described above are diagonal ones. Many instructors start by using lateral aids, that is right rein and strong right leg (for off fore leading), and change to diagonal aids later on. It would appear to be less confusing to the horse, and possibly for the rider, to start as you mean to go on, using diagonal aids from the outset, which was the opinion of the late Henry Wynmalen (*Equitation*).

Once the horse is thoroughly obedient to these aids in the manège, he can be taken out into the open, and cantered and galloped over all sorts of country: up and down hill, over ploughland, if it is the right time of year. There is nothing like it for conditioning the horse, strengthening his muscles, and perfecting his balance. Also give the horse variety. 'After a time,' says Lyndon Bolton (*Training the Horse*), 'I shall rarely go twice running to the same place to school. I like change, and so does my horse.' And he too emphasises the value of getting a horse used to all sorts of distractions, which will never happen in the seclusion of the covered school.

At the walk and canter, the horse nods his head as he steps along, oscillating it backwards and forwards, which is why it has already been said that the hands must follow the movement of the horse's head and neck. They should go backwards and forwards, keeping always a light play on the bit through the reins. At the trot the horse holds his head steady, and the same should happen to the hands, subject to the delicate nuances of contact through the fingers. The horse has become used to going free on a loose rein at the walk and trot, and he should also do so at the canter.

It is true that 'on the bit' is the watchword of the horseman, but too often it is interpreted as a steady hard pull on the reins. Watch any dressage test. The horse, provided he has been properly schooled from the start, can be on the bit through the weight of the reins alone. The skilled cutting horse can be effectively on the bit without one in its mouth at all.

A simple change of leading leg at the canter can be taught quite simply. The mechanics have been described already in Chapter 11. The best way is to make a large figure of eight, making the change at the trot at the intersection point of the figure. Half a dozen strides at first can be reduced to three and two. Then the change is practised on the straight. Finally the horse should be well able to do the flying change. Great care must be taken to apply the aid, which is simply that for the opposite canter lead, at the correct time, so that the signal is felt when the horse is in the state of suspension between strides. Start the sign – diagonal aids – when the present leading forefoot is just about to strike the ground.

The balancing exercises already described will be carried on at the canter as well as at the trot, and, towards the end of this period, the preliminaries to advanced work, flexion and collection, can begin.

17 Flexion, Collection and Suppling

Flexion

If the training up to now has been successfully carried out, the horse should already have begun to flex his lower jaw, and to some extent to collect himself. The supping work, especially the half-halt and the changes of tempo, will have prepared him for greater collection, as described in Chapter 10.

There are all kinds of flexions, of the spine, flexing the hind-legs, as well as of the mouth, head and neck, but specifically the term applies to the direct flexion of the head and lateral flexion of the neck.

Direct flexion is when the horse yields his lower jaw to the action of the bit and bends his head downwards from the poll, thus straightening somewhat the angle of the head to the vertical. Incorrect flexion is when the horse bends his head from the crest of the neck, which accentuates the straightening of the head, causes stiffness and over-bending, and puts the horse behind the bit.

Lateral flexion is the bending of the neck to the right or left.

Elementary flexion and collection can be obtained with a snaffle bit, but for the serious work which must now begin the change to a double bridle must be made. If the horse has become well mouthed, used to playing with and chewing his bit, he should accept the double bit without any difficulty. As when the horse was introduced to the snaffle bit for the first time, extreme care should be taken over this new introduction. Insert the two bits gently into the mouth, and let them hang loosely in the mouth before making the adjustments. The sizes of the bits must be just right for the horse's mouth, and the adjustment of fitting must be carefully made and must be exact. It is not easy to do, and the perfectly fitted double bridle with the curb chain acting in the right place is a rare sight in my experience.

The snaffle bit (bridoon) goes above the curb bit, set just high enough to wrinkle the corners of the lips. The curb bit rests just below the bridoon on the tongue and the bars of the mouth. When it hangs straight down as an extension of the bridle cheekpiece, the curb chain should lie slack just below the chin groove, and it should be turned so that all the links lie flat. While dismounted, hold the snaffle reins above the bits with the left hand, and gently pull the curb reins with the right so that the arm of the curb moves backwards and raises the curb chain into the chin groove. The horse should just begin to yield his lower jaw a little in response to the concentrated action on it of the curb and the chain. The upward pull of the bridoon reins prevents the horse from lowering his head, but allows him to bend it slightly towards the vertical – but nowhere near it – from the poll. Once the response is made, relax and make much of him.

Both direct and lateral flexion can be taught from the ground. James Fillis and Baucher were great artists at this, achieving most extreme flexion, especially lateral, in this way; but modern riders seem to prefer to practise it mounted and can be equally successful. In any case the kind of lateral flexion obtained by Fillis of the horse looking practically at right angles to his proper direction is not required of a modern horse, even in the most advanced dressage. The preliminary exercise described above is really connected with the fitting of the double bit, and thereafter the work can be done mounted.

Start at the halt, holding the bridoon reins in the left hand and the curb reins in the right. The bridoon hand will be held higher than the curb hand, not so much to raise the head as to keep it in position and prevent it from being lowered by the action of the curb bit. As always there should not be a direct pull, but a light fingering action. The snaffle is a simple bit with a straightforward action, so it can be used more frequently and more firmly when necessary than the curb bit.

The curb hand has to make the action of the bit as sensitive and subtle as possible, actuating straight backwards on the bars and against the jaw, so that it will yield slightly, the head nodding from the poll. The legs should act to keep the horse in position at the halt, resisting a possible tendency to rein back. The instant the horse yields his jaw for the first time, relax and make much of him, and let him go forward on light normal contact on the snaffle, the curb rein loose. Repeat this a few times at the halt, which will be sufficient for the first session.

Lateral flexion of the neck can be practised at the same time, still at the halt, by using a direct rein to bend the head slightly to the left, while keeping the horse steady in the halt position with the legs and opposite rein, which yields enough to allow the head to turn but avoids indirect effects on the withers. Bend alternately to right and left a few times, being content with only just noticeable results at first, relaxing the reins between each flexion. There is no need for excessive flexion of the neck, but enough to make the horse obedient to the aids and to supple his neck and jaw muscles.

Once the horse responds easily and gently to these exercises, flexion can be practised on the move; walk and trot at first, later the canter, on turns and circles and serpentine as well as on a straight line. It is a good exercise in finesse to ride with a loose bridoon rein, and the lightest of contact with the curb, so that the horse will respond to the slightest restraining action of it. Obtain halts this way; the transition must be gradual at first, especially at trot or canter, but, according to the way the horse has responded to training, they can become quick. Yield the hand immediately after each response.

A useful flexing and suppling exercise, which was recommended by Harry Chamberlain (*Training Hunters, Jumpers and Hacks*) is the half-turn and half-turn in reverse. For the half-turn, assuming you are on the left rein, and going straight along the side of the manège, or in the open for that matter, at the corner of the manège, or a selected point in the open, make a half circle to the left, using the left opening rein and the right indirect rein (Chapter 8), and the right leg, the left (inside) leg acting to control the quarters. The head is flexed to the left. Proceed diagonally at an angle of about 45 degrees back to the original line of march, but in the opposite direction.

The half-turn in reverse is done in the opposite circle. From the original line of march on the left rein, veer off from the straight at an angle of about 45 degrees, using the left direct opening rein, the right indirect rein and the right leg. Proceed in that direction five to ten yards, then turn right on a half circle back to the side of the manège or the original line of march, but of course going in the opposite direction and now on the right rein. In this case the right opening rein is used with the left rein supporting, the left (outside) leg asking for the turn to the right, the right leg keeping the haunches under control. This teaches obedience to the reins, activates and lightens the quarters, helps to put the horse on the bit, and promotes the flexing of the jaw and the neck, supples the spine, and begins the flexing of the poll; it is also a preliminary to the shoulder-in exercise to come. These exercises are best done at a slow trot sitting.

The horse's head carriage should be stabilised now in the position described on page 170. The bridoon and curb reins can be separated in each hand as before, or the curb rein can be held outside the little fingers of each hand, the bridoon inside. This rein then holds the head in position, while flexing and vibration of the fingers actuate the curb bit, impulsion being increased by leg action. The horse should yield his jaw completely, which will be accompanied by a nodding of the head from the poll. Immediately yield the hands to give the horse the reward of instant relief for his obedience. The head should go forward into the normal position and the mouth close. A horse which keeps its mouth continually open shows that this flexion has been overdone and that contact has become too harsh. Revert to the snaffle and a free rein. In obtaining flexion of the poll the hands should, if anything, be held a little higher than usual; holding them too low will make the horse lower his head and arch his neck from the axis instead of from the highest point of the head, which is totally incorrect.

As has already been said (pages 170–1) successful flexion depends very considerably on the conformation of the horse's head and neck. It is a waste of time to attempt any more than the most elementary flexion, if that, with a horse that has a short thick neck and a coarse tied-in jaw. On the other hand difficulties will also arise from a horse with a long slender neck, which will tend to become rubber and overflexible, encouraging the horse to successful evasions. In this case approach flexion very cautiously, and practise it at a trot, at which pace the head and neck are held more stiffly by the horse than at the walk and canter.

During this period it is well worth teaching the horse to go freely with one hand only holding the reins, in other words to become bridlewise. The influence of formal dressage competition has almost destroyed this art amongst modern riders, except polo players and mounted soldiers, who have to use one hand for other purposes, but I hold that no horse is fully trained (or horseman for that matter) until he can be controlled as easily with one hand as by two, and go nearly as well. A horse which in the course of this basic training has come to accept the effects of the indirect rein will quite easily and willingly become bridlewise, and be an even greater pleasure to ride because of it.

Collection

Collection follows flexion; and here we come to a parting of the ways of the outdoor (*campagne*) school of riding and what is now particularised as dressage riding. Collection has been defined on pages 109–10. It is generally accepted now that some kind of collection is necessary for an outdoor horse, even if you call it engagement of the quarters, but also that it can be kept to a minimum. The tests for the dressage phase of a three-day event do require collection, but as the use of a snaffle is optional, it need be of only very low degree. For novice and intermediate grade one-day events in England no collection is asked for.

The preliminary to collection is the *ramener,* the correct placing of the head in preparation for the signals that will ask for engagement of the quarters and lightening of the forehand. This is in fact the flexion of the poll, which has already been obtained. In the first degree of collection the head should be in the normal position between 45 degrees and 30 degrees to the vertical, jaw slightly flexed. For greater collection the head will be nearer to the vertical, *but never behind it.* It should be emphasised that flexion and collection can only be obtained at slow speeds. On the other hand there must be no loss of impulsion in collected gaits (see the definitions given on pages 108 and 110). What happens is that instead of the legs moving extended horizontally they move just as actively but more vertically and with more elevated steps. In the extreme case you have the *passage.*

The horse learns natural collection all through his early mounted training in the constant repetition of transitions of all kinds, already described in Chapter 16. The method is the close and subtle relation of the hand and leg aids; the legs provide the driving force, while the hands restrain and, as it were, canalise the energy produced upwards instead of forwards – *without, however, losing forward impulsion* – compressing the horse like a steel spring.

It cannot be repeated too often that these exercises should be carried out for short periods only, alternating with plenty of relaxed movement with free extension of head and neck. Even if the horse proves to be an apt pupil and appears to enjoy doing collected work, the rider should strictly limit the amount.

Suppling

All this work, properly done, should have a continuous softening and suppling effect on the horse's muscles, especially those of the neck and shoulders and back, at the same time as they are being developed and strengthened by the gymnastic exercises, which is what in fact they are. But the supreme suppling instruments are the half-halt and the shoulder-in. Both of these have been described on pages 164 and 117 to 120. They should be used regularly in training and school work, and, more intensively, for remaking pullers and spoiled horses. The use of the half-halt for suppling has been meticulously described by A. d'Endrody in *Give Your Horse a Chance.* The process was regularly used for the training of polo ponies. It can also help show jumpers to achieve the speed and handiness which is demanded of them nowadays.

The method is the application of repeated half-halts on a wide circle (school diameter) at the trot and canter, mostly the latter, using a snaffle bit. The work can be direct or lateral, this in the case of horses that are one-sided naturally, or have been allowed to become so by excessive work on one rein. As a preliminary do two or three circles at the walk with a half-halt every few steps, then carry on at the trot first and then at the canter, alternating half-halts with full halts, and turns across the circle to change the rein. Using this as a refresher for a trained horse, there will also be turns (pirouettes), on the haunches, of 180 degrees. The frequency should be about two movements per circle, and the length of the lesson for one horse should be about fifteen minutes.

For one-sided animals work at first at the walk on a straight line, alternating the aids – left rein left leg, right rein right leg – in a series of half-halts. Then work on a circle, using the lateral aids according to which rein you are on. Stiff horses are inclined to carry their heads low and to be on their forehands, so that there must be an upward action of the reins. If the horse tends to throw his head up, apply the treatment described on page 169.

The second suppling exercise, the *shoulder-in,* can run concurrently. The wall to the wall routine is a good preliminary exercise for the shoulder-in, but the best way to move into it is by way of a turn at the corner of the manège or a half-turn as described on page 114. In the first case the horse is not asked to straighten up along the side of the school when the turn is completed but allowed to continue the movement until his forelegs are off the track. Taken at the walk on the right rein, the horse's head will be bent slightly to the right, and he will be checked from going any further on the turn by the left (outside) rein, and the right (inside leg) will act to move him along the side of the school, stepping sideways with his hindlegs on the track and his forelegs just off it, at angle of about 45 degrees to the track. The right rein will act to keep his head flexed to the right (inwards). Before the movement the horse will be positioned on the long side of the school with a half-halt and moderately collected. The right (inside) feet must cross over the left (outside) ones. Two or three steps will be enough to start with. Then the exercise is repeated on the opposite rein.

Using the half-turn, the shoulder-in will begin as the horse is about to take the diagonal direction back to the side of the school, making the way back with a shoulder-in instead of on a straight line. Two or three times per session will be enough for a few days, after which the number of steps can be increased, and the lesson varied with the travers (quarters in), and renvers (quarters out). Gradually progress to exercises at the trot and canter.

18 Turning at the Halt, Lateral Work, and Pirouettes

Turning on the forehand at the halt has already been practised, as an instruction in aid application and recognition (described earlier), and the horse should now be balanced and light on the forehand, and so ready for the half-turn on the haunches, which is the prelude to turns on the move or pirouettes, which come within the range of advanced equitation.

Notes on Dressage, issued by the British Horse Society after World War II, described the movement as follows: 'In the turn on the haunches, the horse's forehand is moved in even, quiet and regular steps round the horse's inner leg. The inner hindleg, acting as a pivot, should remain as nearly as possible on the same spot.'

The turn can be quarter (90 degrees), half (180 degrees), three-quarter (270 degrees), or full (360 degrees). With a still novice horse, an eighth (45 degrees) or less is sufficient. For a turn to the right, halt the horse in a collected manner after a collected walk, on a long side of the manège. Pause to make sure that the horse is standing correctly balanced, hindquarters engaged and burdened, the forehand light, rider's body upright, seat well in the saddle.

With a light action of the right direct rein invite the horse to turn his head to the right. At the same time the legs stimulate movement, but with greater strength from the left leg behind the girth. This accompanied by the action of the left indirect rein on the neck, and yielding forwards. The rider braces the muscles of the small of the back, and shifts his weight slightly to the right to pin down the right (inside) hindleg. The shifting of balance will cause the horse to move his right foreleg to adjust it. Then increased pressure of the left leg and action of the left indirect rein will cause the left foreleg to follow it, moving across and in front of the right. The continued action of the right rein and left leg will move the right foreleg across behind the left foreleg, to resume the normal halt position. Once this first step is accomplished, relax the aids and make much of the horse. It may not happen the first time, but patience and quiet application of the aids will achieve it.

As always it is the first step which counts. Call the horse to attention again and invite him in the same way to take the next step. Three steps will be enough for one lesson; next repeat it on the other rein to the left. As the horse moves round his left (outer) hindleg should move round the right (inside) hindleg, which will move as little as possible. A little forward movement is permissible in the early stages, but not backward. At whatever stage you stop the turn move the horse forward in the new direction, bringing him back on to the track with a circle. Every movement in the school should be a piece of planned gymnastic.

The combined centre of gravity will be shifted rearwards, and the head can be a little higher than normal, further to lighten the forehand. The steps should be taken at a regular, cadenced beat. The moment there is a break in the rhythm stop and start again. Gradually the horse will accomplish the quarter, the half – the most frequently used – and the full turn, which requires a considerable sustained effort.

This too is a balancing and suppling exercise, and prepares the horse for turns on the move (pirouettes). The school pirouette, which will be discussed later (page 238 *et seq*), is a slow highly cadenced movement, requiring considerable muscular control on the part of the horse, and skilful guidance by the rider. It is not the same as that performed by, say, a polo pony, whose 180 degrees turn will be one at top speed, in response to violent and sudden aids from the rider, but the principle is the same. So although the pirouette comes into the realms of high school, it is also necessary for a well-trained outdoor horse albeit in a rough and ready form. Apart from polo and gymkhana events, it is a great asset to a show jumper in the modern style of show jumping where speed is the ultimate governing factor.

After the shoulder-in sequence of movements, the next important exercise in lateral movement is the half-pass (two tracks). The details of this have been described in Chapter 11. The essence is that the horse moves diagonally with his body as straight as possible, his head bent slightly to the direction in which he is going. At first this will be across the manège, but later on it should be done out of doors. The outside feet cross over in front of the inside: if going to the right, left over right; if to the left, right over left. This is a collected movement, and the horse should be prepared for it in the usual way. Aids (to the right): left leg, acting well behind the girth, and the right rein softly leads the horse's head to the right; right leg maintains the movement forward, and the left indirect rein on the neck supports the movement to the right. The horse moves sideways and forwards, body nearly straight, at an angle of about 45 degrees to the original line of direction.

Here is the official description:
'The horse moves on two tracks, the head, neck and shoulders always slightly in advance of the quarters. A slight bend permitting the horse to look to the direction of the movement adds to his grace and gives more freedom of movement to the outside shoulder. The outside legs pass and cross in front of the inside legs. No slowing down of the pace can be tolerated.'

F.E.I. *Rules for Dressage Competitions,* Sec. 411 (d). The French term for this movement is *tenir les hanches.*

The original pace and cadence must be maintained throughout the movement. As usual, two or three correct steps are enough for one lesson, and normally only the distance from the side wall to the centre-line of the manège is enough; but for practice, as the horse progresses in performance, the whole distance can be covered.

After working in this way in both directions, the more sophisticated exercise of the *counter-change of hand,* which means changing direction from one side to the other in a zig-zag movement. At first, starting to the right, move to the centre-line of the manège, straighten and change the bend of the head, then change direction, reversing the aids, timing them to coincide with the inside (right) foreleg reaching the ground, so that it immediately becomes the outside leg, passing across and in front of the left (formerly the outside now the inside leg). Gradually the distance can be reduced until the horse can zig-zag alternate steps.

Practise at the walk first, then trot, and finally at the canter; but the canter zig-zag should not be done until the horse is proficient at the flying change. The value of the half-pass is that it is able to 'Develop muscular control. Increase flexibility of the spine. Promote co-ordinated limb action. Improve limb flexibility. Improve balance by lateral variations of the flow of the centre of gravity *in* the direction of movement. Strengthen abdominal muscles.' (*Riding Technique in Pictures* – C. E. G. Hope and Charles Harris.) When accomplished correctly the single alternate step zig-zag is a wonderful suppling exercise, but the horse must be well advanced in his work before it is attempted.

The full pass has been discussed on page 119, and although it is not a school movement it is well worth practising as a gymnastic exercise in obedience and muscular control. Both reins must keep the horse in position, the inside direct rein bending the head in the direction of the movement, the outside indirect rein and outside leg pushing the point of balance in the same direction, and both legs keeping up the impulsion. As always, the outside legs must step in front of the inside ones, but care must be taken to see that the steps are level. Often there is a tendency to overstep or leap to one side, followed by a short and rather scrambling step, the result of inexperience and not being properly balanced, or possibly the signal being given too sharply. If this happens, stop the movement and go forward a few steps, then start again; a procedure which of course applies to all lateral lessons.

As the horse's muscles become strengthened and toned up by all these exercises and his collected work is sufficiently up to the standard required at this stage, i.e. moderate, extended work can begin. The horse will already have achieved some extension at the walk in the preliminary lessons (page 160), but he will not have attempted extended trot or canter.

Going back to the F.E.I. *Rules for Dressage Competitions* the requirements are:

'*Extended trot.* The horse covers as much ground as possible. He lengthens his stride, remaining on the bit with light contact. The neck is extended and, as a result of great impulsion from the quarters, the horse uses his shoulders covering more ground at each step without his action becoming much higher'. (Section 404 (c).)

In a test the extended trot can be executed either sitting or rising according to instructions, but for the trainee horse a rising trot is best to begin with.

'*Extended canter.* The horse extends his neck; the tip of the nose points more or less forward, the horse lengthens his stride without losing any of his calmness and lightness.' (Section 405 (c).)

The object of extended work is to teach the horse to use himself with the greatest efficiency by the strengthening and toning of the muscles, especially those of the neck, back and hindquarters (see pages 160–2), by the lengthening of his stride

179

and by stimulating forward movement. Extension should only be asked for on a straight line. It is better begun in a manège, but can be carried on out of doors.

The essence of extension is that it begins from the back end of the horse with the active and energetic engagement of the quarters. The daisy-cutting pointing of the toes without any hock action, which is so often seen and which appears to bamboozle the judges, is not extension. It is the hocks which must literally *drive* the forelegs forward.

Prepare for the exercise with a short period of collected work, then a transition to an ordinary gait, which leg action will keep energetic and lively; at the walk the hands will follow the movement of the head, but just softly restrain it from being extended too much; at the trot the hands will be steady, keeping the head in a normal position, with possibly a slight restraint backwards. Go down one long side of the manège and across the short side in this way, then start the diagonal across the school, slightly increasing the pace to stimulate as much energy and impulsion and eagerness to go forward as possible. Before the halfway point apply the legs forcefully and at the same time yield a little with the hands to allow the horse to extend his head as he extends his forelegs. The rider should be able to feel the increased drive of the hocks and see the lengthened movement of the shoulders. One, or at the most two, long strides like this will be enough. Then relax the aids and let the horse calm down, going into an ordinary gait and then to a collected gait, before repeating the lesson.

Do not expect a long extension at first; in any case it is the energy of the movement which counts. Strive to have the horse going forwards with his head slightly extended beyond the normal, which requires very sensitive and accurate actions of the hands. Too often a horse is seen doing an extended trot with his head tucked in to his chest to a taut rein. The rein tension has to be firmer than normal, but the hands must be further forward. They can also be held lower down, if desired, to allow the horse to lower his head as he extends it. It is most desirable to have an observer for this movement, if not for any others, to check on its quality, and, if possible, to take moving pictures of it for study at leisure. Finally the horse should be able to start to build up the extension a stride or two after turning on to the diagonal, bring it to its peak in the last two or three strides before the centre, hold it the same distance afterwards, then gradually contract again.

The extended canter needs more space than is usually available in any normal manège; in competitions the minimum is the long side of the arena, sixty metres (65.6 yards); so it is best practised out of doors. The same procedures apply, the extension being obtained from the ordinary school canter. This is a fairly high action, but as the horse's steps extend they will become flatter and also faster. The extended trot, it must be emphasised, is not a *campagne* school movement but purely a training exercise and test performance. Out of doors any increase of speed above the ordinary trot is made by going into the canter and gallop. This, of course, does not apply to high speed trotters and hackneys, whether ridden or driven, who are specialists.

The turn on the haunches while moving, or pirouette, is conventionally a high school movement, but it is also a highly practical, indeed necessary, accomplishment for any outdoor horse (see page 238), so it properly comes in here at the end of basic training.

As usual let us base the work on the official requirements of the F.E.I. *Rules for Dressage Competitions.*

'*Half-pirouette.* This is the half-turn on the haunches. The forehand commences the half-turn tracing a half circle round the haunches, without pausing, at the moment the inside hindleg ceases its forward movement. The horse moves forward again, without a pause, upon completion of the half turn.

During this movement the horse should maintain his impulsion and should never in the slightest move backwards or deviate sideways. It is necessary that the inside hindleg, while forming the pivot, should return to the same spot each time it leaves the ground.' (Section 413 (a).)

This half-turn (180 degrees) is sufficient for all practical purposes, and can be carried out at walk, trot and canter, gallop.

The first lessons are of course at the walk, starting from a collected walk. Towards the end of a lesson, choosing a time when everything has gone smoothly and horse and rider are mentally calm, practise the halted half-turn on the haunches on both reins. Then go into a collected walk on the long side of the manège and at the corner make a sharp turn and continue it round so that the horse goes back parallel to the track and in the opposite direction. Repeat this at the other end, when the turn will be on the opposite rein to the first one. Then gradually shorten the circle until the hindquarters become the centre of the circle, which has the length of the horse as radius. Do not halt, but with the inside direct rein, fully supported by the outside indirect rein and outside leg, lead the forehand round the quarters, the rider's legs keeping up the impulsion and the movements of the hindlegs, particularly the inside one, which should step up and down in the rhythm of the collected gait. There must be no pause when the turn is complete, the horse moving forward at once.

The movement can also be developed from the renvers or quarters out (page 118). Once again start with a collected walk up the long side of the manège; about halfway make a normal turn which will merge into the renvers position, heading back the way you have come, but well off the track. Do the renvers back to the corner, and then make the moving turn from there. The horse will already be in the right position for it, head bent in the required direction, body flexed longitudinally, and the outer feet stepping across the inner.

Assuming that the horse is destined for outdoor activities, great precision is not required, the important thing being instant obedience and smoothness of movement. I would recommend also the increasing use of the indirect rein to make the horse bridlewise, and, ultimately, schooling with one hand. After being practised at the walk and canter, the half-pirouette can be used in the suppling exercises already described (pages 173–5).

With the exception of jumping, which has the next chapter to itself, this brings us to the end of basic training. The horse should now understand the aids and be obedient to them. It should be supple and strong, and able to move straight. It should be well balanced and light in hand. It should be capable of moderate collection. It should be quiet in traffic, and a comfortable and pleasant ride across country. It will have done some preliminary jumping.

This process will have taken anything from six to twelve months, and the horse should be four to four and half years old. It will still be green, very much a novice, but it will have been allowed to muscle up gradually and grow into its adult strength, and be ready for serious work and long spells of riding. It should be possible to recognise by now its potential, whether it has the aptitude for further advances in training and in what direction. These possibilities and the higher training involved will be discussed in Part IV.

19 Jumping

The general process of jumping has already been described above (Chapter 13), and, as we have seen, the horse is on the whole quite willing and able to jump, if he can see any immediate advantage to himself. It is the job of the trainer to make use of this characteristic and direct it to his advantage.

Mounted jumping should not begin until the horse is at least four years old. If the horse has been with the trainer since foalhood or from two to three years old, he can be given a little gentle encouragement by placing a small obstacle on the way to his water supply, or to the gate where his food will come from. If the lay-out of the fields will allow it, this is a good way of getting the young horse to enjoy jumping without doing himself any harm.

Apart from that he should do no jumping until he has progressed somewhat in the lunge work. Then, at the end of the lesson, he can be led over a pole on the ground. Always leave the jumping lesson to the end of the session, when the horse has been 'worked in' and settled down, so that there is less chance of excitement and resistance. The pupil should be encouraged to step over rather than jump it, literally take it in his stride. The idea is primarily to accustom him to an obstacle across his path. When he walks quietly over the pole in both directions, introduce the cavalletti, set first at the lowest and then at the higher position.

This procedure can then be repeated on the lunge. This requires considerable expertise, and everything should be carefully prepared beforehand. Do not stop the proceedings to fix up a jump in front of the horse, but have one in position (the usual pole at first) somewhere near the lungeing area. At the right time, towards the end of the lesson, manoeuvre the lunge circuit gradually towards the jump, at the same time making it more of an oval than a circle, until the horse sees the pole on the ground in front of him, crossing his path. As he will have already got used to this in the leading lessons, it should not cause him any alarm, despondency or even excitement. Let us hope that he will take it quietly in his stride as he did

183

when led. The reason for the oval track is so that the horse will approach and take the obstacle on a straight line and not on a curve. Two or three turns over the pole will be enough for one lesson.

It is very desirable that every obstacle shown to the horse after this should be heavy and solid and fixed. Peg the cavalletti into the ground for these lessons, and, later on, have the higher fences as solid as possible. The young horse must definitely know when he has hit it, and so be all the more inclined to miss it the next time. It will be useful to have an assistant waiting beyond the jump to give the horse an immediate reward, before he continues on the lunge circuit. The reward should not be given if he hits the obstacle. So deterrent and reward will combine towards the desired end. The great thing is to face the horse with obstacles that are well within his capacity at any given stage, not to over-face him at the start. If the horse runs out, circle him round again to approach the jump and assist him at the last moment with the lungeing whip above his hocks. If he persists in refusing, lower the jump and make him take it at a faster pace. A tendency to rush at a fence should be checked at once, by moving back with the lunge rein and guiding the horse past the jump. Then circle him a few times to steady him down, and approach the jump again at a walk.

Jumping on the lunge can continue progressively but slowly until the horse will go calmly over heights of up to three feet, by which time he should be ready for jumping with a rider on his back. Always put on a neckstrap when ridden jumping work is to be done, and use it when necessary, to avoid any risk of interfering with the mouth at this early stage.

Begin again at the beginning, over a pole on the ground at the end of a normal lesson. A few times over it at the walk and trot should be sufficient, after which the cavalletti can be brought into use progressively at the three heights. Schooling on the flat is the essential preparation for jumping. The pre-jumping lesson should be steady work at the walk and trot, with circles, halts and half-halts, and rein-backs, so that the horse is stepping out well and light in hand.

If you have an assistant, at a given signal from you he will place the cavalletto, at its lowest height first, across the track. If you are on your own, then you will have to dismount and do it yourself, or arrange to have it put in position beforehand in a separate manège. If you have had to do it yourself at the time, circle round one end of the school once or twice, then go

large and approach the jump at an energetic trot, the legs acting to make the horse use his hocks. In spite of the fact of
having seen this thing many times before when on the lunge,
the presence of a rider on his back may change everything, and
he will try to have a look at it, or get fussed and lose his cadence,
not being able to make up his mind actually to jump or step
over it. At this stage you want him to stride over it, so hold
him fairly firmly between hand and leg and push him forward
without any alteration of your position. Repeat until he goes
over smoothly without losing cadence. Make much of him
once he is over.

When he is thoroughly practised at all three heights of the
single cavalletto, introduce a second one; both should be at the
lowest height and three or four yards apart. Once again approach them at walk and then trot, and then at the middle
height, six to eight inches. Then close them up, once again back
at the lowest height, to one step apart, four to five feet (this
distance depends on the size and normal stride of the horse).
The horse should step over the two quietly without interrupt-
ing its stride. This is really a gymnastic exercise, to make
the horse use his hocks, balance himself, and pick his feet
up. Once he does this well at the middle height at walk
and trot, repeat it over three and then four cavalletti in
series.

The horse should then be ready for higher jumps, for which
a post-and-rails will be more suitable. The bar, heavy and solid,
should start at eighteen inches, and should be placed in front
of the uprights, not behind them, making it more difficult to
dislodge, and the uprights should be pegged into the ground.

Warm the horse up over a twelve-inch cavalletto and carry
straight on to the post-and-rails at a steady trot. Squeeze with
the legs three strides before the jump, lean forward and say
'Up!' Pat him once he is over, but do not pull up, or else he
will get the idea of always stopping after a leap, which could
be ludicrous as well as annoying. Pay great attention to making
the horse go straight at the jump, not wandering off to one side
or the other, which might be an incipient refusal. Wings can be
useful, but, if the poles are reasonably long, at least eight feet,
it should be possible to dispense with them, unless the horse
continually runs out. But the more likely tendency will be
to get excited and rush at the jump. Two or three cavalletti
in series about ten feet from the jump will have a steadying
effect. The horse should be exercised in taking the jump from
both directions; but alter the pole so that it is more or less

fixed. Don't forget to have a pole on the ground underneath the upper rail to act as a ground line.

If the horse knocks this low jump, it is probably due to a badly timed take-off and slack movement. Place a pole about two feet in front of the jump, and use the legs more strongly at the approach to increase impulsion. If he persists, lunge him over higher fences than the ones for mounted work, and exercise him over a series of cavalletti as before.

When the horse takes the first low jump calmly and smoothly, without hitting it, raise the pole to two feet. After that point is reached, free jumping practice in a lane can be introduced. An oval lane, as described in Chapter 13, page 128 *et seq* is the best, partly because of greater facility of control and partly because the corners prevent rushing and improve balance.

Push up the stirrup irons to the bars, knot the reins, and lead the horse into the lane; point the horse at the first fence and run with him towards it, then get into the centre of the lane with a lungeing whip. Hesitation on the part of the horse will probably be the least likely trouble; but if he does stop, use the lungeing whip on his hocks. If the horse seems nervous, put a trained horse in beside him and let them go down together. If an assistant is available, the task is made so much easier, the trainer remaining in command of the operation in the centre of the lane, the assistant leading the horse in and greeting him with a bowl of corn at the exit, and leading him quietly in a circle for a few minutes.

One circuit of the lane a day is sufficient. The fences will be upright at first, but gradually they can be varied by the introduction of spread fences, and double combinations or in-and-outs. The lane jumps will always be higher than the ridden jumps. Ridden work can now follow the pattern of the liberty work in the lane but always at a lower height.

To introduce a spread jump when ridden, start with two cavalletti at the top height of twelve inches close together, and gradually separate them to two feet. In the lane the horse will be jumping a spread of three feet, two feet high. After the cavalletti, two post-and-rails up to eighteen inches high and two and a half feet apart will be introduced. The dimensions in the school will increase proportionately to those in the lane up to a limit of about four feet.

This, of course, will take time, first of all because the amount of jumping each day should be strictly limited in the beginning. It is possible to proceed more quickly, many people do; but the horse is still young and comparatively immature, even at four years, however strong he may be, and there is always the danger of strain on the legs and of the horse getting sour and fed up with it, instead of enjoying the jumping as he should.

The above plan of work does not have to be rigidly adhered to. The important thing is the notion of progressive advancement, and of making no step forward until the previous position has been completely consolidated. 'No advance without security,' as one's bank manager says, and sometimes not even then. Every horse is different and will progress at different speeds; the trainer must keep the principles in mind and adjust their application to his special circumstances and the means available. If a separate jumping lane is not feasible, it should be possible to rig up a temporary one in a covered school, or even in an outdoor manège.

A tendency to drop the hind feet over a jump and hit the pole may well be due to weakness or laziness, and consequent lack of engagement of the hindquarters. More oats and more intensive schooling on the flat could be the answer. A thin iron bar or tube placed on top of the pole can often help; it is not harmful or damaging, provided it is passively used, but the different feel of it and noise will surprise the horse, who will try to avoid it in future. Exercises over cavalletti in series will also strengthen the hindleg action and make it more elevated.

Rushing can be dealt with in various ways. If the horse's intention is noticed in time, some distance from the fence, nip it in the bud with a quick halt, then proceed at a collected trot to within three strides of it. The introduction of two or three cavalletti about ten strides in front of the jump will also have a restraining effect. If the rushing starts at the last minute, turn the horse away from it, circle once or twice, then start again. None of these remedies will probably be effective the first time; it is calm and patient repetition which does the trick.

In the lane the horse will almost certainly go at a canter, but in ridden work up to a height of two feet six inches all the work should be at a trot. Most of it can be out of doors, and the jumps varied a bit – oil drums, hurdles with a pole on top, a wall – and they will generally be upright. With the jumps still at two feet six inches, start cantering up to them. Trot to within ten strides, then break into a canter. Use the legs and hands to create enough impulsion without increasing the pace, and give the horse absolute freedom at the take-off, holding on the neck strap. If he has not had the benefit of the lane to prepare him, practise him jumping at the canter on the lunge.

From now on the obstacles can be progressively raised in

height and varied in shape and spread. As has already been mentioned (page 128) timing is all important, and the great difficulty lies in judging one's position at some distance from the obstacle so that one can arrive precisely at the critical point, three strides in front of the take-off point. By trial and error on a trained horse that point can be fixed for every fence in the field, with an allowance for the extent of the take-off zone, and that point can be marked with a stone or flag or something. This will greatly help the trainer to place the horse at, say, ten strides from the fence so that he will come correctly at the end.

More practice can be given now over spread jumps. Begin with the triple bar – the staircase type of fence – which is actually the easiest of all big fences. Start with a simple post-and-rail construction. If the highest pole is two feet six inches, the lowest pole can be a ground line, the middle one eighteen inches, and the total spread three feet six inches; dimensions will increase in roughly these proportions.

For the more difficult parallel bar type, start with a false parallel, i.e. with the front pole lower than the rear one, so that the horse can see both poles clearly. Making the highest pole three feet, the near one should be two feet six inches, and the distance between them three feet six inches. Have a low cavalletto just in front of the front pole to make a ground line and encourage the horse to spread himself. In the true parallel bars, both elements of the fence will be the same height.

Another variation is the open ditch, which is in fact a triple bar with the middle element removed. The pyramid type again starts as a triple bar, but with the lowest element removed, and with a pole behind the centre element the same height as the one in front; also known as a double oxer, from the old type of country fences designed to keep cattle in, having a centre post-and-rails (or wire) fence with a hedge on one side only (oxer) or on both sides (double oxer). The spread will be the same as for a triple bar but distributed equally on either side of the centre element. There will of course be a ground line. The elements can be varied almost infinitely so far as training and competition jumping are concerned: a centre wall with brush fences; a centre brush fence with rails or walls; the rounded 'pig pen' seen in American competitions and at the team Olympic jumping at Stockholm in 1956; plain rustic poles, and so on. In training, always put a pole on top of, or just behind, a brush fence, so that the horse will not be tempted to take a chance with it.

Have plenty of colour. Paint the poles red and white, blue and white, green and white. The horse is now known to be sensitive to primary colours (page 59), so the more he can be accustomed to the different colours that will face him in all future competitive activities the better.

One of the great, if not the greatest, jumping problem is water. It is not all that difficult to find natural water obstacles in the English countryside, but somehow horses never seem to like them. As in every other field of equine education, getting horses used to jumping flat ditches on the ground is a matter of progressive training. It should be possible to provide three ditches in the jumping paddock – two feet, five feet, and ten feet wide. Existing ditches in a field can often be adapted for the purpose.

A water jump is a spread jump, and the horse's first introduction to it can be in the manège over two poles or low cavalletti placed two feet apart. Approach with plenty of impulsion so that he will take it in his stride. Widen the gap gradually to four feet, and raise the near cavalletto to six inches. Next, widen the gap to six feet and put a twelve-inch cavalletto in the middle, which will encourage the horse to jump a little high as well as wide. The approach to this sort of obstacle should be a collected canter with the maximum of impulsion; the horse should be accelerating as he takes off. Three strides should be measured back from the lip of the jump and a mark placed there to guide the take-off. More than anything else jumping water successfully is a matter of exact timing.

The real thing can then be tackled in the open. As in the manège, line each edge of the ditch with a pole, so that it will appear familiar to the horse. There need not be water in the small ditch, but there should be in the two wider ones, showing a proper expanse of water not just a shallow puddle. If the horse persists in putting his foot in the water, or in refusing, put a post-and-rails, up to about two feet high in the middle. The jumpable width of the ditch can be increased by setting back the take-off fence a foot at a time up to three feet; but the horse should also be practised in jumping without any guide fence. The wider the fence the faster, within reason, the speed of approach, but there must always be something in hand to accelerate at the last three strides. The one thing to avoid is to come at the jump at a flat-out gallop, almost inevitably slowing up for the take-off.

The last type of obstacle the horse should get to know is the bank. This obstacle is more often found out hunting or on cross-country courses than in the show-jumping ring, except at a few permanent grounds like Dublin, Hickstead or Lucerne. I do not count the 'Derby' bank, which is not a bank in the ordinary jumping sense of the word. A training bank could be about three feet six inches high, with a small ditch on either side. Banking is a good education for the horse, even if he is not likely to see many of them in his career. As Paul Rodzianko said, 'it teaches the horse not to jump wildly but to think'. (*Modern Horsemanship*.) To take a bank well, the horse must stand back from it, which the ditch encourages him to do, leap well up so that he lands comfortably on the top, collect himself, change legs and spring out and down to the other side. A post and rails on the far side (the pole free to fall) will encourage him to do this. The trainer must take great care not to interfere with the mouth when banking, moving his position well forward and using the neckstrap.

The combination of two or three fences in a single series of jumps (double or treble) is a difficult problem for both horse and rider, and the former must be thoroughly fit and well muscled before these are attempted at any height. As always the beginning is with cavalletti at twelve inches high, set at first far enough apart for three jumping (canter) strides. The rough and ready method of calculating the distance between the two fences, from ground line to ground line is to add the height of each fence to the length of the number of jumping strides required. The latter is a variable, according to the size of the horse and its speed, but an approximate length for most purposes is about eight to nine feet. In the case of the cavalletti the minimum distance would be three strides eighteen feet plus two feet for the heights of the two obstacles, total twenty feet. This can be adjusted in the light of experience. There should be no sort of difficulty over this, and the gap can be narrowed to two and then one jumping stride. After that the fences are raised, the interval opened out again, and so on as the horse gains in experience. Then a third fence can be added to make the treble. At first let the distances be equal, but in time they can be varied – two and three jumping strides; three and two; one and two; one and three, and so on. So far use only upright types of fence, but finally the types can be varied – a spread and then an upright, two spreads, one upright and a spread; it all helps to increase the strength and agility of the horse.

In jumping combinations, the rider must help the horse as much as possible, first by keeping resolutely with the movement, and then by really *driving* the horse forward with his legs to work up the maximum impulsion and acceleration for the last part of the combination. At the same time he must not let the horse over-jump the first fence, or he will come wrong at the second, finding himself say one and half strides away, instead of two. An experienced horse will get the team out of trouble by putting in a short one, but one wants to avoid this in the early stages of training.

In the final stages of training the jumping will be all in the open, and the horse can be practised in getting away quickly after the landing. The rider must be ready, when the hindlegs come to the ground to lean forward with his weight off the quarters, and apply strong leg pressure so that the horse goes forward without losing either its balance or impulsion. In this way it is ready within three or four strides to face another jump or change direction; there is no loss of concentration.

In the jumping paddock there should be jumps in a straight line, in pairs if there is no room for more, at distances of five to ten strides apart, and fences at each end which have to be approached after turning a corner, and some at different angles in the centre of this framework. At first jump only two at a time, first in straight line, then changing direction. Gradually increase the number of fences jumped, until eventually all the jumps are taken as a specific course. In this practice keep the jumps low, three feet to three feet six inches, although you may have got up to four feet over single jumps. The risk of over-facing is a very real one at all times during training; once you *know* that the horse can easily jump higher if required, do not ask it of him too often.

In all this work the horse has always come straight to the fence, if possible to the centre of it. Now jumping at an angle can be practised, and the procedure is the same as when practising a rider (page 127 *et seq*), going back to cavalletti, singly then placed as double and treble combinations.

Give the horse a change from these artificial fences on the flat by taking him for an occasional run across country over as natural jumps as can be found or made up. Take him with an old hand to keep him company and, at first, to give him a lead and confidence. There is nothing like this in all stages of jumping training, provided you have a reliable horse 'tutor' to the novice.

If the horse starts knocking the fences, or refusing, he is probably being over-faced and having too much of it. Go back to lower fences and less jumping. It is impossible to say how much jumping should be done, but the trainer should err on the side of discretion. At the very early stages two or three jumps per session are sufficient, increasing at the low heights to perhaps a dozen jumps; but when the jumps get higher, reduce the number again, say half a dozen at the end of the normal schooling period.

The time spent on jumping training should be at least six months, and the horse should be rising five, if not older. He should show clearly by then what his true *métier* will be – show jumping, cross-country and eventing, high school. He may have reached his ceiling as a good hack, hunter, or one-day-event horse, and you can call it a day and not force him any higher, remembering the twenty-five centuries-old advice of Xenophon: 'What a horse does under compulsion he does blindly.'

It is time, anyway, to apply all the school work to practical affairs.

The excitement of polo

The speed of polo

The skill of polo

FOUR

Applications

20 Show Jumping

Modern show jumping is a highly specialised professional sport. Except in the Foxhunter competitions there is no room for amateur part-time performers, horses or humans. The horses as much as the riders are professionals. The old idea that show jumping is the image of hunting has died long ago; I doubt if any top show jumper ever sees a hound. It would do him good if he did, but he simply has not the time, with the spread of the indoor competition making show jumping an all the year round sport.

It is ruled in this country by the British Show Jumping Association as firmly and almost as autocratically as racing is by the Jockey Club. Gone are the happy-go-lucky days when show jumpers, mostly soldiers, and judges could make their own rules as they went along. The British Show Jumping Association came into being about 1921, but its writ did not run very far. In India in the 'twenties there used to be a lot of talk about B.S.J.A. Rules, but very few people, if any, knew what they were. Before World War I there used to be a picturesque custom, whether universal or not I do not know, of the winner of a jumping competition doing his 'lap of honour' actually over the jumping course. I recall at the Bath and West Show about 1913 when a rider was placed first and second and third in the big competition, whatever it was, and he rode one horse and led the other two faultless over the course. The rider was Harry Buckland, father of Mrs Betty Skelton, famous in the post World War II years as a producer of show ponies. Which goes to show that the modern show jumper has no monopoly of horsemanship or showmanship.

Apart from the greater sophistication of the fences and courses, which of themselves make the problems of today's riders and horses so much harder, the great difference between now and then is speed. In the old days there were no time limits; riders could, and did, take their time over a jump, not having to jump unless they felt everything was right. The whole thing was much more deliberate and precise, slats – the thin, easily detachable laths of wood placed on the tops of jumps

– putting a premium on accuracy, right up to the first years after World War II. The jumps were on the whole no lower than they are now.

Now the clock rules all. In any ordinary competition there is a time limit for the first round, and sometimes the second, but a race against the clock for the final jump-off. Some competitions are judged on time from the start. This has altered the whole pattern of show jumping, requiring new techniques and attitudes of mind from the participants. For a number of years it afflicted the horses with a pile-up of tack on their unfortunate heads – drop nosebands, gags, martingales, check reins – you name it they had it, all with the object of stopping the horse quickly. The drop noseband, a training device for correcting faults of head carriage and head shaking, became an instrument of torture by being lowered to the nostrils and tightened almost to the point of suffocation. The breathing of the horse so maltreated could be heard all round the ground. Happily, it began gradually to be realised that more and better training on the flat could be more effective in the long run than these gadgets. The B.S.J.A. also banned the use of a standing martingale with a dropped noseband.

For both the novice rider and the novice horse the last preparatory work for the show ring follows the same lines: practise in jumping with and against the clock, and over higher fences, up to four feet six inches. The latter lessons will be progressive, needless to say, and the top height jumped very sparingly.

For the former, the jumping field should be laid out as a jumping course with its distance measured. Start with the fences at three feet six inches, and, with the aid of an assistant with a stop watch, time yourself at different speeds. The minimum speeds, that is with the maximum time allowed for the round are laid down for all types of competition, both national and international. The B.S.J.A. Rules cover national competitions, the F.E.I. Rules international ones. Both codes provide for two types of competition, designated Table A and Table S under the former and Table A and Tables B and C under the latter. Would-be show jumpers must of course make themselves familiar with these rules, and they are summarised below.

B.S.J.A.

Table A1 In the event of equality of faults for first place in the second jump-off the prize money will be divided.

Table A2 In the event of equality of faults for first place in the second jump-off time will decide, i.e. the final jump-off will be against the clock.

Table A3 In the event of equality of faults for first place in the jump-off time will decide.

Table A4 In the event of equality of faults for any award in the first round of the competition time will decide. In the event of equality of faults and time for first place there may be a jump-off at the discretion of the judge.

Table A1 is used when there is no automatic timing, or unless otherwise stated. Table A2 is used in Foxhunter competitions and in B.S.J.A. championships, unless otherwise stated. Table A3 is used in Area International Trials. Table A4 is only used in special types of competition which do not concern us here.

Table S covers all speed competitions, and penalties are measured in seconds. Every time a fence is knocked down eight seconds are added to the total time taken on the round. Refusals penalise themselves by loss of time, except that the third refusal, as in every type of competition, eliminates.

The time ratings for Table A competitions vary according to the standard, and are based on the speed of yards per minute: 300, 328, 350, 382, 436 yards. The time allowed without loss of time penalties is calculated by the distance to be covered in a round; for a 600-yard course at 300 yards per minute the time allowed will be two minutes, and the time limit, after which a rider is eliminated, is twice that or four minutes in this example. At the top speed of 436 yards per minute the distance to be covered in two minutes is 872 yards.

In Table S competitions the speed is always 436 yards per minute for adults and 350 yards per minute for juniors. The penalty for being over the time allowed in every case is one-quarter fault for every second over.

Under F.E.I. Rules (*Rules for Jumping Competitions,* Chapter VIII), the normal speed for international competitions is 350 metres (382 yards) per minute. In speed competitions it is the same, and for nations cup competitions it is 400 metres (436 yards) per minute. For a puissance competition the first round speed is 300 metres (327 yards) per minute, with no timing thereafter.

Both the B.S.J.A. and the F.E.I. obligingly supply tables of times, distances and penalties in their Rules.

Another necessary piece of information is the minimum heights for fences. Under B.S.J.A. Rules (Para. 20), the the lowest height is three feet six inches for the first three fences and three feet nine inches thereafter (all these figures are for first rounds only); the maximum starting height for Grade C is four feet; for Grades B and C is four feet three inches; for young riders and Grade B four feet six inches. For ponies the Grade J.C. height is three feet nine inches and for Grade J.A. four feet three inches. In international competitions the heights of fences start from 1.30 metres. (Four feet three inches.)

The inside distances for combinations vary under both rules from twenty-three feet (seven metres) to thirty-nine feet five inches (twelve metres). The distance between the starting line of a course and the first fence varies under B.S.J.A. Rules from seven yards to twenty-seven yards, and under F.E.I. Rules twenty-five metres (eighty-two feet) and six metres (twenty feet); and the distance from the last fence to the finishing line is seventeen to twenty-seven yards and fifteen metres (forty-nine feet two inches) and twenty-five metres respectively.

Incidentally, the actual rate of progress at 300 yards per minute is 10.3 miles an hour, and at 436 yards per minute it is just under 16.5 miles an hour. Obviously the horse will be travelling a good deal faster than that at certain periods during the round; and jump-off speeds against the clock will be greater still.

Another point to be considered is the distance between non-combination fences, for the modern course builder, following the lead of the late Jack Talbot-Ponsonby, will vary these distances with quite diabolical cunning. Apart from combinations, successive fences can be unrelated and treated quite separately by the rider, or related and considered together as one problem. The key distance given by Talbot-Ponsonby ('Testing by Distance', *Light Horse*, May, June, July, 1962) is eighty feet, and simple distances were fifty-five, sixty-five and seventy-five feet. Problems are created by shortening these distances, for example to fifty-one, sixty-two and sixty-nine feet respectively. These are slightly less than six, eight and nine strides, and the rider has to make adjustments accordingly. In a competition the rider is able to walk the course, during which he must check all such distances carefully, without which knowledge he cannot make a coherent jumping plan.

Another problem arises from the siting of successive fences. They can be in a straight line and reasonably straightforward, or they can be set just off the line, requiring a change of direction. The basic shape of a jumping course is oblong or elliptical with a figure-of-eight design. Fences placed on the short sides or on the centre diagonal can be placed so that the rider can go straight on after the previous jump and make a normal turn or circle, or, by slightly altering the angle or moving nearer the longer line of jumps, they can demand a deviation by the rider, which has got to be planned for in advance.

These and similar problems can be prepared in the practice course and worked on first at lower heights and slower speeds, until the horse and rider become really proficient. It would be wise for the rider to practise walking the course on his home ground, for, other things being equal, the correct assessment of distances beforehand is at least half the battle in jumping competitions. The rider will have already learnt in his preliminary training how to estimate speeds at various gaits, and, if a sand track is available, he can work out on the ground the actual stride lengths of the horse, or horses, he is dealing with. This will enable him to deal with the distance, problems already posed above, and all sorts of other ones.

The solution, of course, is to vary the length of the stride between the obstacles so that the horse will reach the further one correctly placed for the take-off. The usual way is to shorten the stride, making seven, nine and ten in the above instance. Shortening makes things rather easier for the horse than lengthening, the action of the driving leg aids and retarding rein aids causing strong engagement of the hocks and so producing greater propelling power. Take care that there is no reduction in speed; this is not quite the same as an exercise in collection, although the previous training in collection will certainly facilitate the operation.

Sometimes, in a speed competition or if the horse has overjumped, lengthening the stride may offer better chances of success, so it as well to practise it too over these same lower fences. Here the aids are as for the school extension: driving action of the legs, and yielding forward of the hands slightly, then steadying. Very often a horse, particularly in a combination, will lengthen his stride of his own accord.

Bearing these methods in mind will give a new significance to practice in walking the course, even if you happen to have laid it out yourself. Watching the methods of top show jumpers will also be a fruitful exercise. Get used to making your own walking strides an exact yard in length, and always pace out the course on the route that you propose to take, so that you can translate it into strides of the horse. All of this requires great concentration, but the standard of modern show jumping is such that any kind of success is impossible without *preparation* and *concentration* all the way.

There is no need to spend too much time on the ring work; the real training comes with experience in actual competition, and I cannot repeat too often the necessity to avoid over-jumping or over-facing the horse, making him bored or sour. Take him out hunting as a recreation. The company of large numbers of other horses and people will prepare him for the excitements of the collecting ring and the general atmosphere of competition. The thrill of a hunt, which undoubtedly is felt by horses, can well liven up a too placid temperament. In the summer a few one-day events in novice classes or with riding clubs can also be a useful preparation. A few horses graduate to show jumping from this sport, a notable example being, of course, Merely-a-Monarch.

The education of rider and horse does not end with the first show-jumping competition; in a sense it is only beginning. Competition, especially with the speed element, makes tremendous demands on both. The good style of the rider, easy enough to maintain in the quiet conditions of the manège and jumping field, may well go to the winds from the stress and strain of it all. All professional show jumpers – and, let us face it, irrespective of money rewards, show jumping is a professional sport – develop their own characteristic styles, because the taking of big jumps at speed and odd angles requires unusual efforts, not to say contortions, of the body; but correct basic training will always show itself. And two things will always be noticeable: the freedom of the horse's head, and keeping of the body weight well off the quarters.

Choose for the first formal debut a small local show, one if possible where the opposition is not likely to be too strong, not worrying about the prize money, which anyway will be small. Make the first class a Foxhunter or Grade C, or both if they are available. If you and the horse have been able to gain experience in riding club events so much the better. Nowadays riders go quickly into high grade competition, perhaps using the various young rider competitions as stepping stones; many come up through the junior classes. With an experienced horse the more competitions you can go in for, and so the more experience you can gain, the better; there is really no limit except your purse and the stamina of the horse. The novice horse, however, should be taken on quietly in his first season, no matter how much promise he shows. Hold him back the first year, then he will really go places the next.

A lot has to happen before the first adventure in the ring. Check all equipment very carefully at home beforehand, make sure that nothing vital is left behind; and always take spare parts, especially girths, stirrup leathers and irons, bits, reins, straps. Prepare everything the day before you actually start for the show, leave early, and don't forget to send your entry before the closing date. There should always be a vet and a farrier available at any show, but take your own first aid kit all the same.

The routine before a class is well established: exercise, warming-up, studying the plan of the course, weighing in, walking the course, waiting in the collecting ring, and then into the ring, and out again two minutes later.

The plan of the course has to be posted conveniently to the collecting ring, and the first task is to study it carefully, noting the various distances between jumps and their positions and make a preliminary plan of campaign, subject to the final inspection of the actual course.

The time spent warming-up depends on what exercise has been done before that. If the class is a very early one – as Foxhunter and Grade C classes usually are – the two can be combined.

Warming-up is the process of loosening up the horse, and suppling and exercising the muscles to be used in jumping. Begin with fifteen to twenty minute walk and trot on a loose rein; then about the same time doing suppling exercises on a circle; half-halts, turns, rein-backs, all with the purpose of making him obedient to the aids, and getting him alert and on his hocks; finally about ten minutes of jumping practice.

Shows provide practice jumps of the post-and-rail variety, officially placed in the exercising area, which often coincides with the collecting ring, where there is always a milling crowd of show jumpers in various stages of exercising and warming-up. Most of them seem to jump incessantly, but with a novice horse it is better to do three or four jumps, lower than those he will meet in the ring, perfectly and leave it at that.

All this work should be timed to end about fifteen minutes before the class is due to start, and the riders pour into the ring to walk the course. This process has already been explained, and practised, and there is not much to add except to stress the need to concentrate on the distances and angles to each other of related fences, including doubles, noting especially the positions of jumps following the end of one line. You have to plan your line one or even two jumps ahead, so that the horse will make an easy circle and come straight at the next jump; as you go over a jump you will always be looking in the direction of the next fence, wherever it may be. During this inspection time you can also take note of possible short cuts in the expectation – or pious hope – of getting into the jump-off. This is the last chance of a close inspection of the course, so make the most of it.

If you are high up in the jumping order, on your return to the collecting ring, weigh in, have a final check of the tack, mount, and walk the horse round quietly until your number is called. If you are low down in the starting order, you may have an hour or more to wait. In this case your warming-up plan can be modified, carrying it out after you have walked the course instead of before.

It is customary on entering the ring for your round to salute the judges, or the V.I.P. watching, if there is one, not likely at 9.00 in the morning. Then canter round quietly until the signal to start is given, taking this opportunity to see how your plan made on the ground matches up with the different look of things from the saddle. Have a good look at the fences, in case a pole is not properly down in its cup, or a gate has not been adjusted after the previous round, which could tell against you in your own round if not corrected beforehand. You have the right to tell the jump stewards and have it put right.

The tension of being in the ring and eagerness to get on with the business may tempt you to pass through the starting lights before the signal to start is given, when of course you will be eliminated. Not to worry. Better riders than you have done that in bigger competitions. It is just one of those things. Sometimes, however, with all the competing noises outside the ring, it is difficult to hear the signal, and and you may not be sure whether it has been sounded or not. If in doubt, ask.

Once the 'go' signal has been given, you are finally on your own to put all the long period of training to the proof. The horse does the jumping; the rider's part is to guide and restrain it whenever necessary, so that its movements between the fences and coming up to them conform as closely as possible with the plan you have made. Things of course do not always go according to plan, and may not do so the first time; so be prepared to be opportunist and adjust your own actions to the changed situation.

The great thing is to try to keep the horse in regular rhythm, especially before and after the approaches, and to steady him if he has knocked down a pole, or even rapped it hard, which always excites a horse for a few seconds and throws it out of balance. The clatter of a rapped pole has an ominous sound, but resist the temptation to look back; it takes away from concentration on the next jump, at the least. Even if the pole has come down and you are out of the hunt for that competition, in the interests of the horse help him to recover and regain his balance, so that in spite of that one unfortunate mistake he jumps a good smooth round. At this time maintaining regularity and preserving the confidence of the horse are more important than a clear round, though of course it will be nice to do one.

Once over the last fence accelerate as much as possible up to the finishing line. You are being timed in this first round, though not actually racing against the clock, and you do not want to risk losing time faults. Once past the automatic timing lamps, slow down gradually, circling the arena if necessary, calming the horse with the voice and giving him a congratulatory pat, and leave the ring at a quiet trot. If you have no further interest in the competition, walk quietly back to the horse lines, off-saddle, inspect legs and mouth for any bumps or cuts, put a rug on, give him a drink, and have him walked round and let him have a quiet graze. Then put him in his box with a feed, and go back to watch the rest of the jumping. There is always something to be learned from other people's performances and mistakes.

On the other hand you may have had a clear round. In this case, on leaving the ring, dismount, loosen the girths, put a rug on, and have the horse walked round quietly, while you take stock of the situation. Supposing there are forty starters – as there can easily be in Foxhunter or Grade C classes – and you went twentieth, there are twenty more to go, which means about an hour to wait for the jump-off. There may be fifteen clear rounds, which could mean another twenty-five minutes if you were the last in the draw. Assuming you have the full time to wait, rest the horse for about twenty minutes, then spend forty minutes warming-up, on an outside exercising area if possible, concentrating on quick starts and halts, and achieving good acceleration for short gallops, and turns and small circles. Then take him three or four times quickly over practice jumps. For the last twenty minutes before you go in have him walked round briskly while you look at the course. It is not allowed to walk the course for the jump-off, but you can inspect it from the ringside, noting the fences that have been removed, and the new circles and turns that have been introduced as a result; if you are not early in the draw, you can watch those who are and see how they go, noting what sort of times are achieved and the speed required to do it.

If you went very early in the first round, say among the first ten, you can take the horse back to the box for an hour and let him relax completely. If you went last, there is no time for anything but one or two sharp gallops to work up speed. You have to be entirely flexible and adjust your plans to the situation; but the great thing in show jumping is that it is as nearly precise in timing as it is possible to be, and you can tell almost to the minute when you will be required. The order of starting is always drawn for in a timed jump-off, and naturally the best place from every point of view is the last. The first rider in a jump-off rarely wins. Sometimes the course is left as it is, but more often it is shortened by cutting out some of the fences, most of the remainder being raised in height.

With a novice horse do not attempt to push him too much or cut corners too sharply; you do not want to over-face him with impossible jumps and consequently dishearten him. Be content with only a slightly faster speed than normal, and try to gain it by a lengthening of stride thus covering more ground at the same speed. At the same time he will need more impulsion for the higher fences. Steady him before the fences, and take generous circles at the corners, concentrating on a clear round before anything else; it can usually bring you into the money.

A novice rider on a trained horse can take more chances – though remember that a Grade C horse is bound to be inexperienced too. But he should also take things steadily; it is not flat-out galloping that wins jumps-off against the clock, but handiness and balance. A mad gallop at a big fence can end in disaster, for the horse will come at it unbalanced and out of control, liable either to refuse or to take it by the roots. Quick starting, stopping, turning and accelerating again, so that you cover the shortest possible distances, taking fences at angles with short approaches, are what brings success. A speed round well ridden is very exhilarating for the rider and spectacular for the onlooker.

When all is over there should be a post mortem. Every rider, in his early days at all events, should have a trainer or mentor with him to watch his performance and comment on it as mercilessly as he likes. It is only by intelligent and fair criticism that one gains experience and improves. Did you lose impulsion at this jump? Or push him too close at that one? Did you turn him too sharply and face him too suddenly at a fence in the jump-off? Did you get left behind during the double? If photographs were taken, they can be studied later to see how they confirm, or otherwise, the observations of the day. How did the horse go at each fence? Which ones did he find difficult? All this deep self-questioning can help to iron out weaknesses in both horse and rider.

Things will not always go as easily, according to plan, as described here. The horse is not a machine, but a thinking, sensitive creature. He will have his own ideas about what is possible or impossible; if he has been well trained he will often valiantly attempt the impossible, or he will decide definitely that he has been presented wrongly or unfairly at a jump and refuse it. Recriminations are pointless; he must be circled out of the way and re-presented, and nine times out of ten he will take it without difficulty. Other times a horse can feel out of sorts, his legs may be tender, he may have a touch of colic without you knowing it, or anything, and he will decide that he has had enough and refuse point-blank to jump. It is impossible to fathom all the motives of a horse, however well trained he may be, however courageous. Bow to the inevitable and take him out; but you are allowed to jump another fence after being eliminated so that you and the horse can end on a good note. Choose an easy one in the direction of the exit.

Bad crashes can occur, especially over spread jumps. If the horse has decanted you, no great harm has been done; but if the horse has fallen, perhaps entangled with poles, then trot him out quickly before remounting, and if he shows any sign of lameness, retire. It may only be a momentary tenderness, but it could be something worse. Give him the benefit of the doubt.

All this and other idiosyncrasies of the horse in the ring can be madly irritating, but nothing is worse than showing it, either publicly in the ring or outside it. Do not, as I have seen people do, flog your horse in fury out of the ring, or dismount and thrash him in the collecting ring or at the horse box, or pull his mouth about. In the first place, such 'punishment' has no effect, because it has no direct relationship to the offence, if it was an offence. Experienced riders can sometimes correct a horse sharply after a refusal, or give him two or three cuts with the whip because they think he has become sluggish; it may be effective, but it never looks well. In any case the jumping ring is not the place for correction, schooling or punishment, so the rider bent on making show jumping his career should school himself to the discipline of patience and complete control of his feelings.

Charges of cruelty have often been made against show jumpers, sometimes well founded, sometimes not. The demands and the high standards of modern show jumping, the rewards that can now be won, and indeed the dedication of riders to the sport, have resulted in all sorts of questionable methods being used in all countries at some time or other – rapping, the use of spiked poles, the deliberate bringing down of a horse over a fence, turpentine on the legs – and they have all been condemned by both national federations and the F.E.I. The B.S.J.A. and the F.E.I. Rules are very clear, and both these organisations have now stipendiary stewards to enforce them at national and international events. There is no doubt that the effect of both official action and public opinion has been salutary.

Meanwhile the novice rider and the novice horse have before them the choice of pursuing the path of show jumping fame and achievement to its ultimate limits by becoming dedicated professional devotees, giving their whole lives to a most demanding sport, or of simply enjoying themselves at the lower levels with limited appearances, as not a few do. The latter has the advantage of not being restricted to one sport; he can dabble in one-day events, hunter trials, and even dressage and combined training competitions and have a great deal of fun. The former must specialise, and every event he goes in for from now on will add to his experience and skills, provided he has the firm foundation of basic training.

21 The Outdoor Horse — Cross-Country

The simplest application of the training of an outdoor horse is hunting. The training requirements for a hunter were, and often still are, considered to be modest in the extreme – good manners, willingness to gallop, ability to jump, and reasonable stoppability. But under the influence of dressage training, particularly in horse trials, it has been realised that a hunter is all the better for a good degree of basic training, such as has been described. From another point of view, hunting is part of that basic training; most horses who take part in competitive outdoor sports, except perhaps polo and flat racing, start their career as hunters.

As far as the rider is concerned, the more training he has had and the more secure seat he has established, the happier he, and his horse, will be in any of these pursuits. It will be especially valuable for him, if he plans to go in for riding and producing show horses, whether hunters, cobs or hacks.

Showing hunters and cobs looks a rough and ready sort of business, but a considerable amount of work and skill goes into it. The horse has to be amenable and move well at normal paces, walk, trot and canter, and to be unmoved by crowds and noises. He also has to gallop full out in a comparatively restricted area, for even the biggest show ring is not exactly a wide open space, and the horse must be well balanced and controlled to get round the corners. In addition he has to stand up well when being inspected for conformation, and to trot freely in hand. Finally, he must stand quiet to be mounted by a stranger, the judge, and then go well for him; though it is noticeable that many horses go better for the judge than for their own riders, the former being usually very fine horsemen. All this is nothing but basic training applied to special circumstances.

The hack is an outdoor horse, indeed all the best hacking used to be done in the country, while the elegant social riding in the Row or the Bois was near-dressage. The hack was the horse on which farmers rode round their farms, or which carried hunting men to the meet while grooms walked the hunters well in advance, a practice which was commemorated in the old show category of 'covert hack'. This was a rougher, sturdier type than the other category, the 'park hack', which had to have the elegance and élan to show off its rider to his girl friend in the carriage and pair, and stand still while he flirted with her under the eyes of the chaperon.

The modern hack is rarely seen outside a show ring – or a dressage arena, and is mostly ridden by girls anyway. The training of a hack used to be very advanced indeed, two-track movements and flying changes being included in the repertoire, and in the past they were nearly always ridden with one hand. To watch men like Jack Hance or Horace Smith or Sam Marsh or Robert Orrsich showing off hacks was both a pleasure and an education. For lightness and handiness, as well as steadiness, a well-trained hack was hard to beat. Polo ponies, as I recall, made excellent, quiet hacks, though not usually show ring animals; perhaps it was, as Brigadier Lyndon Bolton has suggested (*Training the Horse*), because of the galloping they had to do. Owners of restive dressage horses might take note of this.

Modern show hack riders, under the influence of competitive dressage, ride firmly with two hands, and the old lightness and elegance is sadly lacking in most cases.

All this is by way of an introduction to the real present-day career of an outdoor horse (excluding show jumping), which is competitive cross-country riding. The basic, and oldest, form of this is *hunter trials*. With this one might include drag-hunting and paper-chasing, which are means of having good gallops over unseen country without undue waste of time and without the disappointments of blank days. They, in fact, can be an excellent way of preparing a horse for the more complicated competitions of hunter trials and *horse trials*, which is the general English term for the sport of the three-day and one-day event, known variously abroad, where they really started as the *Military*, because it was originally a competition for soldiers only and for troop horses and officers' chargers, the *concours du cheval complet d'equitation*, *Vielseitigkeits-prufung*, and so on according to the language of the country.

Hunter trials have all the image of horse trials without their complications. They are galloping competitions over prepared courses of varying distances up to three or four miles and up to thirty fences of various types, which aim at being as natural as possible. Most of the fences are solid, but a certain number have top poles which can be knocked down for the usual penalties. There can be half a dozen or so classes in a meeting for different types of horses, for riders going singly, in pairs, or in teams of three or four, in which case they are also judged on the style with which they approach fences together. All competitions are timed. A high degree of training is not required, but the more carefully a horse has been trained to jump, especially out of doors, the better. A horse that can gallop on and achieve a paddock jumping height of four feet or so should have no trouble.

Hunter trials can be used as a preparation for horse trials, or they can be competed in concurrently, or used as a relaxation from the more rigorous discipline of the latter with its triple aspect of formal dressage, cross-country and endurance, and formal jumping. As with all these far-flung events, hunter trials require careful organisation and good intercommunication, and a fair army of devoted voluntary helpers as judges, stewards, etc., which does not concern us here. They are exceedingly popular, with hundreds of events every year, mostly organised by hunts, riding clubs, Pony Club branches riding schools, and for the rider whose ambitions or purse will not carry him further they can provide enormous fun.

The horse trial is a sterner test altogether. It is, really, the apotheosis of all training, the comprehensive exercising of horse and rider in three contrasting, yet complementary, modes of horsemanship to produce a truly all-round horse and horseman. The horse must be able first of all to be calm and steady and obedient in a fairly circumscribed arena and able to show that purity of gait and regularity of rhythm at whatever stage the particular test requires up to moderate collection; at the same time he must be able on the second day, or an hour or two later in the case of a one-day event, to gallop at speed and with boldness over a cross-country course, with or without a steeplechase course, of varying length and severity; finally he must be capable of turning out fit after these exertions to behave as a Grade B show jumper.

The training process described in Parts II and III should have taken both rider and horse well up to the level of training in each department, indeed beyond it. The horse should be up to the standard of medium dressage tests, though he will of course start in the novice grade; he should be ready for Grade C show jumping; and he should be well practised in cross-country work. The job is to weld these accomplishments into one all-round horse.

The decision to enter a horse for horse trials may well have been taken very early in his training, but it is as well, before actually embarking him on this career, to consider the essential qualities for success in this sport. First of all the horse must be bold and eager, and he must be fast. As in show jumping the old enemy is Time. Throughout a horse trials competition the clock is ticking against you. There is a time limit for the dressage test, and you lose marks if you exceed it; the time allowance is liberal enough, but it is still there as a factor to be reckoned with. In the second phase, called the 'speed and endurance test' or the 'épreuve de fond', there is a time set for covering several miles of field and woodland ('roads and tracks') at a normal exercising pace, and so you have to watch that. On the steeple-chase course (about two and a half miles) a fast speed is required, something over twenty m.p.h., and over the cross-country course (four and a half miles) the speed is rather less, a bit over fifteen m.p.h., both circuits full of hazards which can delay one, and many marks can be lost. In the third show jumping phase there is quite a stringent time factor too; so you are virtually against the clock from start to finish. To keep up with it the horse must go at a good racing pace for an appreciable part of the time.

Then, to cope successfully with the dressage part of the test, and not jump out of the arena as some horses have been known to do, he must have a calm temperament. Finally, he must be sound and fit. The latter quality is the business of the rider, and will be considered later in Part V. If a horse has all these qualities in good measure, he should go far.

It is not a bad idea, in his fifth year to try the horse out in a few point-to-points. It will encourage a sluggish horse to gallop, get him used to taking fences at speed, and will give a very good idea of his maximum capability. By the same token point-to-point riding is an excellent preparation for the event rider. Besides giving him the necessary experience of jumping biggish fences at racing speed, it enables him to estimate distances before fences and judge his actual speed, which will stand him in good stead when riding against the clock on steeplechase and cross-country courses. Most successful event riders have ridden in point-to-points and/or hunter chases, and many more nowadays are taking it up both for preliminary practice and as a continuing kindred sport.

For the horse, however, this racing practice should not be overdone, there being a fundamental difference between the two skills of racing and eventing. The former – and hunting for that matter – is done in company with other horses, whose

210

presence round our novice both stimulates and reassures, conforming to the inherent gregariousness of his nature. The latter is done alone.

The difference is not so marked in a one-day event, when the various phases are quickly got through, the longest being the six minutes or so of the dressage test, and there are always intervals between that and the cross-country and jumping. In the three-day event the second, speed and endurance phase, consists of about ninety minutes of solitary riding, over fourteen and twenty miles, partly plodding along, partly hurtling over a steeplechase course and over a tricky cross-country course. It is quite a psychological challenge to the horse to ask it to do all this on its own, to move about in an isolated arena (the habit of relegating the usually sparse audience to a line twenty yards or more from the arena accentuates the isolation) and to face strange and often alarming obstacles by himself. All this has to be taken into consideration in the training of an event horse.

As always the preparation should be gradual and progressive. Begin at the riding club or Pony Club level with, separately, dressage competitions (preliminary and novice tests), and jumping competitions; then link them up with combined training tests, which are dressage with jumping. The great value of competition at this level is that it is usually light-hearted and so without the nervous strain of serious events.

However, the preliminaries for all these competitions must be taken seriously, and they should be carried out more or less as prescribed for show jumping (page 200 *et seq*), i.e. preparation and checking of tack, timing of arrival, preliminary exercise and warming-up, limited and adapted, of course, to the end in view. The great thing to remember about warming-up procedures before any kind of event is that they are exactly that – warming-up and suppling-up – not last minute attempts to school the horse. But the performance of your horse in these elementary tests will give you a clear guide as to his potentialities, and to strong and weak points, which can be improved upon or corrected.

The next step, obviously, is the one-day event. There were over fifty official ones organised under the auspices of the British Horse Society in 1971, and the number seems to be steadily growing. There are also several hundred slightly lower grade events during the summer organised by the Pony Club and riding clubs, which form the primary school of the sport.

The order of action of the one-day event is that it starts with the dressage test, which will be one of those prescribed by the

British Horse Society for that standard of event, preliminary, novice or elementary, copies of all the tests being available from the Society. One of the first actions of the aspiring eventer should be to join the Combined Training Group within the British Horse Society, which controls and co-ordinates all activities of this kind. After the dressage test there follow the cross-country and jumping phases, but not always in that order. Sometimes the jumping phase comes first and the cross-country phase last.

There has always been a division of opinion about this, but the consensus seems to be in favour of the latter order, although it is not strictly according to the general intention of the horse trials competition. The reason given, and it is a valid one, is that if the cross-country phase is run first, horses may have a long time to wait before their jumping turn arrives, in which chills can be caught, horses stiffen up, and general inconvenience caused. The jumping, being a lesser effort, does not cause such difficulties. The answer lies in proper horsemastership, but you must be prepared for either arrangement.

As in the case of show jumping, a great deal depends on your place in the starting order, and you should be told this before the competition starts. Unless you live close to the venue of the event, and are in the second half of the starting order, it is best to come the day before, and as early as possible on that day, so that you can follow the preparation procedure adequately. Sometimes, because of the number of entries, the dressage tests begin on the day before the actual competition, in which case you may have to come a day earlier anyway. Another problem caused by the popularity of this sport is that the event may not be able to accommodate all the entries and you may be balloted out of it altogether for one or more events. This makes it even more important to gain as much experience in riding club and other events.

The amount of time you give to warming-up depends on the individual horse, but it should not be less than hour, and should be timed to finish about fifteen minutes before you are due to go into the arena. Always begin the warming-up with some relaxed riding on a loose rein, to calm the horse down. But the whole process should be done as calmly and smoothly as possible; do not try to teach the horse something at the last moment, or get involved in any kind of argument with him. Let the atmosphere be as peaceful as possible.

Many, if not all, of the problems of the dressage test and the preparation for it, spring from a surfeit of oats unrelated to the work done. Stuffing a horse with oats is not necessarily making him fit; it fills him with energy, it is true, but to the point of intoxication, so that he is almost literally 'jumping out of his skin', as they say, and has to be worked for hours in order to calm him down sufficiently to get him into the arena at all. A balanced conditioning process is described in Part V.

After the warming-up process go into the collecting ring and walk round on a loose rein, with a rug on if it is chilly, until it is your turn. You are usually allowed to walk round the arena before actually going in, and those few minutes can be spent doing a few quiet suppling exercises and transitions. When you get the signal to go into the arena, do not rush it. Take your time to adjust the horse from whatever he was doing to the pace and attitude of mind appropriate to the entry. Take a wide circle at the far end of the arena so that you can come straight to the entrance from a good distance with the horse settled down at the appropriate pace, usually a trot. If you feel the rhythm is wrong, go round the arena again.

Once inside concentrate on the horse. 'Ride the "horse" during the performance and not the "test",' says Colonel d'Endrody most aptly (*Give Your Horse a Chance*). You will have memorised the actual test and practised all the movements with your horse, separately as well as combined in the test, which should not be done too often, as it tends to make the horse too familiar with the routine and bored. Now, with the order of movements fixed in the background of your mind, aim to present the horse to the judges in as brilliant and accurate performance as possible.

The official novice test is a very simple one, consisting of the basic gaits; walk, trot, canter; transitions and large twenty-metre circles and half circles three to five metres – in reverse, and of course the halt at the beginning and end of the test. The entry is at the trot. In the Pony Club championship the serpentine has been introduced into the test with excellent results. The aids for these movements are simple, straightforward ones, but they must be given very definitely and clearly, a stride before the point in the arena at which the change is required, so that the transition can be smooth.

After the entry there is the halt at the centre of the school. Start slowing down two or three strides in front of it so that the horse flows easily into the halt without a sudden jerk. The moment he stops yield the hands very slightly, so as not to be obvious to the judges, to tell the horse he has done rightly and to prevent fidgeting. If you feel him start to rest a hind foot, shift your weight and press with that heel and spur. Transfer the reins to the left hand and with the right hand remove your cap or hat with a generous sweeping movement, carry it down to the side, pause an instant, then replace it in the same way. If you are a lady, lower the right hand to the side, and bow from the hips. If you are a soldier, drop the right hand to the side smartly, hold it for a second, then raise it in a correct salute, lowering the hand briskly to the side directly after it. Then, in every case, take the reins in both hands again with a precise unhurried movement, pause a second, then move off. You are now being timed until the final salute. First impressions are very important, so spend time in training on the entry, halt and salute, and on the final movement and salute. It can gain you valuable marks.

Try to ride as relaxed as possible. Any tension of the rider will convey itself quickly to the horse. Keep the head erect but not fixed with a stiff neck. Other points of stiffness are the wrists and ankles; keep the hands and fingers always slightly in play, encouraging the horse to chew at the bit as he goes along, instead of having his mouth wide open through being pulled against. A little faster tempo than required, provided it is regular, will give an impression of eagerness and élan. If you have to make corrections or adjustments, try to do them with the hands and legs on the far side from the judges, and, if possible, at the more distant end of the arena from them.

The time from the end of the test to the start of the next phase will be short, so loosen girths, put on a rug and walk the horse round, changing tack if necessary. If the jumping comes next the same formal clothes are worn as for the dressage test; if it is the cross-country, the jacket is exchanged for a pullover, or some such, with the large back and front number flaps put on over it, and a proper crash cap.

Somehow or other time must be found to walk the courses. If the jumping comes after the dressage, there is time to walk that course then and there, and the procedure for show jumping applies (page 200 *et seq*). Walking the cross-country course takes longer and is more important. Its inspection is best done at leisure on the day before the event; on the day, if there is a long enough interval between the phases.

The length of the course will be between one mile and one and three-quarters, with sixteen to twenty obstacles, with a maximum height of three feet six inches and a maximum spread of nine feet. They are all fixed, and should be solidly built. The minimum speed for a novice course is 575 yards per minute, or just over nineteen and a half m.p.h. No marks are gained by exceeding this speed, but penalties at the rate of one per three seconds are incurred for going slower. For the Advanced and Intermediate classes the distance is two to two and a half miles, the heights and spreads of fences are – Advanced to three feet eleven inches and twelve feet, Intermediate three feet nine inches and twelve feet, and the speed is 656 yards per minute or just under twenty-three m.p.h. The number of fences will be between twenty and thirty.

There are two main problems here. First, how to approach and deal with the various fences; second, how to get the best speed over the course as a whole. The first problem is in fact the easiest to solve. Most of the obstacles will be straightforward, even if they look big, and it is comforting to remember that an obstacle is always more terrifying to the man on the ground than to the horse with his loftier viewpoint, which is why the observer is so often wrong in his diagnosis of the possible effects of various obstacles. The chief points to be decided are the angle of approach and the speed, and, in the case of alternative presentations of a composite obstacle, whether to choose the more difficult and quicker route or the safer but slower one. With a young and untried horse choose the latter. Each fence on the course must be considered in detail in this way.

The other problem is a time and motion one. In order not to lose time faults you have got to average nineteen and a half m.p.h. You will advisedly consider this too fast for a completely novice horse; so accept the fact of penalties, and settle for an average speed of eighteen m.p.h. Take for example the novice course of the Crookham Horse Trials at Tweseldown in 1968: 2,750 yards long, with a minimum time of four minutes forty-seven seconds. At fifteen m.p.h. this would take six minutes fifteen seconds, which would give thirty time penalties; fair enough for the first go.

Now look at the map of the course, which will show you that between some jumps there is quite a considerable distance, some of it, actually, at Tweseldown, on the racecourse itself, and that other fences come in groups of two or three, others at more or less regular intervals. There will be some sharpish turns and also some good wide circles. Obviously on certain parts of the course you will be able to go at a good gallop, sufficiently faster than fifteen m.p.h. to make up for the parts where you will have to go slow, a case of the swings and the roundabouts. Then with a rough idea of your riding plan in your head you set out to walk the course.

You will find, of course, what the map does not show, that

the course is hilly, sometimes short sharp climbs, sometimes a long hard pull up with several fences, some downhill going, and a few nice long spells on the flat. By pacing out the course and noting the distances of various parts of it, and the intervals between fences, you should get a fair idea of the variations of speed that will be more or less forced on you, where you must go slow, where you can make up time. Perhaps there will be 1,000 yards of fast galloping country, 1,000 yards of moderate speed, and 750 yards where you will have to go slow, for instance between closely related fences, up steep ascents, round sharp corners and so on. As in the case of a show jumping course, you may be able to note fences which you can take at an angle to save distance.

With these facts, and your own knowledge of your horse's speed and length of stride, you should be able to work out a riding plan for the whole course with reasonable accuracy. This can be a pre-determined average of fifteen m.p.h., you would have to aim at speeds of twenty, fifteen, and ten m.p.h. respectively. Whether you can achieve this time will show, and it will be extremely instructive to see how close you can get to the time for which you have planned.

The point of all this careful preparation is that by studying the ground closely in this way, you will acquire a very accurate knowledge of it, the type of going and the variations of contour. This will enable you to anticipate the various changes before you come to them, so that you can change gear, as it were, with the minimum delay, saving yourself the possibility of over-shooting a fence by coming at it too fast and having to haul the horse back on to the line, or of not being ready to accelerate directly you come to a fast galloping section. You will also be able to go the shortest way. All this will save many seconds on the round – and every three seconds saved is one penalty the less and reduce unnecessary wear and tear on the horse.

Your riding plan will tell you where you ought to be at certain times, so wear a wrist watch when you start out on the course and time yourself. It is always possible to save a few seconds by speeding up, but it is no use trying to make up large amounts of time lost by refusals or falls. You will always hope to have none, but the unforeseen always happens in this game, and you just have to accept them. Write off the lost time and carry on according to your riding plan.

This system of preparation applies to every level of event up to championship and international three-day events. It is described in considerable detail, together with many other aspects of horse training by Lieutenant-Colonel A. L. d'Endrody in his book, *Give Your Horse a Chance.*

The routine for a three-day event is more complicated than for a single day; the effort required of a horse is immeasurably greater. If possible get to the venue two nights before the event starts, so that the horse can have one full day of normal exercise to get over the effects of the journey, especially if it has been a long one. This is not so necessary for short journeys of up to half a day, but it is as well not to ignore the effects of travelling on horses, and to work on the principle that the more time a horse has to recover after a journey the better.

On arrival, give the horse half a pound or so of glucose in his drinking water, which will help him to overcome the stress of travelling; otherwise treat as usual. Also give normal feeding and exercise the next day. On the first day of the event, make sure that any feed is given at least two hours before competing. This may be very early in the morning on the dressage day, depending on your place in the starting order. Reduce the amount of hay to not more than ten pounds daily during the event.

The amount of work done to 'ride him in' before the dressage test depends entirely on the individual horse and on your method of training, but it is best for it to be plain simple exercises as already described, rather than any schooling with a risk of conflict, when harmony is essential.

The three-day event test is longer and more complex than for the one-day event, but not really more demanding, if the horse has been carefully schooled up to that level. The present F.E.I. test generally in use was introduced in 1963 and is still current at the time of writing. There are nineteen separate movements and the time allowed is seven and a half minutes. The more advanced movements required are two tracks (half-pass at the trot), rein-back (six steps), counter-canter, and some moderate collection. The use of snaffle or double bridle is optional. The practice riding of the full test should be done as much as possible on a horse other than the competition one, who should only do the full test a comparatively few times during the preparation period.

Many riders opt for the snaffle, and, unless the horse is exceptional, usually put up very dull performances without true lightness, for, as already pointed out, (page 108), proper collection cannot be obtained with a snaffle. I would always recommend that this test be ridden in a double bridle. In a test it is always better to make the movements slightly larger than life.

Smooth and easy transitions from one gait to another are essential, but also there should be a sharp distinction between them; between, say, an ordinary trot and an extended trot, and an ordinary trot and a collected one. The effect of the curb lightly used, and with a great deal less effort, will make the collected movement much more of a contrast from the ordinary one, and will so catch the judges' eyes. Before an extension, very light and imperceptible aids can produce a slight slowing up of the ordinary trot before going into the extended trot, again highlighting the contrast. Aim at achieving maximum extension towards the second half of the diagonal across the school; it is better to have three or four strides of full extension than double that amount of an insufficient movement.

After the test, a short gallop as a pipe opener is desirable, followed by a walk to cool off, a rub down, then bed him down and feed. Allow the horse a good two hours rest, then groom thoroughly, water and feed, and leave him alone, except for a check up of feet and shoeing, until the last night feed. This is a good time to check all saddlery, especially stirrup leathers and girths before the endurance phase.

On the second day, give a short feed and water at least two hours before the time of starting, but no hay or chaff. To avoid risk of his eating his bedding the horse should be racked up after his first feed.

You will have inspected the course the day before, and the procedure for planning the cross-country ride has already been described, but this will naturally be a bigger and more complicated business, with a four and a half mile circuit and over thirty fences to cater for. There is also the steeplechase course to be treated in the same way. Aim at completing the two rounds in exactly the time needed to gain a maximum bonus *and no more.* This means that you have to plan the ride as carefully as you have done for the cross-country. You do not want to extract one ounce more energy from your horse than is absolutely necessary, for he still has a long way to go. Mad, uncontrolled galloping can lead to disaster later on.

The two roads and tracks sections are easy to plan, but they *must be* planned. The first section will be between three and three-quarter and four and a half miles, the second between four and six miles. Divide up your time between walk, trot and canter, so that you start and end with a walk. As a sample, take the 1970 Badminton figures, and assume that you know that your horse walks at four m.p.h., trots at ten m.p.h., and canters quietly at fifteen m.p.h.

The first roads and tracks were three miles 484 yards, total 5,764 yards (5,280 metres), and the time allowed was twenty-two minutes, an average speed of just under nine m.p.h. You gain nothing by being under the time allowed but lose one fault for every second over, so you cannot afford to dawdle.

At the above speeds your riding plan could be something like this:

Walk 220 yds at 4 m.p.h.	1¾ min.
Trot 2,640 yds (1½ m.) at 10 m.p.h.	9 min.
Walk 220 yds at 4 m.p.h.	1¾ min.
Canter 1,760 yds (1 m.) at 15 m.p.h.	4 min.
Trot 800 yds at 10 m.p.h.	2¾ min.
Walk 124 yds at 4 m.p.h.	1 min.
Total 5,764 yds	20¼ min.

You have one and three-quarter minutes in hand, and you will probably need it. This sort of timing can be practised during training.

Make a similar riding plan for the second roads and tracks, and, of course, the plans for the steeplechase and cross-country sections. Another reason for going to all this trouble is that it is illegal to rely on having friends and relations posted at strategic intervals to signal information about how you are doing. The F.E.I. Rules are clear and explicit on this point. Among other prohibitions it is forbidden 'To be followed, preceded or accompanied, on any part of the course, by any vehicle, bicycle, pedestrian, or horseman not in the competition.' And, 'To post friends at certain points to call directions or make signals in passing.' (Rule 336.)

In the stables give a final check to everything, then hack or lead the horse to the Box – the starting, finishing and inter-mediate halting point, about ten minutes before you are due to start. Weigh in, then saddle up, make sure the girths and sur-cingle are tight and correctly adjusted, mount and give the horse a little short pipe opener to get him on his toes for the start, which is a standing one. Then walk round until your turn comes.

After the first roads and tracks you should have time for a quick check of girths, etc., before starting round the steeplechase course. Work out your second roads and tracks plan so that you have about two extra minutes in the Box for the veterinary inspection. There should be a well-rehearsed routine for the ten minutes' inspection and rest in the Box, so that not one second is wasted.

The moment you have passed the time keeper, dismount, and while the inspecting panel is looking at the horse, off-saddle the horse. As soon as you have passed the panel, take the horse to one side where the groom will be waiting. Stand the horse facing into the wind, while the groom sponges out his mouth, swabs down the face, neck, flanks and between the thighs, then scrapes the water off with a sweat scraper. Dry him thoroughly after that, with a vigorous hand rubbing, to tone him up. Examine the legs and feet thoroughly for any wounds, cuts, bruises, and to check that the shoes are all right. Saddle up with the girths loose, lead the horse around quietly for the remaining minutes to let him relax. Three minutes before the 'off' girth up, two minutes before mount, one minute before move up to the starting point. You may find lots of people willing to come and help you in the Box, but allow nobody near the horse who has not been well drilled in this procedure.

Ride the cross-country course according to your plan, and let us hope that all will go according to it. If it does not, it is just one of those things. As in the case of show jumping, have a careful post mortem the same evening, while everything is fresh in your mind, to find out what went wrong, or rather what you did wrong. You may not have assistants on the course, but there is nothing against having observers, who can tell you afterwards how things looked to them as you passed, how the horse took difficult fences, and so on.

After the last fence gallop as fast as you can to the finishing line, decelerate gradually after that and return to the collecting ring. Off-saddle, and weigh out while the groom puts on a rug. After weighing out, replace the saddle, put on the light rug again, and, if it is a fine day, walk about for fifteen to twenty minutes to allow him to cool off, then take him back to the stable. If it is wet, get back to the stable as soon as possible.

There give the horse two mouthfuls of cold water to encourage him to stale, then give him a bucket of water with the chill off and with half to three-quarters of a pound of glucose in it. Give him a hay net to nibble at, while you massage the body and legs with straw until dry. Pick out his feet, dry his body thoroughly and remove the worst of the mud from the legs, then wrap them with gamgee and woollen bandages, rug up, and give a light feed of warm bran and oats to which a little cold linseed tea has been added, and leave the horse to rest in peace.

Two or three hours later, take the horse out and walk him about to remove stiffness and to check for lameness; carefully examine for any cuts or bruises, any thorns picked up, shoes loose, or any strain of tendon or ligament. If there is the slightest fear of bruised tendons, apply a cooling pack, such as the following: white wine vinegar and whiting made into a paste and smeared on to a piece of lint to a thickness of half an inch, applied to the legs and covered with the bandages. Then a short period of grazing will help him to relax and freshen up, and act as an appetiser for his last meal.

On the third day there is a veterinary inspection in the morning, so have your own inspection at least two hours before it, and warm him up before the official one. Apart from this revert to normal routine.

The last part of this contest, the jumping phase, takes place in the afternoon. The pre-jumping arrangements will be the same as for show jumping (Chapter 20). In Britain your order of starting will be changed from that of the previous two days. In 1966 I suggested that, to give the final phase more tension and excitement, riders should go in the reverse order of their positions at the end of the second day, literally the last should be first and the first last. This was tried out at Badminton in 1967, and has remained in force in this country, but not yet abroad. Perhaps one day it will be adopted by the F.E.I. for international use. There is always a parade of all those who have got through to this last test before the jumping starts.

All this procedure should be practised constantly before the event, and all grooms and helpers should know exactly what their job is at any given time, so that there is no last minute rush or panic, which is bound to have an adverse effect on the horse. *Always allow plenty of time before the start of the event or any part of it.*

Obviously the whole preparation of horse and rider for a three-day event is a long, arduous and exacting task, requiring in good measure the qualities of patience, perseverance and technical know-how, together with the necessary material factors of space and equipment. In modern conditions it is beyond the reach of many horse owners, but those who do make the effort can, and do, gain success.

22 The Outdoor Horse — Polo

The modern version of the ancient game of polo (the present name derives from the Tibetan word, *pulu*, a root, from which the ball was made, usually willow) is possibly the most difficult ball game in the world. In addition to the usual three elements of a ball striking game, the ball, instrument, and the striker, a fourth, often unpredictable one, is added, the horse, always known as a 'pony' whatever his height. Another element, common to all ball games, the playing surface, is an extra complication, for the polo ground is no billard table, 'The ball no question makes of Ayes and Noes, but Here or There as strikes the Player goes...'

Curiously enough, experience has shown that good horsemanship is not an absolute condition for reaching the top levels of polo, although naturally it is a very great asset. More important, however, is that combination of wrist, hand and vision which makes 'a good eye', what polo players call 'a stick-and-ball eye'. But superlative training of the vehicle, the polo pony, is the prime essential. Opinions of the relative values of horse power vary from 75 to 90 per cent. So let us begin with the pony, and we will continue to call him such, although he has risen in height from thirteen hands (which was about the height of the immortal Maltese Cat and his colleagues (*The Day's Work*, by Rudyard Kipling)) to sixteen hands and over (but modern players after experimenting with failed racehorses up to 15.2 hands, have found the optimum height to be 14.2 to fifteen hands, and the best ponies to be Argentinians).

The making of a polo pony is largely empirical, once he has acquired the basic training of Part III. The final answer is the test of the game itself. Everything he does has to be at speed, two-tracks when he rides off another pony, flying changes whenever required, deceleration from thirty m.p.h. to nothing in a few strides, pirouettes in one motion, leaping from a standstill to full gallop. On top of that he has to be smooth-going for ball hitting and staunch to face oncoming ponies and riders. Until you take him into a game you do not know how he will fare.

So all the movements that the horse has learnt in the school must be progressively quickened up. He must become bridle-wise, to be ridden with one hand. Nearly all the work must be done on a loose rein; and most of the schooling and suppling in a snaffle. I would reserve the curb bit for the actual play itself. After preliminary suppling exercises, the pace for the later stages of schooling should be an easy moderately collected canter. If the horse tends to poke its nose – which many polo ponies do – change to a mild double bridle, and work mainly on the curb. An equal tendency is for the head to be raised extra high when stopping and turning, and the only remedy for that in a game is a standing martingale. Instead of leather, a broad strip of muslin-type cloth (in India, where this kind of martingale originated, it was pagri cloth as used for the winding of turbans) has a slightly elastic 'give' in it, which cushions the violence of the effect of the sudden retarding aids applied at full speed.

The quick stop and the 180 degrees turn are the key to polo tactics, and it has to be faced that in the full heat of a game half measures are useless. The aids of leg and hand must be applied strongly and violently and the hand equally suddenly released. The halt obtained, the turn follows without a pause, usually right-handed: neck reining with the left indirect rein, strong left leg, and the weight of the body helping to swing the pony round on its haunches in one uninterrupted movement; then strong driving aids with both legs, the body forward, to make the pony strike off immediately at the gallop. On hard grounds with little topsoil, this method of stopping and turning is the only one to be used. On English grounds, where there is good holding turf, it is equally effective to swing the pony round in a very small circle. In this case there is no stopping, only a slight check, half-halt, to steady the pony and give him a chance to change legs, if necessary, then using the outside leg and neck rein and body weight guide him round at an accelerating speed in as close a circle as possible.

There is considerable unavoidable wear and tear on the pony's mouth during a game, which must be counteracted as much as possible by slow loose rein schooling and suppling in a snaffle or a bitless bridle. There is no little strain on the legs too, so supporting bandages should be worn by the pony for all schooling.

This is all basic schooling applied to a special purpose; but it is all to no purpose if the pony will not accept the polo stick in the rider's right hand and the ball in front of it. One preliminary practice recommended was to hang a few polo sticks up in the green pony's loose box, so that he could get used to the look of them and, occasionally, the feel of them. Whether this was effective I do not know.

The normal way is to start riding the pony about with the stick held in the right hand, at first held upright as a sword at the carry, and then dangling vertically to the ground. Next, hold it out in front of you past the pony's face so that he can see the head of the stick (mallet) in front of him. Then swing it quietly backwards and forwards. Having done this on the off side with the right hand, change hands and repeat on the near side. The pony may shy away from it at first, but most seem to get used to it very quickly. The final stage is to introduce the ball. Place it on the ground in the field, and have the pony walk up to it, while the stick is hanging down, the head practically trailing along the ground, so that it will hit the ball as the pony passes by. The slight click of ball on mallet may make the pony start, but carry on forwards after the ball, which will have travelled a little way, and let the mallet hit it again. Progress from there to combining a swinging of the mallet with the striking of the ball, until, eventually, you can take a full swing at the ball without the pony flinching. If the pony is going to be permanently ball-shy, it will show the symptoms early on; but the majority seem to accept the situation. The difficult practices are the shots on the near side, whether forwards (near side forehander, although it is actually a backhand stroke) or backwards (near side backhander, although it is actually a forehand stroke, but directed to the rear), and shots under the pony's neck, whether from the off or the near sides. Always use a loose rein when practising these shots and hold on to the neck rein, which every polo pony should wear, whether it has a standing martingale or not. Needless to say you practise all these shots at the walk first, then at the canter. The trot does not come into the polo pony's vocabulary.

Riding off is a lively exercise in two-track work. Begin by getting the pony used to half-passing to the left and right at the canter and then at the gallop. The angle of the diagonal movement should be fairly flat, for there are stringent rules about coming in at too sharp an angle, but the pony should be thoroughly used to obeying the aids. After that, you must have another (trained) horse and rider. First of all at the walk ride close together side by side and gradually ease the pony inwards against the other pony, so that they definitely jostle each other as they go along. If the pony shows willing, separate to a yard

The increasingly popular style of Western
riding is demonstrated here

The elegance and control of dressage riding, note that there is no bridle
used

Two fine examples of the revived interest in driving

or so apart and then half-pass him into the other pony, still at the walk, letting them meet with quite a bump. Progress from there to canter and gallop.

When doing this, aim your pony's shoulder just a bit ahead of that of the other pony, so that your knee makes contact in front of the knee of the other rider and just in front of the saddle. This enables your pony to head the other off from the line of the ball. Most ponies seem to enjoy this rough and tumble, but some will not take to it at all.

Another necessary exercise is to pass another pony at a gallop, and to stand to face an oncoming pony. As before, work with a trained pony, passing first at a canter, then at a gallop, the riders swinging their polo sticks as they do so. When the pony is used to this, make him stand still while the other pony gallops up to and past him. Make sure that the pony is absolutely straight for this. Ponies are seldom, if ever, absolutely still during a game of polo, but often in defence a player must turn to meet the ball and the attacking player following it up, a manoeuvre requiring a good deal of nerve and steadiness at first.

The pony's education then continues in slow chukkars, an essential practice for both mount and man, when everything is done in slow motion, as it were, galloping being frowned on if not specifically forbidden. It used to be a term of abuse among polo playing soldiers to say of somebody that he was the sort of man who would gallop in a slow chukkar. Again, however apt the pupil may be, it is best not to hurry things, and even in fast practice chukkars to take him quietly. But, if a pony is going to be any good at all, he will soon show it; and, starting in slow chukkars at the beginning of the season, he should be ready for tournament polo by the end of it.

As for the rider, the more basic schooling he has had the better. It is true that moderate, even indifferent, riders have excelled at polo, by virtue of courage, balance, skill at other ball games, particularly rackets, but the aspirant to polo who has not had much riding training would be well advised to go back to school and acquire a firm independent seat and mastery over the application of the aids. (Part II)

Special training for polo consists in learning to hit the ball from all angles, at all speeds and in all directions. First of all, the implement. The *polo stick* (called *mallet* in U.S.A.) is in fact a mallet, a cylindrical or cigar-shaped piece of wood, sycamore, ash or bamboo, the latter being sometimes covered with vellum, eight and a half to nine and a half inches long, one and five-eighths to one and thirteen-sixteenths inches diameter, and weighing six to seven and half ounces, attached to a springy cane with a racket grip at the other end, fifty to fifty-four inches long. The cane is either Malacca or Moonah, or a combination of the two spliced together. The whippiness of the cane shaft can vary considerably, from quite stiff to extreme flexibility. The type used is very much a matter of personal choice, but it is a fair generalisation that somebody with a strong forearm, who relies on muscular strength to get length from his strokes, and also perhaps has a slightly slower eye than the next man, will tend to use stiffer canes, while the player with supple wrists and quick eye, will rely on swing and perfect timing to achieve a long shot, with as whippy a cane as possible. The length of the shaft will also depend on several factors: the length of the player's arm, his manner of riding, the height of the pony, and his position on the field, a back, having to hit more backhanders than anything else, will usually prefer a longer stick than forward; but the general principle is that the polo stick should be as short as reasonably possible, so that the player has to get down closer to the ball for his shots.

The normal grip is flat, broadening towards the head, which has a raised rim designed to prevent the handle from slipping through the hand when the full palm grip was used. This very comfortable grip has largely been superseded by the finger grip, in which the little finger goes over the rim, its great advantage being that it facilitates the keeping of arm, wrist and stick in one line at the moment of impact with the ball. A modern grip, known as the *Parada*, has a kind of pistol grip, which gives added security. Two types of normal grip are the O.H.K. or Rugby and the Lloyd or Racquet. Every grip has a sling attached to it, to enable you to retain possession of the stick if it is hooked by an opponent.

The head presents a great variety, but the basic are the cylinder and the cigar. The ball, be it understood, is struck with the long face of the head not with either end as in croquet. The cigar head has its weight and bearing surface concentrated at the centre where it joins the shaft and where the head should hit the ball. The cylinder has the weight and hitting surface evenly distributed, so, although it is not so concentrated at the critical point, it can nevertheless have some effect even if perfect accuracy is not achieved. Both types can have a slice taken off the heel (the inner end, nearest the pony) to make a reaching-out shot from the off side of the pony, or under his neck and tail, easier, or one each taken off both heel and toe (the outer end, furthest from the pony) to simplify close-in shots.

The great debate used to be on the values of the large head (greater diameter) and the small head. The large head was stronger, with more driving power, but the small head had the valuable lofting power through getting more underneath the ball. This was resolved in the 'thirties by the invention by the Royal Naval Polo Association of the elliptical head, which combined both effects very successively, without adding or sacrificing weight. It is known as the R.N.P.A. Head.

Marco (now known to be Earl Mountbatten) in his book, *An Introduction to Polo* sets out league tables of the various qualities of the different parts of the polo stick. Top of the shaft league is the spliced Malacca and Moonah; the best head for drive is sycamore, but it is low down on the durability rating. The vellum-covered bamboo gets ten for durability but is low on drive, although I did not find this to be the case on Indian polo grounds. Moreover, it has one slight advantage: if the head breaks, the vellum cover keeps the thing together until you can change sticks. This book was, and brought up to date in 1950, still is, the last word in instruction for modern polo.

Having chosen your weapon, you start to practise hitting the ball. The accepted training instrument is the wooden horse at the centre of a sort of crater with sloping sides and a netting screen all round. The diameter of the base circle, where the wooden horse is placed, can be about ten feet, and of the top of the crater anything from twenty to thirty feet, depending on the space available. The wire netting screen should be divided into panels about six feet wide, numbered consecutively from the front panel directly in the way of a straight forehand drive from the horse. The horse itself can be entirely rudimentary, provided it is firmly based and can take a saddle. Reins are not necessary, because the beginner should learn to make all his shots without recourse to the reins, but a neck strap can be used if necessary in the early stages.

The late John Board in his *Polo* which has an added value for his graphic and inimitable illustrations, recommended a preliminary to the polo horse and pit in the shape of a packing case 'standing about two feet six inches off the ground and of substantial construction'. The pupil stands on this in braced position, feet about two feet apart, knees bent, and practises swinging the stick, forwards and backwards, timing the swing so that the head of the stick reaches the ground in front of him, about where the pony's fore foot would be when it reaches the ground in that phase of the canter stride, off or near depending on which side you are swinging. When the straight swing has been acquired, the ball can be introduced. The packing case, or a firmly fixed low table, can be an economical substitute for a wooden horse; but a properly made polo pit is essential.

Hitting the ball at polo is like boxing the compass. There are four cardinal points or shots: off side forehand, off side backhand, near side 'forehand' (in fact a backhand shot forwards) near side backhand (a forward shot backwards); then, on either side, there is every direction of the compass, for each of which a special approach and swing is required. In every case the ball should be struck by the centre of the head.

For the straight forward and backward shots the head of the stick must be at right angles to the line of movement. For a cut shot to the right it must be at a wide angle to that line, i.e. more than 90 degrees. For a shot across the line of movement, the angle of the head to the line must be less than 90 degrees.

As in all ball hitting games the body must be correctly placed for the shot, and it must be on a secure base. On a pony this is obtained from the stirrups and a firm grip of calves and knees. At one time polo players tended to ride long and sitting down in their saddles; because of this they needed longer sticks and were inclined to hit the ball from behind the saddle, relying more on brute force than timing. The Indian players of Patiala, Jodhpur and Jaipur were not guilty of this; relying on a well-timed swing with flexible wrists and unerring eye, they achieved equal length with much less effort. A book called *As To Polo*, by an American, William Cameron Forbes, emphasised the value of the forward seat in polo, and players shortened their stirrups several holes, with excellent results. Firmly based on their stirrups, they were able to lean forward and down, getting much nearer to the ball – with shorter sticks – and hitting it well in front of the saddle, thus obtaining both momentum and accuracy. The same downward movement paid off for backhand shots, and the difficult near side strokes were made that much easier by the greater flexibility of the upper part of the body.

Practice with a polo ball should begin in the pit with a standing ball. Make sure the stirrups are correctly adjusted for your height and for the length of the polo stick, fifty-two inches say to start with. Place the ball alongside on the off just about level with the front 'legs' of the 'horse'. Sit upright, the left hand in the position of holding the reins, the right hand holding the stick vertically upright in the normal 'rest' or 'carry' position, which is where you keep it during a game when you are not actually using it to hit the ball or to hook an opponent's stick. Now make your swing for a forehand drive.

The first, and last, lesson of all ball games is *'Keep your eye on the ball'*. So, bend your body a little forward, eyes looking down at the ball. Tighten your grip on the handle of the stick, so that you have the correct, strong finger grip, thumb round the handle. Simultaneously bring the left shoulder forward, so that the body bends over the plane of the ball, sloping the stick slightly forwards, and raise and straighten the right arm backwards and upwards, taking the stick with it, until the hand is as far back as possible and above the shoulder, the stick making a direct extension of arm and hand. Then swing downwards – slowly in the initial practising – so that the head follows the stick and hand in a large and ever-accelerating circle, which should be at its peak of speed when it hits the ball. Four things impart length to the ensuing shot: flexibility of the wrist, resilience of the cane, both giving that extra flick at the last instant, correct moment of impact, and the speed of the pony. Practise this swing many times before putting a ball there to be hit. Your own body and head will bend forward and down so as to give your hand the correct distance from the ball, which is the length of the shaft.

For an off side backhander, you have to shift your grip, so that the thumb is along the rear side of the handle. Bring the right shoulder to the left as you raise the right arm upwards and backwards over the left shoulder, bending your body over to the right and downwards, again looking down and at the ball. At the start of the swing the elbow will be bent, but straighten it about halfway down. The head of the stick should come to the ground just about level with the stirrups. As before, bend the body down as far as is necessary. In every case after a swing, follow through until the stick is held out horizontally in front of or behind you as the case may be. Many players, especially Indian and Pakistani ones, make a double backhand swing at the ball, which can be very effective in imparting greater length to the stroke; but there is also more chance of the stick being hooked during the swing. It is worth while practising this double swing, so as to be able to use either according to the situation.

On the near side, the action is more or less reversed. For the 'forward' stroke, take the reverse grip, as for the off side backhand, lean the right shoulder well over to the left, so that it is over the line of the ball, head looking down, body braced, as before, on stirrups, calves, knees and thighs, and leaning forward and down as far as necessary. Extend the right arm, with the stick, backwards over the left shoulder, and bring it down straight in the same plane as the ball. This, with its variants, is the most difficult shot of all and requires a good deal of practise.

For the 'backhand' stroke, keep the forward grip, raise the right hand as high as possible above the right shoulder, the stick swinging slightly off the vertical; then rotate the shoulders, so that your right shoulder is over the ball, and swing down towards it. In every case, at the moment of impact shoulder, arm, hand, stick and head should be in one vertical line.

If you have hit the ball correctly, it should go straight as a bullet into the netting panel immediately opposite you, or behind you, as the case may be. You will *feel* if your timing has been right.

Concentrate first on the off side strokes, getting the forehand drive as perfect as possible with a stationary ball before changing to the backhand. Then the near side forehand stroke, which is a great deal more tiring to execute than the off side shots; so avoid overtiring yourself by too much repetition at a time. Practise when your arm and wrist are tired can only do harm. After a few near side shots, change over to the off side for a rest. Remember that, if the ball at any of these shots goes off to one side or the other, instead of straight into the target area, you have it wrong. You may not have hit the ball true with the centre of the head, but with one side or the other, causing the ball to go to the right or to the left. You may have sliced it, by hitting it with the head not at right angles to the line of the ball but turned outwards; or pulled it by the head being turned inwards.

Other faults are topping the ball, caused by not getting down far enough and by raising your eyes off the ball; or hitting the ground in front of it, the result of a faulty swing and pressing by relying on strength not swing and timing to hit the ball correctly. It is always best to have an instructor to point out these faults to you, but in default of that these indications will tell you when, and where, you are going wrong.

When you are reasonably sure of accuracy at these four strokes at a sitting ball, progress to a moving one. Whenever you have hit the ball up into the netting surround of the polo pit the force of gravity will bring it back to you, more or less straight, if you have hit it straight in the first place. In this case, make your swing, timing it to meet the ball as it arrives in front of you; if you have mishit and the ball is coming down at you from an angle, stop it and take another standing shot correctly, we will hope. Only when you are able to hit the straight moving ball straight back again into the target area, should you tackle the ball coming from angle.

This should happen when you have practised angle shots, into panels of the netting screen to the right and then to the left of the centre one. To the right they will be cut shots, to the left pulls. To make this change of direction, the stick must be brought down so that the head is facing in the required direction, still at right angles to the line of the ball. To do this successfully, the ball must be struck further out from the side of the pony than was necessary for the straight forehand drive; the same applies for the backhand stroke on the near side. The wider the angle of the cut the further out the ball has to be, and more to the front in the case of the forehand shot, and to the rear for the backhand; and the same on the near side.

The whole secret of success at polo is accurate and reliable stroke play, and the only way to achieve it is by constant practise, remembering two instructions:

1. Keep your eye on the ball.
2. Aim every shot at a mark.

A third point to remember is not to keep on hitting at the ball when tired.

Mounted practice follows the same course as in the pit on a wooden horse. Practise your swings on both sides, first of all without a ball, then with it. Variations can be introduced; half swings, tapping the ball along, which makes one at ease with the stick and strengthens the wrists; and the ability to control the length of one's shot is of great importance.

The following form of mounted practice is of great value in acquiring accuracy of timing and direction. In a field, set up a pair of flags, four yards apart or half the normal width of the goal. Get as many polo balls as you can up to a dozen, and lay them in line from right to left about sixty yards from the goal, five or six feet apart. Canter round in a circle on the right rein, so that you come up to the first of the balls opposite the goal. Aim to get it through the goal with a slow easy swing. Then move the circle so as to approach the next ball, and so on. Do not attempt to hit the ball into the next county, let the swing, your wrist and the momentum of the pony do the work for you; the great thing is to get all those balls through or into the goal mouth.

Then re-align the balls from left to right so that the right-hand one is directly opposite the goal, and you come at it, still on a right-handed circle, on the near side. Arrange your circle so that you are always on a straight line when you come up to the ball. In due course you turn about and take back-hand shots. Steady practice in this way entails no unnecessary wear and tear on the horse.

This is the time also to practise special shots, for which the tapping exercise will have prepared you. But do not make a habit of this tapping – or dribbling – in a game; you will never get very far if you do; though the occasional single tap to position the ball or to get it out of the way of an oncoming opponent can be very effective. A useful shot is the low push (Marco calls it a 'jab shot' in his *An Introduction to Polo.*). If you and your opponent are about to meet each other, off side to off side, you may find that you are going to do so fractionally later than him in getting to the ball. Bend right down as low as you can, run the head of the stick along the ground with your right hand as far in front of you as you can get, so that the under side of the head hits the ball and pushes it under the opponent's swing.

Many a goal has been scored by tapping the ball under the pony's belly between his legs. The chance usually comes in front of goal when the pony is moving comparatively slowly, and you have no time or opportunity to turn or take a shot under the neck. A quick half-halt will help to position the pony's legs, and you make a swing at right angles to the line of the pony, aiming to hit the ground just before you hit the ball, which will help you to stop the follow through and the possibility of the stick and the pony's legs becoming entangled. Another trick, if you notice that the man behind you is contemplating hooking your stick, is to entice him to bring his stick forward with a dummy shot, break off your swing and beat down the stick, and then make a quick half swing so as to make your getaway. All these things happen very quickly, so very quick reflexes are required.

If you have the pony power, you must have the occasional galloping stick-and-ball practice, before you venture on an actual slow chukkar. Henceforward the difficulty will be to restrain your ardour, but try to do so for a while before really getting into the fast game, which you will find exceedingly bewildering at first, with the other members of both teams shouting at you at once. The beginner is invariably placed at No. 1, the leading forward position, and the one instruction given him will be to mark the opposing back (No. 4) and forget about the ball.

Indeed some military martinets were alleged to have sent their tyros into action without polo sticks at all.

Once you have learned how to hit the ball, you can only learn polo from playing it. To the uninitiated it looks like a mad gallop up and down the ground by people swearing at each other and trying to stop their ponies. One shrewd observer once noted that polo was always played on the opposite side of the ground to the spectator. However, there is a definite pattern in good polo which soon becomes clear.

It is first and foremost a team game. The brilliant individualist looks spectacular, but he ruins the game for the others. I am talking about sides whose players are fairly level; a good player in a team of rabbits has to be a bit of an individualist. The four players of a team are numbered 1, 2 (forwards), 3 (centre-half), and 4 (full back). The back defends, passing the ball up to No. 3 (the pivot of the side), who sets an offensive in motion, either taking the ball up the ground himself or, if he is being interfered with, passing it up to the No. 2 forward, who should be given a clear run by the No. 1 forward marking the back, so as to prevent him from backhanding the ball away from his territory. That is the pattern that both sides aim at, and which both sides aim to disrupt, so the game takes fascinating turns all over the ground, riders placing themselves to receive passes in directions unexpected by the enemy; the anticipation of good players who know each other's ways and capabilities is uncanny, one of the things that makes a high handicap player.

And all the time you have to watch that you do not cross the line of the man who has possession of the ball or right of way. The Rules provide very clearly the various ways in which you can infringe the rights of the man in possession, and prescribe severe penalties for infringement. The would-be player should get a copy of the Rules at the very beginning of his career and read and re-read them.

Polo is a very expensive game. To play four chukkars in station polo or in a match, you must have at least three ponies. A pony can normally play two chukkars, but there must be a reserve. This is why, in any country, only a comparative handful of people can afford to play polo with any regularity or hope of success As in the old mounted cavalry days the cost for impecunious but enthusiastic officers was mitigated by the regimental framework and the use of troop horses, many of which were superlatively good, so at the present time the club organisation, which is pretty universal, enables many young players to enjoy some sort of polo, and, sometimes, to acquire the skill which will get them into a team.

In Britain there are twenty-four polo clubs, and the number of players on the 1970 handicap list was 367, to which can be added eighty-two in the Rhine Army. Many, if not all, clubs have a reservoir of club ponies, which they can hire for a fee of £2 per chukkar upwards (£5 for tournaments.). A limited number of young players come up through the Pony Club. Sex equality is established in theory, but in practice very few girls play polo. The governing body of polo in this country is the Hurlingham Polo Association, though it no longer has any connection with the Hurlingham Club.

The leading polo playing countries of the world are the Argentine and U.S.A., with Australia, Mexico and other South American countries not far behind. Great Britain is unable to take on any of them on level terms. Polo is also played in Eire, India and Pakistan, New Zealand, France, Germany and Italy, Rhodesia and South Africa, Kenya, Nigeria, Ghana, Malaysia, and Jamaica.

23 High School
and Grand Prix de Dressage

By the end of the basic training period (Part III) the horse's potentiality should be fairly clearly discernible: whether for the technically lower, but thoroughly rewarding and skilled, fields of show jumping, horse trials and polo, or for the rarefied heights of *haute école*, which has its highest expression in the performances of the Cadre Noir of Saumur and the Spanish Riding School of Vienna, and, competitively, in the Grand Prix de Dressage.

The four movements, or airs, which mark the change from basic and medium to advanced equitation are the named flying changes of leg at the canter, the pirouettes, the piaffe and the passage. The rears and leaps, levade, courbette, capriole are outside the scope of the ordinary private horseman. The overall requirement for high school is extreme collection (*rasembler*) and, above all, the horse must be *willing*.

There must come a time in the training when the horse will not so much obey blindly the aids but seem to *lead* the way, to want to execute more difficult airs of his own volition. After all, they arise out of work already done, in response to aids already learnt, so that they are part of an exciting dialogue between horse and rider, on much more equal terms than it has been hitherto. The sensitive horseman will recognise this thrilling moment, take the horse on as high as he wants to go, re-train him tactfully from overdoing it, encourage his generosity and at the same time maintain the discipline necessary to add accuracy and precision to natural freedom and brilliance which combine to make the perfect performance. The movements of a horse which is *forced* into them will always appear dead and laboured, unsatisfying to both rider and spectator.

Flying change. The horse should already be able to execute a smooth flying change (pages 115–16), and it should not be difficult to train him to do it as often as required at given points: at every third and second stride, then at every stride, as required in the test of the Grand Prix de Dressage. It is interesting to recall that flying changes now reserved for the highest riding test of all, were once part of the manège test for officers' chargers at the Indian Army School of Equitation, Saugor, in the 'twenties. Only three changes were asked for on the straight, but they had to be done consecutively, and I never knew any horse to make any difficulty over it. I trained a polo pony to make the single stride change by changing the lead of the canter half-pass (counter-change of hand on two tracks), first every three strides and reducing to one. I say 'trained', but he took to it quite naturally once he saw what was required, and seemed to enjoy doing it.

The flying change was reached at the end of Chapter 16 (page 168), but, if it is known by then that the horse will be going forward to advanced equitation, it is advisable not to overdo those lessons until the horse has achieved good collection (Chapter 17). It must be thoroughly supple before being asked to do named changes.

The horse makes the change during the period of suspension, but as the phases of the canter stride follow each other so quickly, the preparation for it must begin well before. First there is the positioning with the half-halt, and the collecting of the horse to the right degree, i.e. so that the horse is well balanced fore and aft, without excessive movement of the centre of gravity to the rear.

The first requirement of a flying change is straightness, the horse not swinging his quarters to the left or right and going on two tracks while doing it, which is of course much easier for him. So begin work in the manège on straight lines, using for a few lessons the tracks on the long sides. Only a *few* times like this, then revert to straight lines down the centre of the school, along the diagonals, or across from one side to the other, 'so that the rider can clearly see how much of the horse's straightness is attributable to its obedience to the controls and be sure that the horse is kept from growing accustomed to securing moral support from the wall'. (Zeunig, *Horsemanship.*)

Start by making a few transitions from trot to canter, followed by a few simple changes, then prepare it as above for the final effort. Assuming a change from the left lead to the right canter on the right rein; position the horse as soon as possible after turning the corner from the short side; when you feel the horse is going smoothly and quietly and is ready for the change apply the aids for the canter with the right lead before the left leading leg comes to the ground, when the horse will be on the diagonal; near hind, off fore. This will give time for the change to take place during the ensuing moment of suspension. Apply the left leg behind the girth, while activating the horse with the right leg, the weight of the body shifted to the left by a movement of the seat bones, the right rein meanwhile asking for a slight bend to the right, supported by a slight yielding of the left rein. The moment the change has been made, relax the aids, slow down to walk and make much of the horse.

If the horse fails to make the change, or gets into a disunited canter, do not attempt to force it into the movement. Relax back to a trot, and try it on the other rein. If you are successful on that rein, try again from the original direction. If there are still difficulties, try working on a figure of eight. Consider whether you have been too rough and abrupt with the aids, applying them too late, making it impossible for the horse to obey, however willing he may be. It is worth recalling another piece of advice from Waldemar Zeunig: 'Lymphatic and plump horses should be spared all instruction in the flying change for they should not be tormented with the demands of higher dressage, since they lack the required congenital verve.'

It may take two or three sessions to obtain correct – smooth and straight, flying changes, or they may be achieved the first time. In any case do not overdo them, but gradually bring the horse to an easy freedom in, and even liking for, the movement, before beginning changes at named positions and in given rhythms of strides.

In the high school tests the flying changes are done on the diagonals across the arena, so make your practice along them, not necessarily all the time, but certainly to begin with, so that they will not come as a surprise to the horse when he eventually meets them both in preliminary schooling for and in the actual tests. Place a couple of marks at odd distances on each diagonal, which can remain there during ordinary schooling sessions, so that the horse will get used to their presence. When next you have a flying change practice, make up your mind at which mark you will make the first change, position the horse for it, and apply your aids so that the change will be made exactly at that spot. Knowledge of the horse's stride already acquired will help to obtain accuracy.

Having done the change correctly on one diagonal, change the rein and execute it at a chosen mark on the opposite diagonal. Then call it a day. For the next three or four lessons make the changes at the same spots, but the next time ride the full lengths of the diagonals without asking for any change, just to prevent it from becoming a habit on that one spot. Following that, ring the changes for the chosen positions, still making only one flying change on each diagonal. In due course obtain two changes on one straight line, say six strides apart; and from there progress to a change every five, four, three and two strides.

Vary the flying changes with transitions from canter to walk, and from halt to canter, and of course plenty of relaxed periods as a rest and reward. If a horse can go directly to a walk after five canter strides, he should be able to make a flying change smoothly after six strides (Zeunig), and so on downwards. At the same time the aids should become more subtle, the rider's seat more immovable – or apparently so to onlookers and judges – especially judges. Once the horse has got the idea – and some will get it very quickly, the lightest combination of the aids will be sufficient to achieve the final gymnastic effort of the flying change at every stride.

If any trouble should arise, from boredom or for any other reason, restart from an earlier stage and work up again. On the other hand, the horse may take to it so well that his changes will get out of hand, so care must be taken to keep him always to the exact number and kind of changes required. Profit to the full from his willingness but always retain the ultimate command.

The *pirouette* is the hardest of all the high school movements to do well. Here is the official definition.

> This movement is a small circle on two tracks, with a radius equal to the length of the horse, the forehand moving round the haunches. At whatever pace the pirouette is executed, the horse should turn smoothly, maintaining the exact cadence and sequence of legs at that pace.
>
> At the pirouette, as at the half-pirouette, the forelegs and the outside hindleg move round the inside hindleg, which forms the pivot and should return to the same spot each time it leaves the ground. If, at the canter, this leg is not raised and returned in the same way as the other hindleg, the pace is no longer regular. In executing the pirouette, the rider should maintain perfect lightness while accentuating the collection and engagement of the quarters. (F.E.I. *Rules for Dressage Competitions*, Sec. 413.)

The method of teaching the pirouette has been described above (pages 181, 182), and starting from the renvers position is the most practical way of setting about it, for the horse is in the right position for the movement before it begins. As I have said, it can be accomplished by a moderately trained horse in a rough and ready way, as for polo, but for a school horse, the approach must be more gradual. In the first place, the horse must be able to canter quietly, but with a lively high action, in perfect collection. He should be supple, able to halt and strike off at the lightest aids, which is a necessary preparation for the movement. He should be responsive to the lightest aids, so that the rider can sit as still as possible, without trying to make use of his weight or using too heavy rein aids. The less the rider moves the easier it is for the horse.

In the first lessons from the renvers position the turn in the corner should be a very small volte, the essential thing being to maintain the cadence all through. Apply firm driving aids before going into the turn to keep up impulsion, and restrain the horse with the inside leg from trying to make the turn too fast. After one turn, go straight and reduce to a walk. Two turns are enough for one lesson at this stage. If the horse makes any resistance, go back to larger turns, then very gradually shorten them.

The operative word is *gradually*. Four turns, two each way, should be the maximum for a session, and not at every session – say four times a week. 'It takes quite a long time and diligent, systematic work before the horse is in a position to execute correct and cadenced pirouettes.' (Richard L. Wätjen, *Dressage Riding*.)

The *piaffe* and the *passage* are usually associated together as the acme of the training of a high school horse, and for perfection the latter should proceed from the former. As usual let us start with the official descriptions.

> The *piaffe* is a movement resembling the very collected trot on the spot. The horse's back is supple and vibrating. The haunches with active hocks are well engaged giving great freedom and lightness to the action of the shoulders and forelegs.
>
> The neck is raised, the poll supple, the head perpendicular, the mouth maintaining light contact on a taut rein. The alternate diagonals are raised with even, supple, cadenced and graceful movement, the moment of suspension being prolonged. In principle, the height of the toe of the raised foreleg should be level with the middle of the cannon bone of the other foreleg. The toe of the raised hindleg should be slightly lower, reaching just above the fetlock joint of the other hindleg.
>
> The body of the horse should move up and down with a supple and harmonious movement without any

swinging of either the forehand or the quarters from one side to the other.

The piaffe, although being executed strictly on the spot and with perfect balance, must always be animated by an energetic compulsion which is displayed in the horse's constant desire to move forward as soon as the aids calling for the piaffe are discontinued. (F.E.I. *Rules for Dressage Competitions,* Sec. 415.)

One definite mark of a good piaffe is apparent effortlessness. Another is the lowering of the croup, which means that the hocks are well flexed. Laboured, unequal steps, with swinging quarters and swishing tale are marks that the horse has not been correctly prepared.

The piaffe should not begin to be taught until the horse has acquired a perfect trot at all paces, and perfect collection. The use of cavalletti in the early stages of training help to produce an habitual reasonably elevated trot, which can facilitate to some extent the ultimate achievement of the piaffe and passage, but the use of cavalletti at the last moment, as it were, is no substitute for proper and methodical preparation.

Preparatory exercise should be aimed at increasing suppleness, engagement of the quarters and flexing of the hocks, and strong impulsion. They can include the usual half-halts; transitions from trot to walk; collected walk; transitions in the following sequence: (a) halt – trot – halt; (b) trot – halt – trot. (General de Carpentry, *Piaffer and Passage.*) The number of trot steps in (a) may be a dozen or more at first but progressively reduced; and the halt pause in (b) will be several seconds at first, and also gradually diminishing. The trot should be slow but well cadenced, and the halt and depart absolutely straight. Take care in these exercises not to use the hand and leg aids together, but separately and reciprocally, i.e. hand action should be accompanied by passivity or yielding of the legs, leg action by a yielding or steady hand.

The direct depart from halt to trot may not come easily at first, hence the need for several trot steps and for a good period of immobility after the halt, and the very gradual reduction of the trot steps and the halting time. There should be no loss of balance or scrambling in the trot depart. After repeating the sequences five or six times the lesson should end with a longer trot, a longer halt, and then complete relaxation of the reins.

The piaffe and the passage are closely related and they should not be taught or practised in isolation. One proceeds from the other, and they are both included together in the Grand Prix de Dressage test. It is possible, but not really profitable to start with the passage, and most authorities teach the piaffe first. And three good reasons are given for it by Lieut.-Col. G. von Kazslinszky: '1. The piaffe is the foundation of "high school"; 2. With the piaffe one is better able to establish control of the easily evasive hindquarters; 3. The horse which has learnt the passage without previously achieving the piaffe will drag his quarters.' (*Light Horse*, January, 1967.)

The piaffe can be taught direct in the mounted position, but it seems logical to begin on the ground, which is indeed the way adopted by the Spanish Riding School of Vienna, who begin with work on the short reins, followed by the pillars, before executing the piaffe mounted. Not everyone has pillars at his command, or is sufficiently skilled with the long (short) reins to obtain the best results. The method recommended by Richard Wätjen (*op. cit.*) is to start with a leading (lunge) rein, using it as a substitute for the hand-held reins, and a whip as substitute for the leg aids. Side reins, and a cavesson nose-band should be worn. An advantage is that the horse, 'without being burdened by the weight of a rider... learns more easily to engage and bend the hocks and bring the hindlegs well forward.'

Starting on the left rein, place the horse beside one wall of the manège. The side reins must be adjusted to keep the head in the position of maximum collection, a little in front of the vertical. The leading rein, attached to the cavesson, is held short; the whip is in the right hand. The gentle action of the whip on the hocks encourages the horse to move forward, but the restraint of the leading rein in the left hand holds him back. The horse will start to lift his feet, to mark time as it were. Go on repeating this exercise until the horse starts to make more elevated and quicker movements of his feet which will amount to a trotting action. It is permissible to let the horse go a little forward at the beginning of these lessons, but he must not be allowed to move his quarters off the straight line. If he does so, let him go forward at the trot, and start the exercise again. One or two steps are enough to begin with, and the lesson should not exceed about five minutes at a time. Unauthorised attempts to go forward can be restrained by quick halts with the leading rein. After a few steps done well, relax and reward the horse, and give him some normal uncollected work.

Very gradual progress is essential, and it is best to concentrate on getting the movement perfected on one rein before changing to the other side. The movement must always be on the trot diagonal, and the back should be kept as supple as possible, which is best achieved by not overdoing the lessons to the point of boredom, irritation and resistance. The whip aid should be intermittent, not applied continuously during the movement. Once got into the rhythm of the piaffe the horse should be allowed to free-wheel, as it were, without constant application of the aids. When the whip (or the legs when mounted) acts, the hand should be steady. Over-collection is to be avoided, and care must be taken to see that the horse keeps on the bit, not getting behind it. If the horse tries to rear, he should be driven forward immediately. The probable cause is too much of the exercise at a time, making the horse sick of it. It must be remembered that the piaffe is a most strenous gymnastic exercise, for which the horse must be carefully and progressively prepared.

If this preliminary ground work has been thoroughly carried out, it should be possible to proceed direct to mounted work. Repeat the preparatory exercises and include rein-backs after halts.

The essence of it is a series of alternating back and forth movements controlled by alternating aids. Apply the hand aids without the leg aids, and directly the horse obeys yield the hand and act with the leg, using the whip at first, as on the ground, and gradually supported and supplanted by the legs. Never let the horse become completely immobile. After two or three alternations of this kind relax the horse by going forward at the trot for a few strides then halting. The cadence of the diagonal trot movement must be maintained throughout. The forehand must be raised slightly, the croup lowered. The reins should be taut but light, which can be detected by the position of the curb bit; this should be at a very narrow angle to the vertical. If the cheeks of the bit are drawn back to an angle of 45 degrees or more the rein tension will be too great and there will be stiffness of the back.

The raising of the foreleg is obtained by shifting the weight so that one foreleg is pinned down momentarily while the other is released. Do this by the action of one rein on the neck, so that the weight shifts to the shoulder on that side, e.g. action of the right rein will tend to burden the right shoulder and release the left. This should be done when that leg is on the ground, and to balance itself the horse will raise the opposite (left) leg. The horse must bend his neck willingly to the aid, and must remain quite straight. If any resistances occur, either insufficient bend or too much, break off the movement, trot forward, halt and start again. When the horse responds well to one side, repeat the exercise on the other.

The rider should be able to *feel* the movements of the legs under him, all this being part of the feels of riding without which it is not possible to gain full success at this art. The rein aid should be little more than a closing of the fingers as the leg comes to the ground. The action must be very delicate, so that the forelegs are not raised too high, which is as bad a fault as not being raised enough. Once more the gradualness of the progress must be stressed, and the imperative need not to overdo any part of the training. One perfect, or near perfect, step is enough to begin with. There is no saying how long the process will take; it entirely depends on each individual horse.

The passage can proceed from the piaffe, or it can be developed from the collected school trot. As usual let us start with the official description.

This a measured, very collected, very elevated and very cadenced trot. It is characterised by a pronounced engagement of the quarters, a more accentuated flexion of the knees and hocks and the graceful elasticity of the movement. Each diagonal pair of legs is raised and put to the ground alternately, gaining little ground and with an even cadence and a prolonged suspension. In principle the height of the toe of the raised foreleg should be level with the middle of the cannon bone of the other foreleg. The toe of the raised hindleg should be slightly above the fetlock joint of the other hindleg.

The neck should be raised and gracefully arched with the poll as the highest point and the head close to the perpendicular. The horse should remain light on the bit and be able to go smoothly from the passage into the piaffe and *vice versa*, without apparent effort and without altering the cadence, the impulsion being always active and pronounced. (F.E.I. *Rules for Dressage Competitions*, Sec. 414.)

It is the rhythm and the slight dwelling in the air and pointing of the toes of the raised diagonal which are the charm and delight of this movement at its best. The sideways swinging of the quarters, seen in circus displays, can be impressive but is a fault in classical high school riding.

If a good effortless piaffe has been achieved, use firm driving aids to make the horse step forward, but maintain the elevation with the hands, so that only a little forward ground will be made but more upward movement. Two steps like this are ample for a start. Relax into an ordinary trot and halt. The same can be done from a good collected school trot by elevating aids with the hands, which must be as light as possible but definite, followed by driving action with the legs. Again the angle of the curb bit is a good guide to the correctness of the aids. If horse and rider have become accustomed in the pre-liminary training to the delicate control by finger action, rather than by rigid movement of wrist and forearm, the progress to these elevated gaits will be greatly facilitated.

The piaffe and the passage can be taught on the long reins, or the short hand reins as is practised and displayed by the *reiters* of the Spanish Riding School of Vienna, the whip acting as the leg aid. The procedure is a gradual slowing down of the trot until the horse is trotting on the spot, though a slight advance is permissible, to avoid constricting the horse and stiffening its back. The piaffe is then perfect in the pillars.

The principle of this is clear enough, the horse, wearing side reins, being restrained by reins from the pillars attached to the cavesson noseband, so that he is prevented from going forward or back and is encouraged to elevate his steps at the driving aid of the whip. The application is not so easy, requiring very great care, first in introducing the horse to the pillars, then the application of the aids and the maintenance of straightness. The help of a trained assistant is essential. The horse may get excited or frightened at the restraint of the pillar reins and the trainer must wait patiently, soothing him with voice and hand, until he settles down before applying the driving aid of the whip, and then only very softly.

It can take a year or more before a sufficient piaffe and passage have been obtained to warrant entering for high level competitions; but of course the horse can gain experience by progressing through the lower levels of competition.

Riders should try to gain experience by riding older horses that have already been trained in the high school movements, so that they can get the feel of them before trying to impart them to a novice horse. This is easier to come by in Germany and elsewhere on the Continent, where there are more trained horses about and also high school instructors. In England really expert high school horses are few by comparison. However, a start was made in this direction by the introduction, at the Henley Horse Show in 1969, on the initiative of Mrs Julia Wynmalen, of a special class for novice riders on horses trained up to the level of the higher tests short of Grand Prix. This innovation proved very popular and seems already to have the effect of bringing young riders on and so swelling the ranks of those capable of producing high school horses.

The other problem is the horse. The plan of this book has tried to show a young horse developing from foalhood onwards to the highest levels of equitation, but I hope it has also been made clear that the process is not an inevitable one. The truth is that, whatever the branch of equitation, the top horse is exceptional; he is usually found by accident, especially so in the case of the dressage and high school horse. The skill of the horseman often lies in recognising the latent ability of any horse to begin with, as well as in exploiting it.

As the Rule says, all horses are different and individual, and their training programme must take that fact into consideration all the time, 'the same passage cannot be of all horses ... some horses have a more rounded and longer action, others a more lively shorter action'.

Heredity may have something to do with the production of a high school horse. It must certainly be born and bred into the very bone and spirit of the Lipizzaner; but even in his case there are many rejects. The German Hanoverians, Holsteins and Trakehners seem to have an inbred docility which makes them good material for the high school rider. On the other hand, James Fillis preferred Thoroughbreds to all others; perhaps, in the right hands, they can be brought to great heights of elegance, power and brilliance. One thing is certain, they cannot be forced into it.

The horse learns from his trainer; the horseman learns from every horse he rides, and there is no end to it.

FIVE

Additional Considerations

24 Racing and Western Riding

Racing
There are sundry equestrian activities, of considerable importance and world wide, which are outside the main streams of
orthodox teaching described so far, and which, indeed, appear
to be contradictory to them. For instance, while orthodoxy
emphasises the role of the rider's body weight, the action of the
muscles of the small of the back, and the function of the 'driving
seat' to produce and preserve impulsion, we find the fastest
horse on earth – the racehorse – being driven forward from start
to finish without the rider ever touching the saddle with his
posterior. And there is no doubt that, ever since British jockeys
abandoned the long-legged seat *on* the saddle in favour of
Sloan's forward position, racehorses have galloped faster and
faster.

This was also the essence of the Caprilli revolution some
seventy years ago, and it certainly produced startling results
within his limited range of requirements for outdoor riding.
Even now, when the then widely separated ideas have coalesced
to a great extent there are two schools of show jumping thought
and practice, as to whether one should sit down in the saddle
for the approach to a fence or keep the seat off it. Both seem
to show equal dividends.

Similarly, there is an apparent contradiction in the riding of
the Western range horse, and in particular the cutting horse
and the riding and schooling of any horse under classical
European principles: on the one hand no, or minimal, contact,
on the other full contact.

Such contradictions may be more apparent than real. Every
horse, whatever his future role, experiences the full force of
the driving seat in his early training; every horse must accept
the bit and contact with the rider's hand before he can learn
to do without it. Every rider learns to use his back muscles
and seat and weight in obtaining impulsion, and in fact continues to use the small of his back even in the extreme forward
position. It is surely the sensible application of Steinbrecht's

dictum with which we started (page 82), 'The normal position does not exist.'

It is also a vindication of equestrian orthodoxy, if such is needed, that both the racing fraternity and the western world have recognised the value of, indeed necessity for, basic training of both horse and man to make more efficient their special skills and performance.

For the first time in the history of equitation a small book has been produced on horsemanship for jockeys, written by John Hislop and originally serialised in *The British Racehorse* during 1970.

The task of the racehorse is a straightforward one: to gallop overall faster than the other horses in the race and to conserve his energy so as to be able to exert his full power and pace at the critical moment. He achieves this through the skill of his trainer in bringing him to the starting gate or stalls exactly fit for that particular task, and under the direction of his rider.

So jockeyship, as John Hislop says, 'is the art of race riding – judgement of pace, tactics, sizing up the way a race is being run and acting accordingly, quickness from the start, riding a finish, determination and gamesmanship – ' but, 'if the highest skill in flat race riding is to be attained, it is essential to master the art of horsemanship before attempting to be a jockey'. And this, perhaps, applies equally, if not more so, to riding over fences, whether under National Hunt Rules or point-to-pointing. For them all the education of a jockey 'comes in two stages. The first is learning to be a horseman, the second learning to be a jockey.'

Jockeys start their careers young, as apprentices, and many of them now, thanks to the Pony Club and the improving commercial riding schools, start with some basic training. Perhaps in time it will become a compulsory qualification for apprenticeship to hold a Pony Club or similar certificate.

Apart from the tactical handling of a horse in a race, there is a great deal more in racing horsemanship than meets the eye. It is not a question of riding with very short stirrups, perched up above the saddle and holding the horse hard by the reins. There is a right and wrong length of stirrup leather, depending on the individual horse and the work to be done, and the necessity of all horsemen to be in balance with the horse. For a slow cantering exercise the leathers will be longer than for a fast gallop; they are better short for a sprint race, and long for a distance one. Long reins and short stirrups may be more effective with a horse that pulls than the other way about.

There is also the use of the whip to be learnt and practised. The jockey must be able to transfer the whip from one hand to the other without disturbing the balance or rhythm of the horse at full stretch, and to use it equally well with both hands. He must of course know when to use a whip, and then not to overdo it, or merely for show.

The jockey's position on the horse at rest is not intrinsically different from the normal balanced seat, except that he has a most inadequate saddle to sit on. He must sit as near as possible to the lowest part of the saddle, back straight and supple, knees into the saddle, lower legs hanging naturally, feet resting on the irons on the inside edge of the footplate, toes to the front, hands in light contact with the horse's mouth. He will be using the muscles of the small of the back and the driving seat constantly for small slow actions, like manoeuvring into position at the starting gate, or urging the horse into the starting stall. The more supple and secure he is in the saddle, the better can he concentrate on handling the horse in the race.

For racing over fences both horse and rider should have basic jumping training. It is surprising how badly many steeple-chasers jump; and how many races have been lost, I wonder, by bad approaches and unbalanced leaps? Admitted there is not much time to make conscious preparation as in show jumping, but patient preliminary training can make these actions instinctive.

Apropos race riding in general, John Hislop makes an interesting statement regarding the introduction of starting stalls in England, that it was 'necessitated by foreign influence and a lower standard of horsemastership among trainers and riding on the training ground and on the racecourse, than was the case before the 1939–45 war'.

Western Riding

Everybody is familiar with the cowboy and his horse. Ever since Tom Mix they have become the folk heroes of eastern youth – and the not so very young either, as the audiences to television 'Westerns' bear witness. Uninformed orthodox horsemen have tended to look down on the apparently rough and ready methods and odd clothes and tack, but at its best the horsemanship of the range was the direct descendant, adapted for special purposes, of all that was best in the Spanish and eastern styles of riding which were brought to the New World by Cortes in 1519.

In recent years there has been a growth of practical interest in Western riding in England, concentrated mainly in the New Forest, with some shows staging Western riding classes, which justifies the inclusion of it in this book.

The tack used in Western riding is a good deal more simple than that for normal Eastern and European riding. The centre piece is the saddle, which although modified in the course of the centuries is basically the direct descendant of the saddle of the later Middle Ages in Europe, when the steel-encased rider was kept in position by a high pommel and cantle and rode with a straight leg. The present-day saddle embodies these features and requires that kind of riding, the seat tending to be located more to the rear end of the horse, above the perpendicular vertebrae (Deering Davis, *The American Cow Pony*). The rider does not invariably sit so straight-legged as his predecessors, but on the whole tends to do so.

The saddle tree is of hardwood with high cantle and pommel, covered with a double thickness of rawhide. Firmly fixed to the pommel is the horn, made of steel covered with leather, over which the rope (*lariat, reata*) is tied or dallied (looped round several times) when stopping and holding a roped animal. The pommel and horn combined have a height of up to thirteen inches, and the cantle is up to four inches. The saddle is lined with sheep's wool, and placed on the horse's back over a saddle blanket. Fitting the saddle to different sizes of horse is accomplished by using more blankets. The saddle is kept in place by the cinch (girth), usually made of soft mohair cords woven together. There are no buckles; on the side of the saddle are cinch rings (rigging, single, centre or double), to which are attached long soft straps (*latigo*), which go through the cinch ring and are wound several times to brace it tight. For security a double rig with two cinches is often used. The cinch has to be strong and secure because in a working outfit it had to take the strain of the rider and saddle weight – 200 lb. or so – and of several hundred pounds of live and protesting beef at the end of the lariat.

The stirrup leathers are wide, with broad sweat flaps (*fender sudadero*), and are attached to the tree. The stirrups are large and heavy, usually made of curved oak, metal bound, the footplates leather covered. There are various local variations, the box type (tapaderos) being general in South America. The object of them all is to give protection to the foot when in the saddle and to give quick release in the event of a fall. Cowboy boots always have high heels to avoid any entanglement. The weight of a saddle can vary from thirty-five to sixty pounds, depending on the amount of metal used in decorating it, which is sometimes considerable and quite a work of art. This substantial weight is distributed by its wide skirts over some eight square feet of the horse's back, instead of being concentrated into the two or three square feet of an English hunting or show jumping saddle, which makes it much less of a burden for the horse than one might expect. Add to that the fact that the shape of the saddle helps to keep the rider still, and one can understand the tremendous distances covered by stock horses without undue damage.

The bridle or headstall is as simple as can be, headpiece, cheekpieces, brow band, throat latch, and sometimes dispensing with both the last named, the headstall kept on by passing one ear through a loop in it, hence called the slit-ear headstall. The Argentine *gauchos* used nosebands, and they are occasionally put on for decoration. The material is rawhide or latigo (soft oil-tanned pliable leather). A halter is sometimes worn over the bridle for tethering purposes. The reins are always single, attached to the curb bit and separated, so that, if dropped, they hang loose to the ground from the bit, all cow ponies being trained to remain halted when they are in that position.

The bit is a straightforward curb, of varying degrees of severity, usually with curved and sometimes highly ornamented cheekpieces. The most severe bit is the spade bit, whose mouthpiece has a broad metal plate to press against the roof of the mouth and down on the tongue, unless the horse holds his head correctly. In theory these bits are not severe because with the Western method of loose rein riding and neck reining the full power of the bit is only exerted very rarely and quickly; in practice not every Western cowboy was a heaven-sent horseman, but could straphang with the best of them.

The training bridle for the Western horse is the hackamore, a bitless bridle, whose name, deriving from the Spanish *jaquima* (pronounced 'ha-kee-mah'), and ultimately from the Arabic *hakma* reveals its ancient lineage. It consists of a head and cheekpieces combined in one strap, attached to a noseband (bosal). This is the operative part of the equipment. It is made of about eight strings of braided rawhide wound round a core of twisted rawhide, steel cable, or braided rope, the former being the most flexible yet giving solidity. It has a thickening in front where it contacts the nasal bone (nose button), and two side grooves to take the cheek and head strap. The ends are joined at the rear in a heavy heel knot, which keeps them in position away from the jaw. The side pieces of the bosal are called shanks.

With the hackamore goes a long rope, called the mecate, made of horse hair or mohair, about twenty-two feet long, half an inch thick, and usually made in two colours, black and white, red and white, sorrel or brown and white. At one end is a smart-looking tassel (*la mota*), which hangs down just in front of the heel knot, adding a decorative touch to the equipment. The other end is wrapped round one of the shanks, then up over the pony's neck and withers and back again to the heel knot to form a rein, knotted in various ways; the remaining twelve or fourteen feet of the mecate acts as a lead rope, coiled up and attached to the saddle strings in the case of a trained pony or retained by the rider if it is unbroken.

The bosal has a threefold action: 1. On the nose and nostrils, by pressure of the nose button, on the nasal bone or on the nostrils if it is fixed lower down; 2. On the jaw by the pressure of the shanks; 3. Behind the jaw, when the heel knot is pulled upwards.

Allowing for difference in equipment, the modern method of training cow ponies is based on the same principles as those already described in Part III: a very far cry from the old rough and ready method of back and buck. Ponies are not left to grow up more or less wild, but handled and gentled from foalhood. They are bitted with a snaffle, but the later training is done with the bosal before the curb bit is introduced.

Ponies are saddled and backed at a year, then left until they are two and half to three years old before beginning ridden schooling. The work is progressive, the preliminary work at the walk doing circles, turns and figures of eight; then at the trot; and finally they are asked to break into a canter from a walk. Nearly all the work is on a loose rein, and the pony is taught to be bridlewise from the beginning. The aim is to make the pony obedient to the simple aids, quiet and good mannered, yet able to look after itself. The rider uses his body weight constantly to guide the horse and prepare him for turns and changes of direction.

Spins or turn-about (pirouettes in fact) are taught by going round in a very small circle, giving aids with spurs and whip, or with two whips, one in each hand, which is preferable (Deering Davis, *The American Cow Pony*, Van Nostrand, 1962), gradually reducing the size of the circle until it is a definite swing round on the haunches. Modern western thought favours the taking of a great deal more time over training than used to be the case; Deering Davis, already quoted, declares that 'if possible a horse should have no gruelling or exhaustive work until he is at least six or even better seven'. Many trainers, led by John Richard Young (*The Schooling of the Western Horse*) have gone over to complete European methods.

Riding a Western horse in a Western saddle, although the basic teaching of riding on the lunge and the securing of a deep, independent seat is an aid to it, requires an almost complete reversal of method. To begin with, anything like a forward seat is impossible in a Western saddle; and the particular Western activities – cattle roping, rodeo riding, cattle cutting – can only be efficiently carried out from a backward position.

On getting into the saddle for the first time, the rider lets his legs hang loose, and the stirrup leather is adjusted until the footplate hangs one or two inches below the ankle bone, which is the general all round length of stirrup leather for normal work. In competition work it may be advisable to raise them by a hole or two. The rider then sits towards the cantle of the saddle, so that his seat bones are over that part of the horse's back where the upper bony processes of the vertebrae are perpendicular – approximately the eleventh or twelfth vertebra. The knees are slightly bent, heels down, upper part of the body erect, reins held loosely in the left hand (usually), which is carried high, several inches above the horn of the saddle.

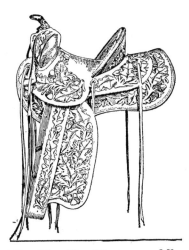

Fig. 16. The Western saddle

From this basic well-balanced position the rider can adapt himself to circumstances, standing up in his stirrups for roping, leaning back for crash halting, and shifting his weight for turning. The rear-placed burden is not so far back as to affect the loins, and in any case the wider bearing surface of the saddle reduces the concentration of weight. This position also gives the forehand and fore limbs greater freedom of manoeuvre, which is what the range pony needs for its work, especially, for example, the cutting horse, who does nearly all his work on the forehand. It will be observed that the muscles of his forearms are highly developed and immensely powerful. From his backward position the rider can conform much more easily to the rapid movements of the cutting horse facing the reluctant steer; or he has a slightly, better chance of staying in the saddle of a professional rodeo buckjumper. An adaptation of this backward seat can be seen in the riding of gaited horses, the rider sitting almost straight-legged and almost on the loins.

Cutting horses are trained in various ways: some start straight away practising on calves as three-year-olds, so that they learn balance and obedience to the rein and body aids as they go; other trainers start with basic training, neck reining, halting and lateral work, before introducing them to their living opponent.

Cattle cutting is unique both as a labour as well as a sport in that the horse, once the preliminary training is over and the rider's controls are established, truly takes charge and works on his own. It seems true, too, that the top-class cutting horse is born not made, witness the case of Sandhill Charlie, World Champion Cutting Horse gelding in 1961, 1962, 1963, who won his first competition as a novice against the professional best. A very 'ornery critter' indeed ('Sandhill Charlie', by Loy Ann Trent in *Light Horse*, January, 1971), he was only amenable to any form of discipline when in front of a cow. Heredity must come into it as well, because the same family lines appear in the pedigrees of many famous cutting horses.

The object of cutting (called cattle draughting in Australia, where it is also a big money sport) is to prevent a selected young heifer from getting back to the rest of the herd, and it will use every sort of trick to rejoin its fellows. The technique of the horse is to keep head to head, anticipating its movements at every step. This requires real power and gymnastic agility and what amounts to an uncanny sense of anticipation. The control exercised by the rider is minimal; his main task is to stay with the pony in all its movements, difficult at all times but impossible in any but a western saddle.

The Western rider's clothes are too well known to warrant long comment. The basic garment is the denim jeans, which first entered the cowboy's life in the 1860s. The point to make is that for comfort and efficiency it must be close but easy fitting, not the skintight tubes that are fashionable in youthful circles today. It should be loose enough to be worn over riding boots, to prevent dust and foreign bodies getting into the boot tops, and to preserve the leather from sweat and other damage. In the open plains of the Argentine the gauchos wear baggy cotton pantaloons (*bombacha*), which are both cool and comfortable. The ends are fastened at the bottom so that they cannot ride up.

Chaps (Mexican *chaparreras*) are over-trousers, made of leather or sheepskin, worn to protect the rider's legs from thorn and cactus. The spreading batwing variety which is universal today was first seen in western America about 1895. Between the wars they were much favoured wear in some polo circles on both sides of the Atlantic.

Western riding boots are rather like Wellington boots, but with high heels, which were introduced in 1875. The object of the high heel is of course to prevent the foot being caught in the stirrup. The heights of boots vary from about ten inches to sixteen inches, and there is a medium size of twelve inches. Nowadays heels are lower than they used to be. The spur has been the badge of knighthood as well as a goad, and the Western variety is no exception, being usually highly chased and decorated.

25 Driving

Driving has been an amateur sport for about 200 years. Horse-drawn transport has been with us since the dawn of history and racing in chariots is practically coeval with it, but the development of driving for pleasure and of the art of handling the ribbons started when the macadamised roads made it possible. At first it was all coach driving, then smaller, more easily handled vehicles were invented, the phaeton, the cabriolet, and so on.

Among the Holy Week parade of some eighteen hundred carriages taken by Society to the Longchamp convent in the Bois de Boulogne on March 26th, 1785, called by one Sophie la Roche who recorded the event 'The pilgrimage of the coaches,' were 'white cabriolets of some of the younger gentlemen... bordered with painted garlands of roses and forget-me-nots'. (László Tarr – *The History of the Carriage.*) A. B. Shone, the historian of amateur driving, mentions a satirical eighteenth century print (c. 1760) which shows a 'New Fashioned Phaeton', a high perch vehicle of adjustable height with its elegant driver making love to a lady on a first floor balcony (*A Century and a Half of Amateur Driving*). *Vive le sport!* In India in the early part of this century, up to the 'twenties, many young officers used to pursue their love affairs in the cosy cabriolet with its conveniently screening hood.

This is not the place for a history of the carriage and its uses, fascinating though it may be. It is enough to point out that sporting driving grew up with the commercial use of the horsed vehicle at the end of the eighteenth century, and in fact survived it. The present flourishing existence of the British Driving Society, which was founded in 1957, is evidence enough of that.

It is a highly traditional sport too. The vehicles themselves are survivals from the past, lovingly resurrected and restored to their pristine elegance, and the accoutrements of the equipage and the principles and conventions of driving have not changed at all.

The details are of the harness as follows:

258

Single. The basis of traction is the collar, the most generally used being the neck collar, which is a roughly pear-shaped loop of thickly padded leather, which lies at the base of the horse's neck in front of the wither and approximately at the same angle as the shoulder. It is reinforced by the hames (from the Dutch *haam*), curved pieces of metal which in grooves on both arms of the collar, linked at the top and bottom by straps; both can be of leather, but the bottom connection is sometimes a chain. About a third of the way up the hame from the bottom is a metal projection with a ring at the end of it, to which is attached the trace on either side of the collar. A third of the way down from the top on either side is a *terret* (Old French *toret*), a swivel ring through which the reins pass.

The collar is put over the horse's head upside down, then turned so that the narrow end is at the top. To be correctly fitted the collar must lie flat on the horse's shoulders, with enough room for the fingers to be inserted between it and the sides of the neck, and for the flat of the hand at the lowest part. It should not be loose enough to rock about, a fruitful cause of galling.

An alternative equipment for light traction where there are no hills is the breast collar, which is a broad padded leather strap fitted across the horse's chest, and held in place by a narrower strap over the neck in front of the withers. The breast strap should be fitted above the point of the shoulder.

The pad is a small saddle set where a normal saddle goes, whose function is to support the pair of terrets through which the reins pass finally before going on to the hands of the driver, and to hold the shaft tugs on either side through which go the shafts. If there are no shafts, it holds the loops for the traces. The pad should be well padded to keep it off the spine, and part of the equipment is of course the girth.

The backband is part of the saddle pad, the strap to which the tug is attached, and going over it with holes for adjusting the height of the tug. It joins the bellyband, which goes outside the traces and over the girth, never tighter than it and usually slightly looser, depending usually on the type of tugs used, particularly Tilbury tugs used on a four-wheeled cart.

From the pad the backstrap runs along the spine to the crupper, a padded loop through which the tail goes. Its function is to prevent the saddle pad working forward. The backstrap also passes through the loin straps which hold up the breeching. The breeching is a broad strap which should hang horizontally between twelve and fourteen inches below the root of the dock,

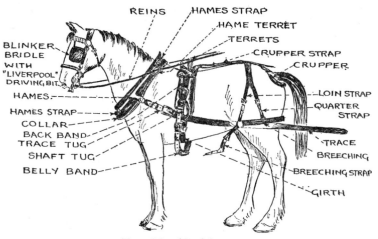

Fig. 17. 'Gig' harness

adjusted to avoid interference with the movement of the horse's quarters. It should be so attached to the shafts that the horse, when brought back against it, should be about a foot away from the cart itself. With light vehicles, unless there is a lot of hill work, the breeching is not essential. The most widely used form of breeching is attached to slots on the shafts between the stops and the front of the cart. Another type is attached to the tugs. When used in double harness, which is not often, the breeching is supported by a strap over the loins and attached to the trace buckles.

The crupper should be tight enough to keep the pad in position, loose enough to allow a hand's breadth between it and the croup. All hairs of the tail should be passed through the tailpiece, which must be kept soft and clean. The traces should be long enough to keep the horse as close as possible to the trace hooks on the vehicle, while leaving the quarters well clear of the footboard or dashboard.

The bridle consists of headpiece, browband, cheekpieces, noseband and throat latch. On the headpiece are attachments for the bearing rein, and blinkers are attached to the cheekpieces. The ordinary canons of bridle fitting apply. The most general driving bit is the Liverpool, which is a kind of Pelham, with four different actions: plain snaffle action on the ring, slight curb action when the rein is attached to the centre bar within the ring, and more severe curb action in the two slots on the cheekpiece below the ring. The mouthpiece can vary as in other bits (pages 63–71). A useful alternative bit to the Liverpool is a double ring broken snaffle, especially for horses with light mouths or of excitable temperaments. A further decorative addition to the browband is a face drop. Made of fancy leather, it is attached to the centre of the headpiece and goes underneath the browband.

The bearing rein has suffered in reputation from frequent abuse, but it is a useful, indeed necessary, counter to a horse that bores and keeps its head low, and commits the crime of getting behind the bit. The driver has no legs to push him forward. However, it needs careful adjusting, so that it is never too tight, and should be completely loosened going up a steep hill. The driving reins should be as soft and supple as possible, thin, and not more than one inch in width, less for small hands and fingers.

Harnessing

There is a regular sequence of harnessing or putting-to. First of all, all the separate items of the assembly must be ready and handy: the harness, the horse in his loose box, the cart outside in the yard – if it is a two-wheeled vehicle, the shafts horizontal, resting on a stand; if a four-wheeler the shafts are in an upright position.

The collar goes on first. Take off the hames and give it a stretch, then, placing the wide end uppermost, manoeuvre it carefully over the horse's head, avoiding any rough contact with the eyes and ears. Replace the hames, buckle up the hame strap, then turn the collar into its right position, the narrow part on top, rotating it with the lie of the mane. The collar should lie closely, but not tightly, along the shoulder; there should be two fingers' space on either side, and a whole hand space between the bottom of the collar and the horse's windpipe. The traces are attached to the harness and looped up loosely in a figure of eight.

Next, the saddle pad with backstrap, crupper, and breeching. Place the pad lightly on the back, behind the correct position, so that the crupper can be fixed; then lift the pad up, move it in front of the normal position and slide it backwards in the same way as putting on a riding saddle. If a martingale or breastplate is to be used, do not forget to pass the girth through their loops before hitching it up. Now take the reins and thread them through the terrets, the buckle end on the near side. Make a loop of them and let them hang over on the off side.

The bridle is then put on with the same care as in the case of a riding bridle. As well as the throat latch, the noseband is usually unbuckled, and of course the curb chain hangs loose. The cheekpieces are parallel with the horse's cheek bones and behind them. The noseband is two fingers' breadth below the cheek bones and should have two fingers' play between the front of it and the nose. The blinkers are fixed to cover the eyes and block any backward view, and are kept in position by two straps to the headpiece. The throat latch is adjusted to four fingers' breadth. The horse's forelock can either go under the browband or over it. Once the bridle and bit are fitted, the reins are then buckled on to the latter, and the horse is ready to be led outside to be put-to.

The vision of a horse with blinkers is very much restricted, so lead him out very carefully and quietly and see that he does not knock himself against the sides of the doors, which should be thrown back wide open.

Place the horse in front of the cart, and run the traces between the belly band and the girth in the case of a two-wheeler, and outside the belly band if Tilbury tugs are used for a four-wheeler, and cross them over the horse's back.

Two-wheeler: Draw the cart, shafts raised high, up to the horse, until the points of the shafts when lowered will be level with the tugs. Pass the shafts through the tugs and forward until the tugs come up against the stops on the shafts. This should allow sufficient clearance between the hindquarters and the front of the cart. The balance of the cart depends on the height of the shafts, which is regulated by the lowering or raising of the tugs. The shafts should be neither too low, nor too high.

Hook the traces on to the cart as soon as the shafts are in position, and make adjustments to the breeching, and kicking strap is there is one. Then buckle up the belly band sufficient to leave a little play of the shafts.

Four-wheeler: The shafts being already raised, the horse is backed into position in front of and underneath them, and they are then lowered on to the tugs. Tilbury tugs, if used, have metal half-loops covered with leather, on which the shafts rest, being secured by straps and buckles round them. The putting-to follows the same procedure as for a two-wheeler, except that, with a Tilbury tug, the belly band is pulled tight.

Personal equipment

It is *de rigueur* to wear gloves, carry a whip, and sport an apron. Dog skin, or as an alternative doe skin, is the recommended material for driving gloves, but woollen or string gloves are better for wet weather, and should always be carried in reserve. The important thing is that the gloves are fairly thick and roomy with nearly an inch to spare in the lengths of the fingers when new.

The whip, usually made of holly wood, sometimes of cherry, is light and well balanced, with a thong, leather pointed, about half the length of the stick. When not in use, do not stand it on its butt in a corner, hand it up on a round or semi-circular block.

A box cloth rug with a V-shaped slit at the top makes a comfortable covering for the knees of driver and passenger, if there is one, in cold or wet weather, and is definitely part of the uniform of the driving 'fancy'. It also protects the clothes. In summer a light linen rug can be used.

Neatness and smartness of the whole turn-out is a must. Harness must be polished, soft and of good quality, all straps well in their keepers, and none of them too long, no strap hanging loose underneath the belly, all brass work shining, and don't forget the carriage lamps. The driver's own dress should be in keeping with the equipage.

Double harness

For driving in pairs, side by side, the individual harness is the same, except for the coupling reins. Each rein is divided at the end into two ends: the draught rein on the outside, which goes direct from the driver's hands to the outside ring of the bit, and the coupling rein, which bifurcates from the main rein, passes through the terrets and is attached to the inside bit ring of the opposite horse. This enables both horses of a pair to be turned to the right or left by the action of a single rein; and it is most important that the coupling reins should be most accurately fitted, so that when in movement the horses' shoulders are level and their heads and necks straight to the front and parallel. The first requirement for correct fitting is that the traces are absolutely level, making a basis for the adjustment of the coupling reins according to the lengths of the horses' necks, which, of course, for pair driving should be as near as possible equal. Reins and traces need to have ample holes for adjustment.

There being a centre pole instead of shafts, the cart is placed in position in the yard, and the horses, already harnessed up as before, are moved alongside, brought forward from the rear, and the coupling pole chains, to keep the horses together, are linked from a ring at the head of the pole to rings on the collars. Then the traces are attached to the roller bolts, the outside one first in each case, then the inside one as quickly as possible.

Other methods of yoking the horses are with the curricle bar, and the Cape cart harness.

'The classical two-wheeled pair horse carriage is the curricle. At its most perfect it belongs to mid-nineteenth century London and, because of the exacting requirements of perfectly matched and stylish horses, with an expensive carriage and harness, it was the perfect medium for a display of ostentation without violating the conventional good taste.' (Tom Ryder, *On the Box Seat*.) The curricle bear is a strong steel bar, with a centre slit, and removable stop nuts at each end. It requires a special strong saddle pad on each horse, with roller bolts securely built in. The bar is inserted between the rollers and rest on them, and so is able to move freely from side to side in conformity with the movements of the two horses. The rollers can be raised or lowered an inch or two according to the heights of the horses. Through the centre slit goes a strong leather brace to the centre pole, to which it is fastened over a spring, to give it resilience. To prevent the pole from tipping up when the back of the cart is overweighted, a strap can be passed under the two horses from trace buckle to trace buckle and over the centre pole.

I cannot think of the curricle and the curricle bar without recalling that delightful poem of Rudyard Kipling's, in which the impecunious young soldier, driving by tonga to Simla on leave, meditates on his chances with the girl he met last season to the beat of the jingling tonga (curricle) bar – with satisfactory results: 'Try your luck – you can't do better!' twanged the loosened tonga-bar. ('As the Bell Clinks,' *Departmental Ditties*.)

Cape Cart: The feature of this is a yoke, a bar of wood, sometimes called a *bugle*, which supports the centre pole, being slung in front of it on a strap from the withers. At the centre of the bar is a leather loop which goes over the pole, giving plenty of play both longitudinal and lateral. Only breast collars are used with this harness, which became popular in England in the 'eighties of the last century.

Tandem: The most spectacular two-horse equipage is undoubtedly the tandem – and driving it is certainly a sporting pastime, not entirely without risk. The harness for the wheeler, the horse nearest to the cart, is the same as for a single turn-out. The driver holds two pairs of reins, the leader's reins passing through the terrets on the wheeler's pad and through rings at the top of his bridle. The leader's traces can either be attached to those of the wheeler or to a swingletree (usually a double one) between the wheeler and the leader.

Four-in-hand

This is basically two sets of double harness but with modifications. The wheel pads have centre terrets for the lead reins, and there are rings for the leaders' reins on either side of the wheelers' bridles. The leaders' traces are attached to swingle-trees, and they should not be too long.

The four-in-hand is the ultimate in driving in the British Isles, and a coach and four is still the most impressive vehicular turn-out on the public highway. To sit on the box of a smart coach, or even a brake, with the reins in your hands, a lively-stepping well-matched team below you, is surely the greatest thrill that the horse can offer. You are literally on top of the world, and the power that surges up the reins into your hands, and heart, is awesome. It is something no one can experience at second-hand. Unfortunately very few can enjoy this privilege.

Driving

The art of driving, even a single horse, simple though it may look, is by no means easy. After all that has been said about hand and leg, collection, light contact and so on, the driver finds himself sitting on a box seat instead of a saddle, his sole contact with the horse being the bit in its mouth about twelve feet away, his only other aids the whip in his hand and the tongue in his head. The clicking of the tongue encourages the horse to go on; 'Steady!' does in fact help to restrain an excited horse; and the human voice does seem to have an influence on the horse. Another point about driving a horse-drawn vehicle is that, like a car, it must be done on a public highway; so, like the 'L' driver, the learner whip should learn his driving from a teacher sitting beside him and showing him exactly what to do with the reins, so that he learns correct handling from the start. There are a few riding schools who also teach driving, and the British Driving Society can also help in this respect.

However, the theory of the art can be learnt from books, of which there are several good modern ones, and practice in handling the reins can be gained in private by rigging up a simple system of pulleys over which the reins, with a weight at one end, go to the hands of the learner sitting in a chair a few feet away. For a single horse practice there will be two reins, each with a four to five pound weight on one end, which will give the hands about the same tension as a trotting horse. For four-in-hand practice there will of course be four reins, each with a four pound weight. The reins are always held in the left hand, and the whip should be in the right as part of the practice. One point of this home-training method is that the left hand and wrist get accustomed to the weight placed upon them when driving; in the case of a four-in-hand it is quite considerable after a while.

Let us now suppose that the single horse is harnessed to its gig, chaise, dog cart, or whatever, and you are about to take charge.

First, make an inspection to make sure that the harness is correctly fitted and buckled up. Then, standing on the off side of the trap, take the reins in the right hand, near rein under the forefinger, off rein under the third finger. Get into the trap, sit down and adjust the rug or apron round the knees, and transfer the reins to the left hand. The whip will be in its socket on the off side wing of the trap.

Position of the reins: Near rein over the forefinger, the off rein between the second and third fingers. The ends of the rein are gripped by the third and fourth fingers. The thumb points to the right, and is not pressed down on to the reins. The forefinger points to the right rear, so that the rein is close to the knuckle, and the horse can be guided by the movement of the hand: turning it upwards to go to the left, downwards to go to the right.

Elbows should be close to the sides, the points almost touching the hips. Sit straight upright, leaning neither forward nor back, feet and knees close together. Wrists should be rounded and flexible; left forearm horizontal; back of the hand to the front and three to four inches from the body.

The whip, which should always be carried when driving, is held in the right hand, grasped lightly at the point of balance with the thumb and last three fingers, the forefinger being extended. The hand is placed at the same level as the left hand an inch or two from it, in front of the body, and the whip is pointing half left across the body. The purpose of the free forefinger is to enable it to grasp the reins whenever necessary to shorten reins or make a loop, without altering the position of the whip.

The whip is there to help control the horse, to give it the office to go forward, to keep it up to the bit, and to support the turning aids of the reins, especially when driving a pair. Even with a single horse great dexterity, and also tact, are needed in handling the whip. As a driving aid, the lash should be applied lightly between the collar and the pad, drawn across from either direction in a sort of stroking movement, the wrist and forearm being kept straight. Except for punishment or as a last resort the whip should not be applied to the flanks or quarters. Greater skill and accuracy is required to wield the whip on a tandem or four-in-hand, so that the lash hits the right place on the leader, and the beginner should not attempt it without a good deal of private practice, aiming at a mark.

Now you are on the road. To start the horse feel the mouth lightly and speak or click to him, or, if necessary touch him lightly with the whip. Yield the hand slightly the moment he starts. The reins should always be held in the left hand, and the off rein should never be taken in the right hand (except in hackney competition driving, and in certain types of driving competition, and if the horse bolts); and at all times the reins should be of equal length. Watch with the fore and aft rig-four-in-hand, tandem, etc., that the leaders' reins do not act before the wheelers. It happened to me once when learning to drive a four-in-hand, and I should have known better. The leaders halted, the wheelers and the vehicle ploughed on, and in a second there was a writhing plunging mass of horses on the ground, hooves flying, and an ominous crack. With great skill the grooms separated the horses and all was calm; by some sort of miracle not a single horse was even scratched. The only casualty was the centre pole of the brake.

With a hard-mouthed horse, or one that begins to take a hold, the left hand can be reinforced by placing the right hand on the reins in front of it, off rein under the little finger and near rein between the second and third fingers. To shorten reins, take the reins in the right hand above the left at the required distance, and slide the left hand up to the right; or it can be done the other way, the right hand taking the reins behind the left hand, which is then moved up as required.

When turning a corner, give the correct signal with the whip in good time. The usual method now is to point the whip to the right or left; or else use ordinary hand signals, temporarily shifting the whip into the left hand. It used to be customary for the driver not to take off his hat to anybody except royalty, but to salute with the whip, held horizontally level with the chin. Nowadays the whip is raised vertically until the hand is level with the brim of the hat; in America drivers transfer the whip to the left hand and raise their hats to ladies.

Continuing with turning, after giving the signal, check the pace, and keep to the near side of the road when turning to the right, and *vice versa*. Slight bends or curves of the road can be dealt with by turning the hand as explained above (page 267). For proper turns, use the right hand to shorten the required rein temporarily by placing it in front of the left hand with the appropriate rein under the little finger, pulling it steadily and without jerking. Release the rein directly the turn is completed. Drive generally with a steady firm contact, not letting the reins sag, and keep a steady consistent pace.

Looping the rein is the process of shortening one rein for a turn and leaving it still in the left hand, so that the right is free to use the whip or to check the horse, especially a green one or one that is inclined to rush or cut its corners. The normal procedure in driving a tandem or four-in-hand or similar equipage of horses in series not side by side, it is not necessary in single horse driving, except for practice.

To take up a loop, shorten the required rein as already described for a turn; then pull extra length back over the forefinger and hold it in place with the left thumb; the right hand is then free for any necessary action.

Always give yourself plenty of time to make any change of direction or before stopping; watch the traffic well ahead, learn to anticipate developments. The slow-moving vehicle will appear to leave you time in hand, but the rapid motor traffic will not. Avoid changes of pace unless they are absolutely necessary. Never jab the horse in the mouth except as a definite punishment.

Go slowly downhill, setting the pace from the top and continuing at a steady even pace. Passengers should shift their weight rearwards if they can. Four-wheel vehicles usually have brakes, but there is no need to apply them until you see the pole chains (of a pair) taking the strain. Release the moment they begin to slacken at the bottom of the hill. The brake, incidentally, should always be on when the vehicle is stationary, and while you are mounting. Up hill, give the horse his head, and get the weight forward if possible. On really steep or long hills get out and walk.

To take off on return to the stable. 1. The groom goes to the horse's head. 2. Put the whip in its socket, and descend from the cart holding the reins in the right hand. 3. Coil the spare end of the reins through the off side terret, so that they lie in front of the shaft stop. 4. Unbuckle the breeching from the slots on the shafts. 5. Unbuckle the bellyband, unhook the traces, knotting them again in a loose figure of eight. 6. Lead the horse forward from between the shafts.

Four-in-hand: The same procedure for harnessing, as with a pair, is followed with the necessary modifications. The coach-man will have two pairs of reins to hold, one for the wheelers, one for the leaders, both in the left hand. The positions are: near lead rein over the first finger; off lead rein under the first finger; near wheel rein between the first and second fingers; off wheel rein between the second and third fingers. The ends of the rein are secured by the second, third and fourth fingers, and alterations to the positions of the reins are made with the right hand. The positions of the forefinger and thumb are the same as with a single pair of reins. The technique of turning is to make the leaders make as wide a circle as possible, starting well away from the direction of the turn, i.e. for a right turn, the leaders will keep well to the left and start turning when they are nearly level with the left-hand kerb of the new road. While the leaders are turned in the direction required, the wheelers are first turned towards the opposite direction, so that they do not follow the leaders too closely or quickly and make too sharp a lock.

Begin making a point or loop of the required rein, see that the leaders start to make their turn; at the same time make a loop of the opposite wheel rein, to lead the wheelers away slightly from the direction of the turn. The wheelers should in fact make their proper turn at about the same spot as the leaders made theirs. When turning to the left the leaders should start the move-ment when they are about level with the centre line of the new road, and the vehicle should move on to the left side of the road as soon as possible. When the leaders have made their turn, the lead loop is released to get them going straight and the wheel loop is reversed, so that the wheelers now follow the leaders round.

Reins are shortened in the same manner as for a single pair, but particular care must be taken not to shorten the lead reins without the wheel reins. The effect is to stop the leaders while the wheelers go on, which can cause the chaos described above.

The whip should be held loosely between the thumb and fingers of the right hand, the thong folded so that a fairly long loop hangs down from a point just below the junction of the stick and the binding of the quill, the remainder of the lash wound round the stick, the end secured by the hand.

To fold the whip, let the thong hang down in a large loop, the end held by the hand; then with a flick of the wrist make the point describe a backward figure of eight, so that the loop folds itself round the whip. Easier said than done! The expert coachman makes it look simple, but only long practice with a teacher can bring the required perfection and consistency in this operation.

The correct handling of the whip is the basis of good coach driving, and no one should attempt to take a four-in-hand on to the roads until he has completely mastered the art of whip control. The general principle is that the wheelers should only be hit in front of the pad, to avoid the chance of them kicking, and the leaders on their hocks under the bars, below the line of the trace.

To hit the wheelers draw the double thong across from the left with a stiff wrist and forearm; or the off wheeler can be hit from the right-hand side. The leaders' reins should not be too long when hitting the wheelers, so that both leaders and wheelers will string off together.

To hit the off leader, move the top of the whip over to the off side of the coach, swing the stick round to shake open the thong, holding the end down with the left thumb. Then swing the stick back to the right until the wrist is about level with the right shoulder, releasing the end of the lash. Swing the stick round to the front with a quick action of the wrist aiming a little in front of the spot you want to hit. To hit the near leader, make the swing of the stick so that the lash flies round on the near side, well above the heads of the passengers, then drop the point slightly so that the lash will swing towards the near leader, while missing the near wheeler's head.

To recover the thong after hitting the off leader, swing the stick up and to the right, then lay it across the left arm pointing to the left, when the thong can be caught by the right hand or under the arm, and then secured by the left thumb, by moving the right hand across to the left. Then it can be transferred to the right hand under the right thumb, and the whip can be folded again. After hitting the near leader, swing the stick to the left in a circular motion and then to the right, when the thong can be caught as before.

The best practice is to sit on the box seat of an unharnessed coach or training brake, with the centre pole in position to guide direction length, and practise swinging, folding and flighting the whip until accuracy is obtained. It is always best to have a definite mark to aim at, which can be contrived by setting poles or stools at about the position of the horse's quarters, and placing ping-pong or similar balls on them. When you can knock a ball down every time, you are doing well.

Competitive driving

The modern amateur coachman mainly drives for pleasure, but the competitive urge is strong, and of course it helps to improve driving skills. The basic competition in Britain is the 'Marathon' (six to eight miles for coaching; four to six miles for private driving), in which the competitors are first examined for condition and turn-out, go out for a country drive on the public highway, and on return the horses are again examined for condition to see how they have stood up to the test.

In 1960 a driving competition was introduced to the programme of the Royal International Horse Show at White City, and has continued at that show (now at Wembley) ever since. It took the form of a race over a set course, which included such hazards as nursemaids at zebra crossings, backing and turning, and driving through markers, and over small jumps.

On the Continent driving competitions are taken very seriously, and are held for every kind of vehicle and equipage, and can be very gruelling tests. A famous one is held at Aachen every year as part of the big equestrian show in early July. In 1970 an official international driving three-day event championship was instituted under the auspices of the F.E.I., in which the competition was divided into three phases, roughly 'dressage' or driving skill, turn-out and endurance. This has now become an annual event.

Competitive hackney driving is a close-knit professional world of its own, derived from the days of the fast-trotting Norfolk roadsters and keeping up the high-stepping tradition. The object is to present a perfectly balanced trotter, with a high knee action in front and strong active hock action behind, yet covering a lot of ground at each stride. The animals are bred to the game, assisted by special heavy shoeing and growing the hooves long; and most of great whips have been born into to it too.

It has of course a technique all its own, the basic difference between it and ordinary driving being that the reins are held in two hands separated. The light, four-wheeled show wagon has a single seat, and is mounted from the near side. The reins are taken in the left hand, the left rein over the first finger, the right between the second and third fingers, the two reins then grasped in the palm of the hand. The driver should sit leaning slightly forwards, the feet firmly braced against the foot bar. The reins are separated, one being held by each hand, the right rein under the little finger of the right hand, which also holds the whip, and a passing upwards to be secured by the palm of the hand. Both hands are held level, slightly elevated, fairly close together, wrists turned inwards, elbows at right angles to the forearms. The whip slopes forward and to the left. The strain of keeping up the high action is very great, and usually the effort is concentrated on the few strides in front of the judges.

Training a horse to harness

Most horses that have had good basic training can be broken to harness, and horses destined for draught only should have basic training. Work with long reins is a very good preparation.

First of all accustom the horse to the harness, by putting it on carefully every day for a week or so, then leading him about in it, and then long-reining him. Progress should be careful, depending to some extent on the horse's receptivity. Temperament plays quite a big part in harness work.

Next, harness the horse to a wooden sledge, with traces long enough to have it out of kicking distance, stand on the sledge and drive the horse about, pulling the sledge behind him, holding the reins and using the whip in the same way as in a cart.

The third stage is the breaking cart, which is an ordinary fairly substantial gig, with extra long shafts, again so that the driver is out of kicking distance. Use a kicking strap then, and when the horse is put to a conventional vehicle. Go quietly at this stage, letting the horse stand still and be made much of when he is between the shafts, then leading him about, so that he gets used to the noise, weight and movement behind him. Finally drive him round the field until he goes quietly and steadily. The strongest resistance will probably come at the putting-to stage, and it should not be attempted singlehanded: the trainer at the reins, and two assistants at the shafts are necessary. Morley Knight wanted the early driving lessons to be in traffic, 'for he will go much better if he sees other things moving about, as they will distract his attention, and keep him from playing tricks on the driver'. (Capt. C. Morley Knight, *Hints on Driving*.) But that was in 1884!

No one can say how long the breaking to harness process will take, but it must be both gradual and continuous, and perfect the first stage before proceeding to the next. That seems to be the abiding lesson which we must have learnt in this book and in all our association with the horse : *festina lente!*

26 Condition and Stable Management

The foundation for all the the work and activities that have been described so far is the physical and psychological fitness of the horse. If the actual education of the young horse has been sympathetically and successfully carried out, he should be mentally prepared for anything, provided his physical training and well-being have marched along with it.

The emphasis in all the training described has been on gradualness; the word over-facing has been used in connection with jumping as something to be avoided. So it is in the physical training: at all times the work given the horse, at whatever stage he may have reached, must be well within his capacity at that time, so that he is never over-faced, but proceeds steadily from strength to strength, as it were.

It is well known that the basics of physical fitness are food, fresh air and exercise. As the horse has a delicate and complicated digestive system, it is well to start with food. I will preface this by stressing the importance of regularity and routine. Feeding and stable work should, as far as is humanly possible, conform to a rigid timetable, which should generate an atmosphere of unhurried calm about a stable, which will in its turn communicate itself to the horse and, amongst other things, aid his digestion and so the regular performance of his normal functions. Few things are so important to efficiency, equine or human, as 'inner cleanliness', as the advertisements say.

The principles of feeding should not have to be enlarged upon. The horse's basic food is grass, which man has adapted, when he requires special efforts from the horse, by converting it into 'concentrates'– oats, barley, maize, bran and other grains and pulses. In recent years this concentration has been further developed by the production of special mixtures of all these ingredients compressed into nuts and cubes.

The main constituents of these grains, or of any food for that matter, are water, nitrogenous matter (of which the muscle-building and energy-producing elements are the proteins), carbohydrates (starch and sugar, which produce energy but also fat, some horses having to watch their calories as carefully as humans), fats, woody fibre (an aid to digestion by promoting mastication) and ash. Over the years, and proved by results, oats has been universally recognised as the best balanced food for horses, containing in good measure the muscle-building and energy-producing constituents.

However, at the present time, some veterinary surgeons think that an excessive amount of oats in a diet can become indigestible and cause liver trouble. Attacks of azoturia which keep cropping up in event horses suggests that too much oats and not enough steady exercise could be the cause. It is well known, also, that oats can have a very intoxicating effect on small ponies, especially of the Mountain and Moorland breeds. Racehorses are fed exclusively on oats, but any harmful effects are absorbed in the sustained exercise they undergo and the great speeds which they have to produce on the racecourse. For ordinary horses, a top limit of fifteen pounds should normally be enough, the balance of food being made up with barley, bran, and possibly flaked maize.

The claims of barley as a primary food for horses are being more and more considered. In many parts of the East it is a staple diet; Indian cavalry horses had it combined with gram, and did very well on it. It is considered also to contain more calcium producing elements, and therefore particularly good for young, growing horses. Specimen diets for various ages of a horse, such as the one whose education we have been describing, based on a balance of grains, will be given below.

A horse must have bulk, of course, which in natural conditions he takes in by constant, unremitting grazing. Under domesticated conditions he must have hay, in quantities of anything up to fifteen pounds, and the quality of this must be a serious consideration. All hay fed must have been cut in early June, when the protein value present in the leaf and seed is at its greatest. In July and August the seed has fallen from the grass, and hay made from it, being deficient in protein, has insufficient food value. Needless to say, all the hay and corn given must be of the best quality.

The concentrated nuts and cubes already mentioned are excellent, and certainly do save labour, but they must not be regarded as a substitute for the hay bulk, which must always be added, or for the best natural grains, if they can be obtained. If nuts are used, they must be introduced gradually, like everything to do with horses, a few at a time mixed with ordinary feeds and gradually increasing. Some horses thrive on them, others do not take to them, and some again get tired of them.

Being a concentrated mixture of the best quality ingredients, they can be too rich for some horses. Feeding is always a matter of trial and error and constant watchfulness.

Nowadays, when for various reasons the natural products of the soil are lacking in mineral and vital content, the disappearance of hedgerows and the nutritious herbs (weeds) that grew there is a great loss to good horse husbandry, the use of additives becomes necessary to put back the vital elements which have been taken out. There are any number of tonics and pepping-up preparations and pills on the market now (even the horse is becoming a pill-addict), and they probably all have some value. Every owner will have his pet energiser which he swears by, but only the horse can give the final verdict.

One valuable additive, however, which must be mentioned is seaweed, which contains many necessary minerals and trace elements, which used to be found in the herbs and plants of the aforesaid hedgerows. It can be obtained in powdered form, and should be a regular addition to any diet, fed in small quantities, say a teaspoonful mixed with every feed. Cod liver oil is another important extra, but see always that the full vitamin content is declared on the label.

Two pressing problems which face horse owners and trainers in the 'seventies are possible shortages of hay, the increasing cost of it and the pollution of nearly all the food that the horse eats, with already unpleasant consequences to young-stock, the cause of which is perhaps not clearly recognised.

In the winter of 1970–71 there was an alarming shortage of hay in some parts of the country, and substitutes were being looked for. One such is sugar beet pulp, which, if fully soaked, can be fed in quite large quantities to a working horse, supplemented with wheat and oat straw, desperate remedies, perhaps, but effective.

The problem of pollution from weed killers, widespread spraying of chemicals, whose total effects are not sufficiently known, as well as industrial pollution, is more serious than many people realise. What was called the 'unprecedented number of deformed foals' in 1970 could well be due to the poisons now present in our fields. Owners of the foals are reluctant to advertise these 'failures' in their breeding, but such reticence does no service to the cause that they must have at heart, the well-being and health of their horses and ponies. And all this toxic avalanche must surely have a bad effect on the performance of the modern sporting horse.

A long-term answer to this problem, as well as to the shortage of hay, is the hydroponic process of growing grass. The word is derived from the Greek *hydor* (water) and *ponos* (toil), and it means 'water-working' by contrast with geoponics (agriculture). It is a method of raising plants without any soil, nourished instead by solutions of water and fertiliser. The first great advantages of the system are its high yield, quality and quick production: 'from the start of the operation to maturity of forage takes only six days'. (J. Sholto Douglas, 'Stable-grown Fresh Forage', *Light Horse*, February, 1969.) The other present asset is that the grower knows where his forage is coming from and can guarantee the quality. The food value is high. Tests on oats conducted by the Wisconsin Research Foundation, U.S.A., have shown that the hydroponically grown green grass had a protein content of 21.99 per cent compared with 15 per cent for dry grain. On a long-term basis the cost can be less than that of conventionally grown forage. This may be a plan for the future, but a future that is not all that distant.

The routine of feeding needs little elaboration: 'little and often' is the watchword, though it need not be overdone, like a cavalry squadron commander I once knew, who tried to take it literally and took handfuls of corn to his own horses every half hour. The optimum number of feeds a day is four, the normal three, and, if circumstances compel it, it can be less. Harry Faudel-Phillips once described how, when running his famous riding school at Temple House, Theobalds Park, near Waltham Cross, Hertfordshire, between the wars, he fed his school horses once a day, a big meal after the morning's work, followed by two hours of absolute quiet for digestion. This last was, of course, the key to it: the horse must have time to digest his meal, whatever its size may be.

The feeding plan, whatever it is, should be based on a six-day working week, with one rest day. This should be a completely corn-free day, on which the horse should have bran mashes to which linseed jelly or Epsom salt, or both, has been added, and some green food like lucerne as well as the normal hay.

One more point about the digestion concerns the teeth. Digestion depends on proper mastication of the food, and efficient mastication depends on the teeth. So watch the teeth at all times. Because of the side-to-side movement of the molars during mastication, the outer edges of the upper and inner edges of the lower row become very pointed, and these rough edges can cause minute wounds to the tongue and cheek muscles, this problem can be prevented by inspection directly any abnormality of digestion is suspected and by the timely application of the file, very lightly up and down each edge; a few movements only will suffice. A great deal of subsequent trouble can be avoided by this small but timely attention to detail.

Feeding plans

The actual amounts of each ingredient at each stage of the horse's growth or training must be as carefully worked out as possible, so as to provide at all times a sufficient and balanced diet. There are no scientific rules for this that I know of; it is a matter of trial and error, based on the size and type of the horse, the work it is expected to do, its present condition, and its own individual metabolism and temperament and the owner's personal knowledge and understanding of the horse.

In the old horse-drawn days, a London omnibus horse pulled one and a half tons for twelve and a half miles at a speed of five m.p.h. six days a week. (W. J. Gordon, *The Horse World of London, 1893.*) He did this on a total daily food weight of thirty-one pounds made up of maize, sixteen pounds; oats, one and a half pounds; peas, one and a half pounds; hay chop, twelve pounds, these figures being supplied by Captain M. H. Hayes in *Stable Management and Exercise.* And the horse lasted for five years.

Few horses do work of the intensity these days, and the bulk of the food given is oats and/or barley. The following specimen diet sheets are offered with the proviso that they are *specimen* only, to be regarded as a starting point, to be modified up or down according to individual experience and the re-actions of the horse.

Horses. 15–16 h.h. and over. Weanlings. Barley (bruised) 2–4 lb. Bran ½ lb. Hay *ad lib.*

Yearlings. Barley (bruised) 3–5 lb. Bran 1 lb. Hay *ad lib.* Increase the barley up to 4–6 lb. by the time he is three years old.

3–4 years (lunge and preliminary training). Oats 2–3 lb. Barley 3–4 lb. Bran 1–2 lb. Hay 10–12 lb.

At maturity, in full work (up to 4 hours daily). *15 h.h.* Oats 8–10 lb., barley 2 lb., bran 2 lb., hay 12 lb.

15–16 h.h. Oats 10 lb., barley 4 lb., bran 2 lb., hay 12–14 lb.

Over EP *h.h.* Oats 12–14 lb., barley 5 lb., bran 2 lb., hay 14 lb.

Additions to this food, as tonic and to give it variety and palatability would be sliced carrots, turnips, potatoes, apples, the outsides of green vegetables; and a teaspoonful of seaweed powder to each feed. To make further variety, flaked maize can be substituted for part of the barley; or the oats can be decreased and the barley increased. This is for the working week of six days.

Ponies of mixed breed need a good deal less corn. Assuming that they are exercised every day for at least two hours, the following could be a starting diet.

14.2 h.h. Oats 2–3 lb., barley 3 lb., bran 1 lb., hay 12lb.

13.2 h.h. Oats 2 lb., barley 3 lb., bran 1 lb., hay 10 lb.

12.2 h.h. Oats and barley 2 lb., bran 1 lb., hay 10 lb.

For ponies working only at week-ends a daily feed should be maintained in preference to stuffing them at the week-end, the above amounts being reduced by half, and the bran to half a pound. The hay ration remains the same. Give the same extras as to the horses.

Mountain and moorland ponies, unless doing fast work; hunting, gymkhanas, or long hours trekking or showing, are best kept to hay and coarse grazing. The lush green pastures of civilisation are bad for them, making them over-fat and causing laminitis, and probably aggravating the allergy affliction of sweet itch.

If the work is likely to be heavy, then they might be given two to three pounds barley, half a pound bran, ten pounds hay daily.

Concentrates in the form of nuts and cubes have the paramount advantage for modern owner-grooms of being easy to feed. The main problem is what is the equivalent. The makers vary in their proportions. The average ratio is about one-third more cubes than the corn ration, e.g. eight pounds of cubes for six pounds of oats. In spite of claims to include the bulk element, hay should always be added. Police horses, doing a daily stint of three and a half hours, carrying sixteen stone and covering twelve miles, receive fifteen pounds of Spiller cubes with seven pounds of hay.

Feeds should always be measured in exact weights, not scoops or handfuls, which can never be guaranteed to furnish the same amount each day. The easiest thing is to have the different ingredients weighed in distributing receptacles such as mugs or small jugs, so that you have a known weight to work from.

Watering

Everyone knows that a horse should be watered before feeding, but there is more to it than that, especially when the time comes to prepare a horse for great exertions.

Cold water given directly on return from hard work when the horse is hot can very easily upset its sensitive bowel. If, as is usually the case, only tap water is available, it should not be given straight from the tap before it has had a chance to become aerated and to rise in temperature. If possible, the water should be drawn about an hour before return from work; or draw it before going out to work.

There is one variation to this treatment. As it is essential for the horse to stale directly on his return to the stable from work, he can be encouraged to do so by being given a mouthful or two of cold water, which will produce minor shock and cause most horses to stale at once. Then the chilled water can be given. If it has been a strenuous day during special training, powdered glucose should be added to the water. You will probably have to break him gently to the glucose; give an occasional small quantity of it in the water to get him used to the taste but not enough to make it a habit; then, after hard galloping exercise put half to three-quarters of a pound into the drink. The glucose so administered acts as a pre-digested food which will quickly restore normal tone to the nervous system upset by the strenuous exercise and the horse will turn out much better for it the next day.

Grooming

It should not be necessary to emphasise the contribution of good grooming to the fitness of a stable-kept horse. (On the other hand, a horse kept out of doors with his full coat, should be groomed very sparingly, so that the essential oils which help to keep him warm are retained.) Apart from the polishing of the coat and toning up of the muscles, grooming keeps the pores of the skin free of scurf and sebaceous material, so that toxins which come into the body with the normal food can be excreted by the sweat. Most of these toxic substances are eliminated from the body by the bowel and kidneys, but the skin is also an important outlet. So grooming must always be vigorous, a good three-quarters of an hour's work, accompanied by the hard wisping which increases the circulation, thereby providing more muscle-building material.

Psychology

The horse, it cannot be said too often, is not a machine, and he is as capable of being bored as his master or mistress. A working horse is kept in a stable, and, if he does three hours work a day, he spends the remaining twenty-one hours in prison, as it were, often in semi-darkness, and virtually alone. No wonder crib-biting, weaving, wind-sucking, stable kicking are endemic vices of the present-day domesticated horse.

He should be visited as often as possible outside feeding hours; taken for a short walk on a leading rein in the afternoon for half an hour to nibble at some grass and to see a little life. It would be better still, if his box could open out on to a small paddock which he could use at will. The physical value of mental interest and contentment cannot be measured, but it must surely be very high indeed.

Bringing up from grass

It is traditional at the end of an active season, whether it be hunting in the winter or eventing in the summer, to turn horses out to grass and give them a rest. Horses are supposed to enjoy it, but it is debatable whether they do or not, or whether it is really good for them. It is of course a great saving of forage, and also of time for an owner-groom. In the old days many grooms in private hunting stables used to be sacked in the summer.

However that may be, the practice still goes on, and the problem arises of getting horses fit again after a good many weeks of grass diet. Fix the date of the first event, whatever it may be, when the horse must be in peak condition for it; ten weeks before that will be D-day for starting training.

Normally the change from the grass to the hard diet is effected with the aid of a powerful purgative, but the best way is to prepare the horse gradually for the change by giving him two pounds of corn – half oats, half barley – daily for six weeks before the training period is to begin. The last four days of this preparation time give him bran mashes, and he will be able to come on to a progressively increased corn ration without any digestive upset or filled legs, and without the administering of the old-fashioned physic dose. This procedure can also be followed if the horse has been out of work for any period during his training. After the mashes, with the corn can be given a tablespoonful of the following powder once daily for ten days: bicarbonate of soda four ounces, potassium nitrate one ounce, powdered glucose eight ounces, Epsom salt one pound.

The normal method of training is a progressive increase of work and food on a week by week basis. The first week should be one hour's walking exercise, with, say, four pounds of oats, one pound of bran, twelve pounds of hay; working up thereafter to the full ration and anything up to three hours' exercise including schooling sessions, which must continue throughout the conditioning period.

The importance of the feet and legs can never be stressed too much, and a good deal of tendon trouble and bruised soles can be avoided if a careful hardening up process is carried out from the beginning. Plenty of road work is essential, progressively increasing periods of long walks with occasional trotting over country roads. After three weeks of this part of the work can be over any uneven surfaces and stony ground that can be found, including walking and trotting over plough, that 'ridge and furrow' work which has already been mentioned above. During this time progressively include up and down hill work, first at the walk for two or three weeks, then at the trot, and finally, at the end of the training, at the canter.

After about five weeks, spells of steady cantering (twelve to fifteen m.p.h.) for varying distances can be introduced two days a week. Start with half-mile stints, working up to a mile and a mile and a half, increasing in the latter half of the programme to three or four two-mile canters. In the last four weeks the speed can be stepped up three-quarter speed gallops at distances varying from half a mile to one and a half miles, and occasional two and three-furlong full-speed sprints. Always have a rest period after each cantering or galloping stint, which will usually be steady walking. This 'rest' period will be long at first, perhaps ten minutes, but will be reduced as the horse gets fitter and is able to recover more quickly from the energy lost through the greater exertion. There should be a certain rhythm of this 'expenditure and income' as it were.

All this is based on the traditional, empirical methods of training, which have stood the test of time; especially successful when they conform most closely to the physical reactions of the horse's body to the expenditure of energy. During great physical exertion the body uses up oxygen faster than the heart and lungs can replace it in the blood stream and carry away the excess of carbonic acid produced by the oxidisation of glucose in the muscles. The accumulation of this acid is what causes fatigue, making the muscles ache and lose their elasticity.

Given time, the heart and lungs can return to normal functioning so that the lost oxygen is replaced. The quicker the rate of recovery the fitter the horse, or man, will be. So, modern scientific training of human athletes is based on a series of strenuous efforts followed by intervals of rest, known as Interval Training. It is not so easy to apply this system to horses as it is to men and women, and perhaps not so necessary, but it has

been done, and, for those who are interested, is fully described by G. N. Jackson in *Effective Horsemanship*. However,
there is no reason why you should not apply this method in a
rough and ready way, which will probably teach you something
else about your horse that you do not know already.

The method is based on the observations of the temperature,
pulse and respiration rates of the horse before, during and after
work (T.P.R.). The first thing to do is to get accustomed to
taking these observations on your horse at different phases of
his progress, so that you know fairly accurately what is the
norm for him.

Then apply it in a simple way to the training programme.
For example, the normal pulse of the horse in the stable at rest
is forty to the minute; after a period of trot and canter a check
will show that it has increased to sixty-five; and after a short
sharp gallop it may rise to 100. Halt, and check the time it
takes for the pulse to recover to sixty-five, possibly about two
minutes. If it takes longer, it would be as well to look into the
horse's condition more closely and modify the training programme. The same procedure applies to temperature and respiration; they both rise with exertion, and they should come
down with relaxation from it at approximately the same rate.

In 1964–65, the Russians carried out extensive tests of the
effect of exercise on horses, and came up with, among other
things, the following figures:

Clinical characteristics of sports horses of different training.

Training	Pulse	Respiration	Temperature (C.)
	At rest		
Well-trained horses	22–34	6–12	37.2–38.3
Undertrained horses	34–44	10–18	37.5–38.3
After proportioned load			
Well-trained horses	54–76	22–32	38.5–39.0
Undertrained horses	66–88	32–48	38.8–39.4
After competitions			
Well-trained horses	108–122	72–104	40.0–41.5
Undertrained horses	96–142	62–100	40.5–42.0

The conclusions drawn from this are that fit horses are more
relaxed at rest than undertrained ones; have less variation of
T.P.R. after moderate work; and do better under the maximum load, than the others. It was also found that the recovery
period was shorter for the well-trained horse. (From a Report
to the F.E.I., by Professor I. Bobylev, Moscow Veterinary

Academy, *F.E.I. Bulletin* No. 60, and *Light Horse,* November, 1965.)

All this is still in its infancy, though it is a signpost to the future; and the well-tried traditional methods still pay off, but not invariably. In every race or endurance test of any kind there are some horses who show peak condition at the right moment, and they reach the top; but there are as many whose training has not worked out just right, and they fail.

The horseman, who has got thus far in the making of a top-class riding horse, should seek more and more precise methods of ensuring that his companion and servant is as fit as possible in every way for whatever task he may be set. That, after all, is horsemanship.

Postscript

It is as hard to end a book as to begin it. The last sentence is as elusive as the opening one. Well, they have been found, and the book is ended. About what lies between them I have nothing to add but the hope that the persevering learner and the practical rider, the serious student of horsemanship in all its aspects, to whom it is offered, will find something of interest, something of help, and something of encouragement; and that the principal beneficiary of all the work that is entailed in becoming a horseman will be the horse. Without him there would be no books to be written – or read! Terrible thought! So let us echo one of the last thoughts of John Board, a great horselover, before he died in 1965: 'Thank God for the horse!'

It now only remains to thank all those who have helped in some way to the making of this book. First of all riders, great and not so great, whose performances in their varied fields have both inspired and instructed. Next, the great equestrian writers, whether orthodox or innovators, who have set out the principles and illuminated the practice of horsemanship for the benefit of lesser mortals. You cannot read too much about horsemanship; there is always something more to be learned. I have quoted from them in the text, and they and others are listed below.

More specifically, I would like to thank—

Captain Edy Goldman, of the Cheshire Equestrian Centre, for reading and checking Part II of the book, 'The Training of the Rider'.

Colonel W. S. Codrington, T.D., M.R.C.V.S., for advising on Chapters 3, 4 and 5, on the Anatomy, Conformation and Mind of the Horse.

Mrs Julia Wynmalen for patiently coping with Part III, 'The Training of the Horse', and making most pertinent and valuable suggestions.

Sanders and Biddy Watney for checking Chapter 25 on 'Driving'.

Needless to say that none of these is to be held responsible for any errors or omissions.

The F.E.I. for permission to quote from their *Rules for Dressage Competitions.*

Bill Luscombe, of Pelham Books, for egging me on to tackle this book and for finding it worth publishing, and incidentally for the great encouragement that he gives to the horse world and to equestrian sports by producing so many excellent and varied books on the subject.

Finally, I thank my wife for reading not only the manuscript but the proofs as well with such care, and for invariably asking the right questions.

And of course I thank the reader for having got this far – if he has.

C. E. G. Hope

Earls Court
June 1970 – January 1971.

Appendix

RIDING SIDE-SADDLE

The general practice of side-saddle riding for women has had a comparatively brief reign in history: say a matter of 250 years, roughly, from about the middle of the sixteenth century to the end of World War I. There was an earlier transition period, and the beginnings of the side-saddle appeared in the fourteenth century, but, generally, women, when they did ride in the Middle Ages, rode astride.

Now the girls have come back to it in modern times, and although side-saddle riding has had a revival in the show ring in children's classes, and the traditional ladies' hunter and ladies' hack classes are still with us, and a few women still ride that way out hunting, one cannot avoid the feeling that it is an elegant irrelevance.

This does not mean that women who ride side-saddle are in any way inferior to their cross-saddle sisters; far from it. They can, or could, achieve equally high standards in many fields. In hunting certainly; they have show-jumped with success in the past; the side-saddle *haute ecole* riding of Elizabeth Schumann in the circus is quite a spectacle.

There is great security in a side-saddle, but to ride in it correctly requires as much skill and practice as, if not more than, ordinary riding astride. The horse, too, has to be specially trained to be responsive to the whip aids on the off side.

The saddle in its modern form is larger and heavier than an astride one, weighing about twenty pounds, but, like the Western saddle, the weight is well distributed. It has a long and broad and flat seat, with no raised cantle. In front are two pommels or leg rests, one sloping upwards, which takes the right leg, the other sloping downwards, giving support to the left knee. The saddle needs to be very securely fixed to the horse, and there is usually an auxiliary strap from the rear of the seat to girth to hold it steady.

The same principles of riding apply, especially the necessity for a completely upright and square position. Balance is a problem, because with two legs on one side the extra load on the near side has to be compensated for.

Mounting

The most popular way is the leg-up, which is not the same as for a cross-saddle (page 79). The difference is that the rider stands facing the horse's head, reins and whip in the right hand, which with the left is holding the pommel. Then she bends her left knee and the assistant takes the left foot in both hands. When ready, the lady moves first, springing off the left foot and straightening her leg; the assistant must hold his hands firm and not lift her until her leg is fully straight. As she is lifted she turns her body to the left, and sits sideways on the saddle behind the pommels. Finally, she swings her right leg over the pommels and turns her body to the right to get into the correct position facing the horse's head. Then she will adjust the skirt, and the assistant will fix the elastic loop at the bottom of the latter under the left foot, to hold it in position; the left foot will be put into the stirrup and the leather adjusted if necessary.

To mount independently, 1. Stand with your back to the horse's head, reins and whip in the left hand, which holds the lower pommel. 2. Take the stirrup with the right hand. 3. Move the left hand to the top pommel and hold the leaping-head with the right. 4. Spring up until the left leg is straight, knee against the saddle, back still to the horse's head. 5. Move the right hand to the back of the saddle, to help the lifting, at the same time press the left knee well into the saddle to lever the foot and stirrup away from the saddle, so that it becomes the pivot of the turn round to the left to face the horse's head. 6. Shift the right hand back to the pommel, move the right leg over the saddle and sit astride. 7. Then, using the pommels as a brace, bring the right leg up over the withers into position. 8. Adjust the elastic loop of the skirt over the right foot.

Dismount

Take off the elastic, pull back the skirt, transfer reins and whip to the right hand, bring the right leg over the pommels, so that you are sitting sideways on the saddle. Take the left foot out of the stirrup and slide down to the ground, taking care not to catch any part of the habit on the pommels.

The seat

On a side-saddle the seat must be upright, with the body

absolutely square to the front. The right knee is crooked over the upper pommel, so that the thigh is as near horizontal as possible, and the lower leg hangs vertically downwards. The left thigh should normally not be pressed against the leaping-head, but leave a clearance of the thickness of the hand. The left leg hangs down in the normal way, foot pressed home in the stirrup and facing slightly outwards, heel down. When extra grip is required, the left thigh is pressed up against the leaping-head.

The rider's hips and shoulders should be in one plane, and at right angles to the line of movement. The posterior should be firmly placed on the saddle, so that the rider's spine is exactly above the backbone of the horse. This relationship must be maintained at all times, whatever the position of the body when in movement, i.e. leaning forwards or back, or rising in the stirrup for the posting trot. The whip is held in the right hand, and it takes the place of the missing right leg aid.

The right thigh, which takes most of the rider's weight, crosses the horse's backbone just behind the withers, and the concentration of the load should be felt at that point. At the same time, in order to counteract the increased burden of the legs on the near side, the rider must work to place more weight on the right seat bone, than on the left; an even balance there will result in an imbalance to the left.

The chief faults of a side-saddle position are: leaning to the right, with the right shoulder dropped and the whole body off the vertical; trying to make an adjustment by leaning the hips to the right but keeping the shoulders straight, which causes an uncomfortable distortion; weight too much on the near side; sitting with the seat bones and buttocks too much to the right; leaning forward with rounded shoulder, or crouching. In fact, any deviation from the position described above is a fault.

To maintain the correct position entails considerable muscular effort and concentration, and it should be practised regularly on a dummy horse, or anyway a very quiet horse. There is no reason why side-saddle riding on the lunge should not be carried out, not without the stirrup, however, for the purchase given by that is an essential part of the position.

Circling and turning conform to the same principles as for riding astride: the body should always remain in the same plane as the horse. The forward seat can be maintained over fences as well as with a cross-saddle; the body moving forward at the approach and the seat leaving the saddle during the jump. The work here is done by the right thigh pressing down on the pommel and the left thigh against the leaping-head, and the brace of the left foot in the stirrup.

The aids act in the same way with hands, leg (spur) and whip, as with hands and legs. A horse that has been trained at the outset to understand the whip aids should be able to come back to the whip aid without difficulty, with careful progressive training, so that he gets used to the unusual combination of leg on one side and whip on the other. The left leg should always have a spur, as extreme leg pressure is not attainable in the same way as when riding astride.

When riding side-saddle the rider's dress and equipment should always be impeccable. Riding habits are simple affairs now of jackets and aprons, but they must still look like skirts when the rider is in the saddle, the right leg covered up by it. The hair should be done up tidily with a bun or hair net, and a top-hat and veil, or bowler hat, with or without veil; whatever hat is worn should be on straight or tilted slightly forward, *never* back.

Whether irrelevant or not, side-saddle riding still remains the peak of equestrian elegance.

Bibliography

There being over 20,000 titles in the English language alone of books dealing with the horse and horsemanship, there is no attempt here even to begin to be exhaustive. It would be pointless anyway, because no one would ever read them. Here, however, is a list of the books that have been quoted or mentioned in the text and some of others of general or special interest which are still available.

THE PRECURSORS
The Training of Horses, by Kikkuli (14th century B.C.)
Hippike, by Xenophon 350 B.C. English translation by M. H. Morgan (J. A. Allen, 1962)
Hippiatrica Sive Marescalia, by Laurentius Rusius, c. 1350
Ordini di Cavalcare, by Federico Grisone, c. 1550
Le Cavalerie François, by Salomon de la Broue, 1594
Instruction du Roi, by Antoine de Pluvinel, 1623
A General System of Horsemanship, by the Duke of Newcastle, 1657
Ecole de Cavalerie, by François Robichon de la Guérinière, 1733
A Method of Breaking Horses and Teaching Soldiers to Ride, by the Earl of Pembroke, 1762
Trait ésur la Cavalerie, by Count Drummond de Melfort, 1776

MODERN
Accoutrements of the Riding Horse, by Cecil G. Trew, Seeley Service, 1951
American Cow Pony, The, by Deering Davis, Van Nostrand, 1962
Ancient Greek Horsemanship, by J. K. Anderson, University of California Press, 1960
Arab Horse in Europe, The, by Erika Schiele, Harrap, 1970
As To Polo, by William Cameron Forbes, Manila Polo Club, 1919

Be a Better Horseman, by Vladimir Littauer, Hurst & Blackett, 1953

Bit by Bit, by Diana Tuke, W. H. Allen, 1965

Breaking and Riding, by James Fillis, Hurst and Blackett, 1902. Reprinted by J. A. Allen, 1969

Caprilli Papers, The, Ed. by Piero Santini from notes of Federico Caprilli, first published in *Light Horse* in 1951, in serial form, and in book form by J. A. Allen, 1967

Cavalletti, by Reiner Klimke tr. Daphne Machin Goodall, J. A. Allen, 1969

Cavalry Horsemanship, by Lieut-Col. Blacque Belair, tr. J. Swire, Vinton, 1919

Century and a Half of Amateur Driving, A, by A. B. Shone, J. A. Allen, 1955

Colours and Markings of Horses, Royal College of Veterinary Surgeons, London, 1954

Commonsense Horsemanship, by Vladimir Littauer, Macmillan, 1954

Das Gymnasium des Pferdes, by Gustav Steinbrecht, 1885

Defense of the Forward Seat, The, by Vladimir Littauer and S. Kournakoff

Dressage, by Henry Wynmalen, *Country Life*, 1953

Dressage Riding, by Richard L. Wätjen, tr. Dr V. Saloschin, J. A. Allen, 1958

Driving and Harness, by Colonel R. S. Timmis, D.S.O., J. A. Allen, 1965

Driving Book, The, by Maj. H. Faudel-Phillips, 1943, J. A. Allen, 1965

Effective Horsemanship, by G. N. Jackson, David Rendel Ltd, 1967

Equitation, by Henry Wynmalen, *Country Life*, 1938

F.E.I. Rules, Brussels, 1967

Forward Impulse, The, by Piero Santini, *Country Life*, 1937

Fundamentals of Private Driving, by Sally Walrond, British Driving Society, 1969

Fundamentals of Riding, by Gregor de Romaszkan, tr. M. A. Stoneridge, Pelham Books, 1965

Give Your Horse a Chance, by Colonel A. L. d'Endrody, J. A. Allen, 1959

Harmony in Horsemanship, by Colonel J. A. Talbot-Ponsonby D.S.O., *Country Life*, 1964

High Steppers, The, by Tom Ryder, J. A. Allen, 1961

Hints on Driving, by Capt. C. Morley Knight, first published 1884, reprinted by J. A. Allen, 1969

History of Horsemanship, A, by Charles Chenevix Trench, Longmans, 1970

History of the Carriage, The, by László Tarr, Vision Press, 1969

Horse and Rider in Equilibrium, by Gregor de Romaszkan, tr. M. A. Stoneridge, Pelham Books, 1967

Horse and the Furrow, The, by Ewart Evans, Faber & Faber, 1960

Horse Breeding and Stud Management, by Henry Wynmalen, Country Life, 1950

Horsemanship, by Waldemar Zeunig, tr. Leonard Mins, Doubleday, U.S.A. 1956, Robert Hale, G.B., 1958

Horsemanship for Jockeys, by John Hislop, *The British Racehorse,* 1970

Horseman's Progress, by Vladimir Littauer, Van Nostrand, 1962

Horse Psychology, by Moira Williams, Methuen, 1956

Horse World of London, 1893, The, by W. J. Gordon, Religious Tract, Society, 1933/J. A. Allen, 1971

Horses in Action, by R. H. Smythe, *Country Life,* 1963

Introduction to Polo, An, by Marco, *Country Life,* 1931/1950

Kingdom of the Horse, The, by Hans-Heinrich Isenbart and Emil Martin Buhrer, Collins, 1970

Know Your Horse, by Lieut.-Col. W. S. Codrington, T.D., M.R.C.V.S., J. A. Allen, 1963

Learn to Ride, by Lieut.-Col. C. E. G. Hope, Pelham Books, 1965

Le Gymnase du Cheval, by Gustav Steinbrecht, published in Germany, 1885, French tr. Comdt. Dupont, Epiac, 1963

Manual of Horsemastership, etc., War Office, 1937

Medieval Technology and Social Change, by Lynn White Jnr, Oxford University Press, 1962 (For the development and influence of the Stirrup)

Mind of the Horse, The, by R. H. Smythe, *Country Life,* 1965

Modern Horsemanship, by Paul Rodzianko, Seeley Service, 1933

Notes on Dressage, British Horse Society, 1947

Obstacle Conduit et Style, by Gudin de Vallerin, Henri Neveu, Paris, 1950

Olympic Dressage Test in Pictures, The, by Gregor de Romaszkan, Pelham Books, 1968

On the Box Seat, by Tom Ryder, Horse Drawn Carriages Ltd, 1969

Piaffer and Passage, by General de Carpentry, tr. Patricia Galvin, Van Nostrand, 1961

Points of the Horse, The, by Capt. M. H. Hayes, Hurst & Blackett, 1893/Stanley Paul, 1969

Polo, by John Board, Faber & Faber, 1956

Pony Owner's Encyclopaedia, The, by C. E. G. Hope, Pelham Books, 1965

Psychologie du Cheval, by Maurice Hontang, Payot, Paris, 1954

Riding, by Benjamin Lewis, J. A. Allen, 1966

Riding and Jumping, by William Steinkraus, rev. edit. Pelham Books, 1971

Riding Instructor, The, by Piero Santini, *Country Life,* 1953

Riding Logic, by Wilhelm Müseler, tr. F. W. Schiller, Methuen, 1937

Riding Reflections, by Piero Santini, *Country Life,* 1933

Riding Technique in Pictures, by C. E. G. Hope and Charles Harris, F.I.H., F.B.H.S., Hulton Press 1956/J. A. Allen, 1968

Saddle of Queens, The, by Leida Fleitmann Bloodgood, J. A. Allen, 1959

Saddlery, by E. Hartley Edwards, *Country Life,* 1963

Saddlery and Harness Making, ed. Paul N. Hasluck, Cassell, 1904/J. A. Allen, 1962

Schooling of the Western Horse, The, by John Richard Young, University of Oklahoma Press, 1954

Side-Saddle, by Doreen Archer-Houblon, *Country Life,* 1938/ 1961

Souvenirs, by General L'Hottt

Spanish Riding School, The, by Col. Alois Podhajsky, Vienna, 1948

Stable Management and Exercise, by Capt. M. H. Hayes, Hurst and Blackett, 1900/1968

Stable Management for the Owner Groom, by George Wheatley, Cassell, 1966

Stitch by Stitch, by Diana Tuke, J. A. Allen, 1970 (Saddles and Saddle Making)

Such Agreeable Friends, by Bernhard Grzimek, André Deutsch, 1964 (For Horse Psychology)

Summerhays' Encyclopaedia for Horsemen, by R. S. Summerhays, Frederick Warne, 1970

Tackle Riding This Way, by Lieut.-Col. C. E. G. Hope, Stanley Paul, 1959/1969

Training Hunters, Jumpers and Hacks, by Harry D. Chamberlain, Hurst & Blackett, 1938, Van Nostrand, 1969

Training the Horse, by Lyndon Bolton, Pelham Books, 1964

Index

295

JUN 2 5 '74	DATE DUE	
OCT 30 '74		
MAY 2 4 1978		